REVITALIZE, DON'T RETIRE

LEWIS D. SOLOMON

iUNIVERSE, INC.
NEW YORK   BLOOMINGTON

Revitalize, Don't Retire

iUniverse books may be ordered through booksellers or by contacting:

iUniverse
1663 Liberty Drive
Bloomington, IN 47403
www.iuniverse.com
1-800-Authors (1-800-288-4677)

Because of the dynamic nature of the Internet, any Web addresses or links contained in this book may have changed since publication and may no longer be valid.

ISBN: 978-1-4502-2731-5 (sc)
ISBN: 978-1-4502-2730-8 (ebk)

Printed in the United States of America

iUniverse rev. date: 5/13/2010

DEDICATION

In memory of Samuel Lewis and Philip Tilkus

I want to thank posthumously Rabbi Morris Lichtenstein, whose focus on character development enlightened my path.

Note: Except for my relatives, the names used in this book are pseudonyms.

CONTENTS

INTRODUCTION: THE NEW RETIREMENT

Retirement may be the longest stage of your life. You want a fulfilling life, feeling valued and needed, mentally challenged, not merely keeping busy.

Men in their 60s today are apt to enjoy considerably healthier retirements than their fathers and grandfathers. Many stand a decent chance of living well into their 80s, if not reaching 90, doing so with a modicum of style. Senior years can be a time of promise, renewal, and revitalization.

This book focuses on the positive possibilities of men growing old in the United States. It seeks to develop role models for wise elders in a rapidly aging population by presenting a comprehensive approach to longevity planning: existential, emotional, physical, and financial. It's part of my legacy to my son and future generations of men to let them know what to expect when they live to age 90 and beyond.

THE TRADITIONAL APPROACH TO RETIREMENT

The word "retirement" comes from the French word, *retirer*, meaning to withdraw. Retirement traditionally meant a withdrawal from one's occupation or business into leisure and not being actively involved. It connoted a descent into the end of life.

The traditional concept of retirement was based on a time when guys quit working because physical demands overwhelmed them; they lacked the physical capacity and could no longer produce. They were worn out cogs not in the best physical shape when they retired and they weren't going to live long.

For most of them, one's work was already achieved, one's tasks were already done, and one's duties were already fulfilled. It was a time to give up one's place to others. It was regarded as not an ideal stage of life. Almost nothing was expected of the elderly except to take it easy, pursue leisure activities, amuse oneself, or just do nothing.

When my stepfather, Manny, a warm-hearted, wonderful guy, retired at age 65, he did it the old-fashioned way. He saw life in a rather linear fashion: going to school, beginning to work, marrying and raising a family, continuing to work, and then retiring. On giving up his dental practice, his period of striving and aspiring ended. His new domain became the couch in front of the television. For nearly two decades, he saw retirement as a termination of productive activity, entering into inactivity and taking it easy. Retirement for him began a great coast. His life became a rather dull monotony, his days settled into an uninspiring, rather bleak procession. The powers of his mind had nothing to do. The days stretched ahead pointlessly. Although he never fell into depression, he became ever more boring to be around from his aimless days.

I often heard him say at age 65 and for years thereafter, "The world is for young people. I am passed the stage of ambition; there is nothing left for me but to retire." His use of the word "retire" connoted a withdrawal from life. When he took on this attitude, he passed a death sentence upon himself, although he "lived" for two decades more. Life for him became a process of vegetation, a period of waiting for the end.

You don't want to flunk retirement, but it's no longer clear what's expected of men in their "old" age. For some, it becomes a rather role-less time. At age 60 or 65, the life map becomes blurry. For most, the path enters *terra incognita*, uncharted territory. The accepted guideposts men lived by have been taken down. The familiar life script—education, career, marriage, children, the empty nest—runs out.

Many men simply don't prepare for a smooth and fulfilling transition from their job, career, or business. They don't have a longevity strategy. The retired Chrysler CEO, Lee Iacocca, put it this way: "You can plan everything in your life, and then the roof caves in on you because you haven't done enough thinking about who you are and what you should do with the rest of your life."[1]

Your job, career, or business provided an identity, structure, purpose, and focus. It probably served as an object of personal ambition and challenge. You may even miss the simple act of performing a job you'd known for so long.

When you retire you lose far more than a paycheck. You lose a community of like-minded individuals, the camaraderie of shared victories and disappointments, a sense of power and accomplishment, and a feeling of personal identity. The relationships most of us have built are for the main part, business- or work-related. Once you retire, the lunches with colleagues, the outings don't happen anymore. How will you fill your days? How will you use two or three decades? Being bored and having nothing to do, is debilitating, emotionally, physically, and mentally.

You probably know someone who retired in good health only to fall seriously ill soon after retirement. It's a feeling of not being needed, of being pushed aside as the world goes by. A life of ease became a life of disease. The challenge of the corporate world followed by an abrupt cut-off in responsibility and a reason for being, often leads to a post-retirement life expectancy of twelve months or so. Charlie, the hard working senior vice president who ran a small bank, had a massive heart attack 11 months after retirement and died. He could see nothing but a void in his life. Charlie didn't replace the satisfaction of his career with another activity that might have provided a similar challenge and lasting satisfaction.

If your capacities do not find an outlet, if your energies do not find an expression, if your creativity shrinks, if your powers of thought lose their vitality, then your enthusiasm and interest in life vanish. Left behind is a sensation of emptiness and restlessness. With nothing to do, life becomes monotonous and empty of purpose. Often facing emotional crises, even depression, such events affect more than the retiree; his family can also be plunged into upset. Physical problems mount, leading to disease and disability.

Some stop looking forward to the future. Things close in on them physically and emotionally. Eyesight is fading; teeth are falling out; hearing is receding. Movement of the body is harder. Joints begin to lock up. Memory starts to decline. Breath struggles after climbing the stairs. Emotionally they're depressed and worn out. Suffering from one ailment after another, the highlight of their week often consists of visits to a variety of health care specialists in the quest for the latest therapies and drugs for an ever-growing list of maladies.

Ask yourself: Are the best years of my life ahead of or behind me? Are ambitions and dreams in my past or my future? What a tragedy if you think you're just biding your time until you die and that life has passed you by.

Some retired to a life of leisure-oriented activities, such as golf. Some ate and drank their way through the country-club scene. Having deferred their gratification, they wanted to take their turn to play.

For the affluent leisure-class, retirement living became a decade-long (or perhaps two) cocktail party. Here's the guys drill nearly every weekday, weather permitting. After breakfast at home, Marty and his three pals met at the club and conversed through the morning. At about 11:15, they began checking their watches because at 11:30 they could have their first cocktail. After one or two drinks, it's on to lunch and a 1:30pm tee time. Then it's home, a new round of drinks, and dinner with their wives, followed by spending the evening viewing TV sitcoms.

They did not search for and thus could not identify their inner calling. They satisfied their craving by devoting themselves to a search for pleasure be it golf or alcohol. Pleasure, they felt, would fill the gap in their life, eliminate its emptiness and give them something to live for. Most found that the fascination with a life of mere pleasure did not last because, generally speaking, a life filled solely with pleasure does not stimulate one's spirit, it does not animate one's mind, and it does not enrich one's personality. Rather, a life of mere pleasure often tires the heart and stupefies the senses and faculties. A variety of even greater pleasures become necessary to make life attractive and interesting. But in the end, those who sought mere pleasure as something to live for, generally met with deep disappointment.

Feeling that their achievements were made, there was nothing left but to wait for the end of one's days. With such an outlook on life, there was no inspiration, no ambition, and no action. Emotions no longer swayed and dreams no longer stirred. Advanced age became a period of stagnation and dreariness, a period of decline and self-resignation, a period of helplessness and wretchedness, a period devoid of effort and creation, a period in which accumulated weaknesses broke out and debilitated the body and mind.

My stepfather and his peers, such as Marty, who followed traditional retirement patterns, failed to see that one must keep on growing, otherwise one withers away. Our being does not tolerate stagnation. They became bored and then boring. Their boredom sometimes led to self-destructive behavioral patterns, such as alcoholism and other forms of substance abuse.

THE NEW RETIREMENT AND THE NEED FOR LONGEVITY PLANNING

Longevity has increased, the aging process has slowed. Men in the United States, who reach age 65 can expect to live, on average, 17.4 more years. You will have a lot of time on your hands. Don't underestimate the length of your "retirement." More and more of us will see our retirements last twenty, if not thirty, years. When you realize that your retirement will last that long you need a longevity plan for the long-term. Don't approach retirement as you would a two-week vacation.

For most of us, the extra years can be productive, not enfeebling. With enhanced existential, emotional, physical, and financial well-being, your advanced years will be far more active and energetic than your father's and grandfather's lives.

Do not regard the period of advanced age as a period of rest. Do not say to yourself: "I have worked enough, now I must retire and withdraw from life." Do not surrender your dreams or passions. Boredom and a sense of uselessness present huge problems in retirement.

Many are creating a new definition of retirement. I call it revitalizing. They view themselves as entering an exciting, new phase of life. They want to be productive, rather than risk being bored. As Jim, age 66, put it: "I want to be useful." They have high expectations about the future and want to tap into their potential. Many want to make the transition to something new, productive, and creative. There may be second and third careers, or a series of volunteer activities. They have no desire for retirement filled with watching television or one soaked in libation.

In the revitalization process, seek balance and set aside time for fun, as you define it. You may continue to engage in outdoor leisure activities, such as golf, fishing, or boating. Or, you may want to travel everywhere, taking cruises and soft adventure trips, such as safaris.

In addition to pursuing these traditional retirement patterns, more and more baby boomers as well as retirees see that life demands that each of us, gifted with powers for action and thought, use our abilities. Retirement is changing, reflecting a more proactive mindset. We look to set new goals, to start new activities, to be involved and productive. Regularly strive to include an enjoyable activity that gives meaning and purpose to your life.

Many of us don't equate retiring from work with retiring from life. To be productive and engage in purposeful activities, activities that provide meaning, we want to remain active, at least on our own schedule, not the 24/7 existence some had been living. We want to think less of recreation and more of re-creation. We want to be free to do what we love for as long as we're able, often combining our weeks with both fun-filled endeavors and stimulating, productive activities. Only you can arrive at the best mix for you.

Phil, at 79, a former public relations consultant, fills his days with: creative endeavors— painting and music; learning—philosophy, foreign languages, and religions of the world; and leisure —working out daily, horseback riding, and scuba diving. Wherever he goes, the young, the middle-aged, and the very old, seek him out. The shared love for various, exciting pursuits provides a common ground. He finds that there aren't sufficient hours in the day for all his interests and involvements. His home is filled with books, paintings, and CDs. His car is crammed with his foreign language and music CDs and tapes. In retirement, he has jammed several lifetimes into one. He expresses the familiar refrain: "I am so busy. I don't know how I ever had time to work".

The great increase in well-educated, more affluent seniors, drives, in part, the desire to remain active, engaged, and vital. Also, the perceived deficiencies in the traditional retirement patterns play a role. We don't want to lead a life of mental irrelevance and intellectual stagnation.

By offering concisely and in one place the four pillars of well-being for men in retirement—existential, emotional, physical, and financial—, this book provides you with guideposts for fulfillment. This book will help point the way for your revitalization—a new you. It will help design a longevity plan for the life you want to live that goes far beyond the typical money-crunching retirement planning. It reflects the need for a more holistic approach to living in your senior years, integrating one's aspirations, emotional and physical well-being, and concerns about money.

You will see how to develop: your existential, emotional, physical, and financial wellness.

Your *existential wellness* focuses on continued productive activity in your quest for meaning in your life. Part of your longevity plan must focus on the purpose for your retirement years.

Ask yourself: Who am I and what do I want to do with the rest of my life that may span decades? How can I discover what I want to do, not what I must do or what others are doing? What will make me happy, what will renew my energy, give me new challenges, and provide me with a sense of purpose? What would I do if I could start fresh? How can I align myself with my life's purpose?

Some know exactly how they want to spend their time. Most, however, need to think about and discover what they want to do. It begins with each of them discovering their dreams or passions in more structured manner. They can then search out their values, strengths, motivators, and personal characteristics so they can achieve their dreams or passions. It may take years to settle on a longevity plan for the non-financial aspects of your retirement. You need to find the intersection between what you're passionate about and what you do really well.

It is never too late to start life over again, by discovering your dreams or passions, thereby finding your life's purpose. For most of us, the traditional retirement activities, by themselves, cannot define the meaning of our life. It is never too late to recharge one's life. When you start over again, you live over again. A new world can stretch before you, filled with new ideas, new joys. When you start all over, you have the opportunity to be remade all over.

With good emotional and physical health, in my experience, those most satisfied in retirement are actively and regularly engaged in one or more meaningful and fulfilling endeavors—work, entrepreneurship, volunteering, learning, or creativity, in addition to the traditional retirement pursuits. However, in most cases, productive activity makes them feel relevant, needed, connected. Wanting to live life to the fullest, your reinvention can be sequential. You can continually revitalize yourself. You have so many choices; the options are wide open.

Your *emotional wellness* centers on being more optimistic about the possibility for positive change—the best is yet to be and looking forward to getting up in the morning, more serene by lowering your stress, anger and envy levels, and more loving and forgiving.

This book emphasizes the mind-body connection, the links between your thoughts and your emotional and physical health. If you're in good emotional and physical health, most of your advanced years will be as enjoyable and productive as your earlier days. It will be a reasonably normal time physically, for a number of years, rather than an extended period of decrepitude. Advanced age can be a time for continued achievement and well-being.

Your *physical wellness* connotes managing your physical health—your body and your brain—through nutrition, exercise, and pursuing an active lifestyle.

Few of us hope merely to survive. We worry about losing our physical health and/or our mental abilities. We want to avoid disease and disability (as well as lessen the risk factors for disease and disability) and maintain high physical and cognitive functioning. Successful aging involves being physically able to maintain our independence, able to move about on our own. Whatever the genetic hand you've been dealt, this book will help you experience many years without infirmity or decrepitude.

We want to remain mentally alert, able to remember, to reason, to express our thoughts and emotions. Longevity is a waste if your body is healthy, but you're not mentally alert and suffer from dementia, in one of its various forms. If the mind becomes flabby, the flesh becomes flabby. When the mind becomes weak, the body becomes weak.

Living healthfully adds years to your life and adds life to your years. You can keep yourself well and able to enjoy life far longer than you otherwise might have.

Your *financial wellness* focuses on implementing a sound investment and withdrawal strategy for your retirement accounts and other investments as well as leaving a financial legacy, regardless of whether you're well-to-do, financially comfortable, or have modest savings.

A secure retirement needs a sound financial base. Many of us worry about running out of money before we run out of life. Decisions you made decades ago determine your current financial status. You've probably come to terms about your financial resources. This book will help you maximize them.

Financial factors play a role in longevity planning. Although money serves as a key part of any longevity strategy, it can't be just about money. Most of us don't want to be glued to financial news channels on television, checking markets online and trading hourly, refiguring one's net worth every evening, another familiar retirement calling. Following the easy, straightforward approaches contained in this book, you can secure your financial well-being. You then can ask (and hopefully answer) a far more basic question: How am I going to use the extra years given to me? What will provide fulfillment and fun over the decades? You must plan for your well-being far beyond your finances.

Although most of us focus on getting ready financially, an important component of this book, you must also get ready emotionally and physically. To a degree, happiness in retirement is linked with the financial wherewithal and preparedness for whatever retirement lifestyle you want. With longer life expectancies, you must focus on the existential, emotional, and physical aspects of retirement, not merely the financial element. Although financial and estate planning is important, successful retirement preparation and implementation of a longevity strategy involves more than monetary questions. Spend as much, if not more time, thinking about your existential, emotional, and physical wellness as you do preparing for your financial well-being. Partly it's about money, but more it's about how are you going to structure your time and live your life.

For most of us, retirement will not simply unfold on its own. Most of us don't have a vision, a dream for our longevity. Retirement is a blank slate. The unarticulated assumption is that once you're there, you'll figure out what retirement is supposed to be.

This book will help you fill the void as you prepare to retire and after you retire. Combining fun with productive activity will point the way to living to a ripe, old age.

As part of a strategic approach to an active life, what I call revitalization in all of its dimensions—existential, emotional, physical, and financial—this book will help you come up with your unique longevity plan, one that is both resilient—able to weather changes—and nimble. Recognize that your plan will evolve as you test ideas, discard things, and as your goals change.

Retirement today describes a time in your life filled with possibilities and opportunities. You will eventually retire in the traditional sense—withdraw from life—but at a much later age and in a more contemporary style with a period marked by physical and/or mental frailty and decline that hopefully will be short.

But for as long as possible, don't withdraw, rather renew and recharge yourself. Have fun and enjoy yourself, but seek a balanced life and strive to revitalize. It's a time for new beginnings. There is no one best or right retirement for everyone. It's your retirement. It's a second chance to rediscover yourself and launch a new you.

I. Existential Wellness: Find Meaning and Purpose In Your Life So You Can Be Young At Eighty and Ninety

Some at sixty-five feel old. They see themselves on the downward slope of life, anticipating weakness and inactivity, becoming irritable, discontented grumpy old men, looking longingly to the past and facing the future with foreboding or resignation. When they resign themselves to their condition or circumstance, they declare their unwillingness or inability to battle it. In their resignation, they surrender their self-confidence, their self-assertion, accepting debility and feebleness as part of their longevity. They see much dreariness in their environment, much weariness in their life.

This approach stems from the erroneous opinions they foster on themselves. It is a misapprehension of age and of human time. Sixty-five, the traditional retirement age, does not represent a landmark of old age. It does not signal the traditional weakness from one's youthful days.

Even at eighty many can remain active, but less so. They settle into a routine, with much of the same activities as in the first phase of retirement, but at a less frenetic pace. Although the body may begin to slow down somewhat, age eighty does not necessarily mark an entrance into a state of infirmity and decrepitude. Life at eighty often continues with vigor and well-being. A new attitude can change the misconception of years, obliterating the difference between one's advanced days and one's youthful days.

1

There exists far more danger in rest then in productive activity. Your energies follow the law of supply and demand. If you do not use your energies, they recede. If you call upon them, they become replenished.

By keeping your interests in life constantly alive, you will be forever young, even at age ninety. By keeping your aspirations constantly in action, your enthusiasm aflame, and your mind at work—you will find nearly perpetual energy.

Your unique human potential can blossom. You can discover and pursue your unique capabilities. You can be active in designing your destiny in your 60s, 70s, and 80s. You can push "old age" out of your lingo.

Ask yourself: what do I really want out of life? What will nourish my spirit? In addition to fun endeavors, most of us want to spend our days engaged in enjoyable activities we find satisfying and absorbing. We want to fulfill our dreams, passions, and values and engage in activities we see as "useful," as each of us defines it. Building on our strengths and drivers, we want to feel we're good at something and motivated. We want to have a sense of purpose—whether it's working, being an entrepreneur, volunteering for a cause, continuing our quest for knowledge, returning to a long-neglected hobby, or fulfilling our creativity.

This part of the book focuses on your existential wellness—your quest for meaning and purpose in your life. You'll ask and answer difficult questions: who am I? Where am I going with my life? Why am I here? What do I want to be remembered for? It's an effort to discover and articulate your purpose and mission in life and claim them. Be patient. Give yourself time. Finding a calling that exists only for you, one that only you can fulfill, you'll be able to say: "I believe that I'm doing the thing for which I was created."

Building a successful retirement turns, in part, on deliberately searching out your dreams, passions, values, strengths, motivators, and personality characteristics. This part of the book will help you devise a longevity plan that is consistent with your dreams, passions, and values; one that puts your strengths to work; one that satisfies your drivers and is supported by your personality characteristics. You'll learn to contemplate the obstacles to your plan and how to work around them. With a flexible longevity plan, it's a time to experiment, free from previous constraints. You can find activities and organizations where you can excel and find satisfaction. Your longevity plan will help you make more effective choices.

Advanced years can be a time of clearer reflection and more acute judgment. Free from the passions which overshadowed one's vision, from the frivolities that disturbed one's judgment, you can rise above your daily environment and take a more panoramic view of life—your life—and take in the higher, more subtle joys of life.

1. DISCOVER YOUR DREAMS, PASSIONS, AND VALUES

What to do next after leaving a job or a career? How can I find enjoyable pursuits that I will experience as meaningful and purposeful? These questions nag many of us both before and after retirement.

Increasingly, what one does—beyond traditional leisure activities, travel, and spending time with family and friends—defines contemporary retirement. Many look to setting new goals, starting activities, being involved. Why? We're living much longer and stronger. If you retire at age sixty-five, for instance, you may look forward to fifteen, even twenty years, of decent health and productive capabilities. With longer, healthier life expectancies you must focus on how to channel your energies. It's a time to experiment and try new things.

The baby boomers on the cusp of retirement have grown up with generally positive images of retirement. They want their retirement to be special. They see retirement as a transition, a moving towards an even better future rather than an undefined something or a period of decline. Many want to be involved in meaningful and productive activities.

When one leaves a job or a career in favor of leisure, after awhile one often lacks intellectual stimulation and challenge. Often missing are other factors that contribute to happiness and satisfaction, such as a sense of purpose and day-to-day interaction with others. You may miss: the challenges and the camaraderie of work; the way you had lunch with colleagues and talked about the ball game or the weekend; the regular, reliable routine; the status and the respect from others; the feelings of importance and usefulness; and the satisfaction from one's accomplishments. Many want to stay active and be meaningfully connected to the world, rather than merely engaging in leisure-oriented pursuits, surfing websites, or playing computer games.

In your search for opportunities that afford self-expression and self-actualization don't envy your neighbor's or friend's retirement. Revitalizing is an individual process. Although learning from others, don't look to others for direction. Be true to yourself.

Self-knowledge represents the key to finding out how to live life to the fullest. Use self-knowledge to discover: your deepest needs; prioritize options; make sound choices; decide what to continue and what to drop; and help define the trade-offs.

SEARCHING FOR MEANING AND PURPOSE IN YOUR LIFE

Nearly all of us seek to find our bliss that will enable us to use to our strengths and motivators to contribute to our personal growth and development as well as attain fulfillment in life. Ask yourself: Do I have a specific mission in life that I have not already accomplished?

Each of us needs to discover his bliss, his destiny. The more clearly you follow your life's purpose—what you understand to be your unique function here on earth: being, relating, producing, and creating—the more your advanced years will have meaning for you. The more successful and happier these years will be for you.

Following the insights of psychiatrist and existential philosopher, Viktor E. Frankl, a prisoner in Nazi concentration camps, we can discover meaning in life by: the attitude we take to unavoidable suffering; experiencing something or encountering something; or creating a work or doing a deed.[1] Frankl concluded that survival was more likely for those who tried living in a meaningful way, even in an impossible situation. He identified survivors of the Holocaust as individuals who had a sense of life-meaning and purpose.

In the preface to the 1984 edition of his classic work, *Man's Search for Meaning*, Frankl wrote that he "had wanted simply to convey to the reader by way of a concrete example that life holds a potential meaning under any conditions, even the most miserable ones."[2] Apart from luck, survival in the camps often rested on finding meaning, even in the senseless suffering where goals in life were snatched away. In Auschwitz, some prisoners were able to discover meaning in their lives, if only in helping one another through the day, however difficult. Those discoveries gave them the will and the strength to endure.

More generally, Frankl wrote, we strive and struggle for a "worthwhile goal, a freely chosen task." Each of us needs "the call of a potential meaning waiting to be fulfilled..." and "the man who has to fulfill it."[3] He continued, "Everyone has his own specific vocation or mission in life to carry out a concrete assignment which demands fulfillment. Therein he cannot be replaced, nor can his life be repeated. Thus, everyone's task is as unique as is his specific opportunity to implement it."[4]

Discovering one's purpose in life has a practical aspect, namely, better physical health. One study that followed 12,460 middle-aged (45-64) Hungarians found that those who felt their lives had meaning had much lower rates of cancer and total mortality than did those who did not feel this way.[5]

Each of us, I believe, needs to discover his own purpose in life. Ask yourself: What is my personal calling, my reason for being alive, my ultimate concern, the meaning for my life, the legacy I wish to leave?

In retirement, you want to live life to the fullest in relation to the people and circumstances around you. You want to make sound choices and seek quality experiences. Formulating your life purpose provides meaning to your life and inspires your life's daily activities. Having a life purpose generates your commitment to the loftiest reaches of your potential. But only you can find meaning in your life. No one can tell you what your purpose is.

Make the effort to articulate your purpose in life. Some examples: your relationship to your wife (or significant other); your relationship to your children and grandchildren; finding creative endeavors; maintaining sound emotional and physical health; contributing by giving back to your community; being grateful and appreciative.

What's your mission—your calling—in life? Some have a genetic aptitude or signature strength so obvious, for example, in sports or music, that their answer to the question—what's your calling—turns on developing that aptitude or strength to its fullest.

Some have found a calling, a purpose in life, so that their daily existence becomes an expression of their loftiest hopes. If your career is so exciting and gratifying and it is what you want to do the most, keep at it. You can banish the word "retirement" from your vocabulary.

Examples abound of those who have found an activity that fulfills their inner life's desires.

Chris, a world-renowned physician, is now 71. At age 66, he phased down his clinical practice by one day a week and became the editor of the leading journal in his medical specialty.

Some professors, like Walt, can't seem to put their yellowing notes or PowerPoints behind them. They have found their life's goal in teaching and research. At age 75, Walt continues to enjoy teaching undergraduate and graduate business students.

Those who are so fortunate want to die with their boots on (or their fingers poised on their keyboards) in a longstanding career. They have found their niche and don't want to leave it. They may continue to pursue their calling, doing as much or as little as they choose.

For others, their careers may not only fulfill their inner desires but also their needs for status and power. Following the die-in-the-saddle model, they too will work until they expire slumped over at their desks.

Roger, an attorney, is now 90 years old. Following his service as a high-ranking, federal government appointee, he founded his own law firm some forty years ago. After his daily morning swim, he continues to go to the office nearly every weekday. Although his billable hours are not as high as they once were, he remains professionally active as a wise counselor-at-law, and in pro bono endeavors. Mentally keen as ever, he also sits on several corporate boards, including one of a major corporation, where he secured an age-waiver to continue his directorship.

Others continue to pursue a career as a source of identity. Bob at age 77 continues as a money manager and wealth advisor. He would expire if he didn't have his career as an identity badge.

Some stay in harness for less noble reasons, for instance, to earn money to pay for spending proclivities. Perhaps they have found their mission in life, but probably not. They remain on a treadmill, never stepping back and asking: "Is this meaningful to me?"

Don, a journalist by profession, gravitated to public relations. Candidly admitting he has no hobbies, no interests outside of work, at age 69 he soldiers on to pay for a new luxury car, extensive home renovations, and costly furniture.

For others, continuing to work may serve as an escape from troubling issues, such as difficulties with their wives. Facing mandatory retirement at age 65 and being forced out of his partnership at a large law firm, Sam went to a smaller firm. A decade and a half later, at age 80, he continues to work five days a week. He does it to be out-of-the-house and escape from his wife.

Some keep working to keep busy and avoid boredom; others for financial reasons. The extra income helps. They continue working part-time to supplement their Social Security benefits and the income from their meager retirement savings, like Carl, a retired UPS driver, who now drives a taxi three days a week.

As nest eggs shrunk, house prices fell, and anxieties about one's financial future grew in the second half of 2008, more of the oldest members of the baby boomer generation put off planning to leave the office. They postponed their retirement from age 62, to 65 or even 70. Working longer will give them more time to rebuild their 401(k) plans, obtain bigger Social Security benefits, and reduce the amount of time they need to depend on their depleted retirement savings. They need a work-life combination that allows them to find the balance they desire, while providing the necessary income for the lifestyle they want.

Some stay, even if their job isn't the greatest, because the accomplishment they derive can provide a limited sense of purpose. However, they experience a passion drift in hanging on for four more years as Ned does to secure a government pension. They feel discontented and lack a sense of mission in their lives.

Others were (or are) fixed in a job they never set out to do. They missed their calling early in life or didn't explore the possibilities. Somehow they drifted into a job decades ago and remained stuck in it. For many, as they approach or enter retirement, it's a time of choice. They want to change careers and do something different and unlock their latent potential. They sense a mismatch between their strengths and the needs of the organizations they serve. They want to be free from the draining drudgery and the stressful tasks. They want to shed their old life, become who they want to be and choose what activities they will engage in. They search for a purpose to be served by living out the rest of their lives. They ask: what is the essence of my life, my inner purpose, the central theme to bind my advanced years around? In addition to traditional leisure-oriented endeavors, such as golf or travel, many want a productive activity on their own terms that not only is interesting and personally fulfilling, but also makes a difference in the world by being of service and contributing to the betterment of others.

At 65, Fred went into mandatory retirement from serving as a president of a major foundation. Today, at age 73, he describes his retirement as grandfather not only for his own grandchildren, but also for the succeeding generations, worldwide. He continues to consult with various foundations, engage in numerous volunteer activities, focusing on environmental sustainability, and write.

Retirement may, if you choose, free you from your well-known identity. You're free to take up a new self and find fresh challenges and connections. You can blossom and open up your untapped resources, for example, by experiencing a burst of creativity.

If you feel your mission in life is a vital one, it becomes an endless one and there is always more before you than you have already done. It is far better (and easier) to do something rather than merely killing time. The purpose of life, at every stage of your existence, is not to rest, but to grow and develop.

You can invoke and stimulate the great and inexhaustible resources within yourself and utilize them. You can come up with your unique personal calling and find a new sense of purpose by discovering your dreams, passions, and values.

DISCOVERING YOUR DREAMS OR YOUR PASSIONS

You want to live a full and meaningful life. Retirement is a major transition. Do not drift. It can be a rebirth of freedom—to a new life—to pursue your heart's desires. You want to live the rest of your life in the best possible way, as determined by who you are and what you want out of life.

Baby boomers and younger generations want and need to continue to pursue productive activities long after previous generations retired. In short, they want what Marc Freedman, the founder and chief executive of Civic Ventures, a San Francisco nonprofit focused on expanding the contributions of older Americans, calls an "encore career." It's not merely a retirement job between the completion of one's working life and the start of retirement. Rather as a significant body of work, entailing perhaps one or two decades, it involves a "search for new meaning and a deep desire to contribute to the greater good . . .but work that people can genuinely look forward to and be proud of — [it] isn't just a financial necessity, but a fundamental aspiration."[6]

Do not retire from pursuing your dreams or passions. For the moment you do, you may shorten your days. You begin to seal your own end when you tell your body and your brain that they have labored enough and it is time for them to lapse into a passive existence. If you're emotionally and physically healthy (topics covered in Parts II and III of this book), your active brain and your creative energies cannot find happiness in inactivity.

You may retire from your job or career, but not from productive activity. You need to continue to be productive and to grow and develop. Put forth your efforts and expand your energies to use your inherent powers towards your utmost growth and development. You attain happiness when you have some ideals to attain, some knowledge to discover, something to build and achieve, something to add to the world. The growth of your mind and spirit is infinite. The dimensions of your mind and the height of your spirit are not circumscribed, whatever your age. There is always a higher level not attained; loftier ideals to be realized and greater knowledge to be mastered. No matter how old you are, you can still grow and develop.

Researchers have discovered numerous links between post-retirement careers and physical health. Those that stay busy and productive in their older years generally enjoy better health. The longer you continue working, the better for your health. A study of men and women born in 1920-1921 shed light on the impact of work on longevity. The participants joined the study at age 70 and were followed for 7 years. Controlling for self-assessed health, education, illnesses, functional dependency, and pre-existing economic difficulties at the beginning of the study, among other factors, researchers found that work emerged as a major determinant in whether an individual was still alive. Those who continued to work at age 70 and beyond were more than twice as likely to be alive at age 77 as those who retired and were not working at the beginning of the study. Work also correlated with better health and greater independence.[7]

If you like your career, try to keep on working. If you don't like your job, find something meaningful that keeps you alive. By finding a productive activity, you will gain health and life.

Most of us don't need to rest in our retirement. Generally, today our bodies are not physically worn out from hard labor. We want to continue our active lifestyle, staying vital, revitalizing, and not retiring in the traditional mode.

We want intellectual stimulation and engagement in life. We want meaningful, productive activities. We want to strike a balance between productive activity and play.

The most successful revitalizers don't give up pursuing their dream, no matter what their chronological age. It's never too late to chase a goal and follow your bliss in a far less inhibited manner than previously, free from convention and less approval-seeking of others.

You may know your deepest needs intuitively or you may need to discover what is meaningful to you in a more systematic manner.

Some have had a clear sense of their calling since their youth that for one reason or another they never pursued. After slogging through a series of dead-end jobs in his twenties, Frank McCourt, a best-selling author, heard a small voice in his head saying, "Don't settle for less. Find what you love and do it." Putting aside his first choice, writing, he settled for thirty years of public school teaching, his second choice. He had no time or energy at the end of the day to write. After retiring, he put pen to paper and wrote *Angela's Ashes* at age 64, the novel he had thought about for years. His book not only became a best seller but also catapulted McCourt into prominence on television. He continued: "The world was shocked to learn that I was 66. Wow! Sixty-six, but not stuck looking at the ocean in Florida! My generation—and the ones behind it—took notice. Look at this guy: 66, touring the country, yakking about his life, working on other books."[8]

McCourt recalled that the idea of writing about his miserable childhood in Ireland was one of the main "abscesses" in the back of his mind for years. He noted, "If I hadn't written Angela's Ashes, I would have died howling." Also, if what happened to him in retirement, namely, writing two best sellers, *Angela's Ashes* and *Tis*, the latter describing his struggle to gain a foothold in New York, and winning a Pulitzer Prize, had happened when he was 35 or 40 years old, he cautioned, "I would be dead on whiskey and fornication."[9]

Others, like McCourt, found their passions later in life. My Uncle Dan retired at age 65 as a national sales manager of a major consumer electronics corporation. After some forty years in sales, he found his "psychic bank account" fully depleted. After recovering from a heart attack, soon after retirement, he rediscovered his passion for animals. He volunteered at a local animal shelter, finding good homes for pets and serving on its board of directors.

To help unearth your dreams or passions, think back to your high school and college years. What were your career interests at that point? Which ones remain unfulfilled?

Between my junior and senior years at college, when the world was bright with possibility, I seriously contemplated four careers: attorney, academic, rabbi, and business executive. Having pursued the first two, the first right after college, and the second, some ten years later, in my early fifties, I focused on the third. I started planning fifteen years before "retiring" (or as I prefer, transitioning) at 65.

My interest in becoming a rabbi stemmed not only from decades of interest in Judaism but several negative factors. Over the decades, I saw what I call neo-traditional Judaism gaining momentum. Even within the "progressive" strand of Judaism, neo-traditional Judaism came to focus on more and more Hebrew in worship services and an increasing emphasis on ritual. Although Hebrew links Jews to their ancient history, it is not our native language here in the United States. While pleasing to a few, worship in Hebrew, in my view, failed to provide a meaningful worship experience for most Jews. Neo-traditionalists also seek to promote the observance of Jewish rituals, both inside and outside houses of worship. They want Judaism to again become synonymous with an almost endless performance of rituals, particularly with respect to observing the Sabbath and the dietary laws. Yet, for most Jews, rituals are the byways of Judaism, not its highways. Finding little value in rules for their own sake, the indecipherable and the rigid rites are for many spiritually choking, an empty shell, resting on tradition, nostalgia, and idealized memories of "the old country" and one's ancestors. Beyond my dissatisfaction, I had a desire to serve others and a sense of calling to try in some way to reorient Judaism from what I saw as an otherwise empty future.

I found a seminary that met my spiritual interests and gained ordination as a rabbi and an interfaith minister. I chose one of the most popular fields: training for the ministry, where experience and age earn respect. I could also pursue it part-time by officiating at life cycle events, such as weddings, funerals, and baby namings, while continuing my academic-consultant-writer career.

You may want to consider paths previously not taken or those you ceased exploring, years ago. Think back to high school, college, even decades ago, what did you want to do? Was it always the same? What other adventures appealed to you? What past activities have given you pleasure, a sense of satisfaction that made you feel at your best? What activities in life have you never had time for, but always wanted to pursue? What do you really want to do now? Try to be as specific as possible.

UNLOCK YOUR DREAMS

Ask yourself: What is my unique dream? What is it I've always wanted to do but thought I couldn't? What is purposive and valuable for my life? What is my visceral yearning? What is my optimal picture for my future years, perhaps combining fun and contributing in a productive manner?

The next exercise will help you unlock your dreams, your fantasies that you would like to fulfill so that you can truly live the life you want.

Unlocking My Dreams: My Perfect Life Exercise

Go to a favorite place where you won't be disturbed, a park, the beach, your car. Relax, close your eyes, let your feelings and thoughts flow, let your mind see what you want in the totality of your life in the future, including your personal life, your key activities, the important people you want to be connected to, whatever is of importance to you now and whatever you feel will be of importance to you in the future.

Imagine what your perfect life would be. Where are you? Who is with you? Who and what will provide you with meaning and happiness? How do you feel?

Listen to your inner self. Imagine your preferred future. How will you be at work, play, love, creative activities? What gives you boundless energy and makes you feel so good, passionately alive, joyful, serene, loving? What are your fantasies that you haven't done? If money were no impediment, what would you like to do?

Write down your thoughts and feelings in as much detail as possible. When an insight comes to you, gently open your eyes and write it down. Do it for yourself. Don't show your dream to anyone else. No one will criticize or evaluate what you write.

Remember that over the course of the next two or more decades, your dreams can change. You may want to do this exercise every five years or so.

What is your dream? In terms of future, productive activities, do you want to: start your own business, go back to school, become an AmeriCorps volunteer, open a bed and breakfast, invent a new product, teach at a college, write a novel. At this point, don't worry about the practicability of your dream or any obstacles.

Two other exercises can help you unlock your dreams.

My Dream Day: A Guided Visualization[10]

Visualization involves focusing your mind on a visual image, a thought directed to a desired goal — here your dream activity (or activities) — to project a better idea for yourself. In forming a mental image, you visualize what you desire to attain and outline in your mind what you want to achieve.

Introduction: You will need some paper and a pen nearby. Close your eyes, sit quietly, calm and relax your body, breathe in and out normally, feeling where the breath flows into and out of your body. Adjust the breaths so that the in and out breaths are the same length.

Imagine you're five years into the future, waking up on your dream day.

After you get up, go to your front door to get the newspaper. Today it contains an article about you.

Prepare your breakfast. Then open the newspaper to the page where the article appears.

In what section of the paper does the article appear?

What is the title of the article?

Look at your photograph accompanying the article. How are you dressed? What is the expression on your face? Are you with people or alone?

Read the article. What does the article say about you? What are your emotional reactions to the article? Write down several words about the article and your emotional response. Do these words suggest anything about your dream activity?

Concluding instructions. Now come back to the here and now. Take time to ease yourself back. Slowly bring back awareness into your body. Feel yourself back in the room and open your eyes.

Try another exercise focusing on the finiteness of life to discover your dreams.

Unlocking My Dreams: Finiteness of My Life Exercise

To help you focus on the important, lasting things in your life, ask yourself:

If I had only three months left to live, for instance, as the result of a rare, incurable disease for which there is no known treatment or surgical procedure, and money would not be an issue, what would I do with my last few months on this earth? What are my highest priorities? Write down your ideas.

What if I had two years to live? What would I want to do? Again, write down your ideas.

Compare your two lists. Note the things you wrote down more than once.

In using these exercises to discover your dreams, think big: People usually don't exert themselves for small goals. Imagine if the builders of the pyramids had opted for little sand castles.

With a goal in mind, you'll be better able to persevere in its pursuit. If your dreams are worth fighting for, be totally committed to them and be one hundred percent willing to jump in, fight for them and sweat it out, if necessary.

FIND YOUR PASSIONS

Although most of us have a dream, all of us, I believe, yearn for a passion, a feeling of a compelling nature. If you can't come up with a dream, what is your passion?

Start with your interests, current or deferred. Can you turn a hobby into a vocation? Do you want to work with your hands, to repair things, to build things?

What things grab your attention? What do you naturally migrate to? What really excites you? What do you care about most deeply? When on vacation what do you do?

Visit a bookstore and see what subjects interest you. Go to a newsstand and scan magazines and newspapers that fit your interests. If you don't have a passion, you may have an interest. Perhaps your interest will evolve into a passion.

What gives you energy? Physical things, mental things, outdoor things, things that involve animals, nature.

What enlivens your curiosity? What do you want to learn?

Who are your heroes? This may tell you about the person you want to be. What qualities or deeds do you admire in them?

Jerry ran a successful public relations firm. At age 62, he'd grown tired of the field. For years he thought about becoming a chef, his passion. He bought cookbooks and prepared elaborate meals for family and friends. Taking the leap, he enrolled at a culinary school, earned an internship at a premier restaurant, and ultimately landed a position at a fine-dining restaurant in his hometown.

Write out your passions for the next chapter on your life.

Discovering My Passions Exercise

To help you find your true calling, put your thoughts in writing. Go back over the key events and people in your life and how they made you feel. What places and things do you feel passionate about? Think about the time you felt best about yourself. What several days stand out in your mind? What were you doing and with whom? What made those instances special?

These lists are for you. You don't need to impress anyone or protect anyone else's feelings. Focus on yourself.

Spending thirty minutes and recording your thoughts and conclusions regarding your dreams or your passions in writing, I have found most useful. After you write down how you would like your retirement to be, step back and analyze it two days later. Is your perception of retirement based on reality? Do your dreams (or passions) mesh with your wife's (or significant other's)? Moving your residence to implement your golfing dream likely will not mesh with your wife's, who doesn't play golf, but desires to remain where you are and keep seeing regularly your grandkids and her friends.

Run a gut check. How do you feel about your calling? Are you emotionally ready to plunge in or are you riddled with doubt?

Set aside quiet time to listen to your inner self. The answer may come from a gentle nudge or intuition telling you to take a new direction. You may have a sense of guilt for not pursuing a childhood dream or passion.

Focus On Your Values

Beyond discovering your dreams or your passions, discern your values. Your values are integral to your worldview. To discover your deeply held beliefs again ask yourself: Who am I? Who do I want to be? What do I want as my legacy? By living true to your values you live true to yourself.

I met Ron, a hard-charging, smart, achievement-oriented, workaholic attorney, a Type-A bulldog, impatient, competitive, with an aggressive personality, when he was 63, facing mandatory retirement from his law firm in two years. He found his dream intuitively, focusing on his values. He was concerned about what he regarded as the "liberal" bias on many American campuses and the lack of intellectual diversity at America's colleges and universities, filled with trendy professors, who encouraged political correctness at the expense of intellectual rigor. Disgust filled his mind when he thought about how undergraduate and graduate school professors sought to indoctrinate students with what he regarded as anti-American, anti-business views.

His challenge centered on how to get tenured professors to re-embrace a culture of reasoned inquiry and meaningful debate. Beyond contributing money to non-profit "counterweight" organizations, Ron wanted to make a difference as a volunteer, before retirement, and later, in retirement. With his expertise in a particular legal-public policy area, he sought out student groups to sponsor him as a campus speaker. He paid his own expenses and did not seek an honorarium. He also began contacting university trustees, emphasizing the need for them to take the lead in assessing the problem at their own institution and coming up with appropriate, practical remedial steps.

Ask yourself: what really matters to me? What do I value most deeply? What activities enhance and nourish me and which do not? Remember: you are the only one on this quest. What issue is so important to you that you want to devote time to it? Do not borrow someone else's values. You want to come up with something you prize, something that has worth to you.

My Core Values Exercise

Create a written list of your five core values and how they relate to your dreams or your passions. Explain each one in a paragraph and rank them in importance to you. What changes do you need to make in your current lifestyle to live your key values?

Here are some values for you to consider:

Relational—family, friends. Do you want to connect totally with those around you, by reaching out, sharing yourself through caring, making relationships with others work? Do you want to be in love and sustain deep intimacy by renewing your marriage (or intimate relationship) by talking, touching, and caring for each other in new ways? Do you want to devote yourself to grandparenting, to loving and caring for your own grandchildren? Do you want to enhance your friendships and your bonds with others? Do you want to develop and sustain your own social network by maintaining relationships with others and building new ones?

Spiritual—prayer, meditation, faith. Do you want to search for meaning through spirituality and/or religion? If so, you want to follow your own spiritual path and develop your personal spirituality, listening to your inner self, or do you want to follow a specific religious tradition and be involved with one (or more) of its institutions?

Physical—your own health, diet and exercise. Do you want to do all you can to promote and maintain your physical health?

Education—study, self-improvement. Do you want to challenge your mind by continuing to learn and taking a fresh look at things?

Creative—self-expression for yourself or the public. Do you want to express yourself through being creative, imaginative, intuitive, original, humorous, curious, childlike, following your feelings? Are you open to new ideas? Do you want to be an innovator (or learning about innovation) in various fields, such as technology, healthcare, or education?

Cultural—visual and performing arts. Do you want to pursue and/or support cultural endeavors, including visual (art, sculpture, photography) and/or performing (music, dance, theatre, opera) activities as a participant and/or an observer?

Recreation—sports, hobbies, travel. Do you want to have fun, devoting yourself to your favorite past-times, such as sports, hobbies, or travel? Are you interested in genealogy? In history? Do you want to fix things, your home, your car? Do you want to devote yourself to gardening? To caring for animals?

Philanthropic—contribute time and money to others. Do you want to have a social impact and contribute to the general good, as you see it, by, for example, improving the quality of life in your community? Do you feel that life is not worth living if you cannot contribute to others' well-being? Do you want to live for the sake of benefiting humanity, by devoting yourself to the task of eliminating suffering, banishing misery, lightening the burden of the despondent, planting love in the hearts of the discouraged, holding out a hand to the distressed? If so, do you want to help and join in a cause (or causes) you believe in, thereby making a lasting contribution to humanity?

Public—community involvement, governmental service. Do you want to make a contribution to the greater good, to something larger than yourself — to your community, your state, the nation? Do you want to focus on developing and sustaining leadership roles for yourself (and/or others) in your community? What are your political-economic-social preferences? Do you favor more (or less) governmental intervention in the economy, more (or less) redistribution of income and wealth through taxation? What about human rights, environmental, racial, and gender issues?

Work—competence, meaningful achievement, excellence. Do you want to prove yourself through productive achievement, by maintaining and reaching clear goals and objectives, working on projects, gaining recognition and money, being purposive and doing? Do you seek validation and respect from others for your accomplishments? Do you feel a person should continue to work for pay or run a business as an entrepreneur for as long as he is able? Do you believe that older people who no longer work for pay or run a business as an entrepreneur ought to contribute through community service or other volunteer activities?

Emotional—kindness, compassion, inner peace, joyfulness. Do you want to give of yourself by being compassionate, doing good deeds (preferable anonymously), passing on your wisdom and knowledge to the next generation? Do you want to mentor, guide, sponsor, share your competence as a professional or businessman with younger persons in your field and/or as a human being with your children and grandchildren thereby linking generation-to-generation? Do you want to emphasize your self-mastery by building your self-esteem, confidence, and courage?

Economic—thrift, stewardship, financial responsibility. Do you want to continue accumulating money? Do you want to impart these character traits to your grandchildren, to others? Do you want to pass on a financial legacy by transmitting wealth to your children and grandchildren?

Personal—loyalty, integrity. Do you want to impart these character traits to your grandchildren, to others?

Ethical—fairness, justice. Do you want to make the world a better place, more equitable, just, peaceful, or environmentally-sound? If so, through volunteer or other activities?

Remember: Try to discover and stay value-driven. Remain anchored in your values. Try to bond with others through one or more organizations that support your basic beliefs.

Try to pull together your dreams (or passions) and your values. In your search for what is meaningful in your life, does a pattern emerge?

In retirement, Eric built furniture. It gave him a feeling of accomplishment. He did it for both self-satisfaction and for others. What started as a hobby for Eric, turned into a profitable business.

Larry, a physician, always wanted to be a cellist in an orchestra. In college, family pressure diverted him from following his dream. At age 60, he had accumulated sufficient wealth, paid for his grandchildren's college education, and paid off his mortgage. He treated his patients mechanically and saw his life as empty. One of his friend's grandchildren went to a summer music camp and played in a symphony there. Hearing about this, it awakened his old dream and he imagined himself there. Disengaging gradually from the active practice of medicine, he began to take lessons. Eventually, he auditioned and found a place for himself at a local orchestra. Although he missed his patients and the excitement of medicine, he found himself happier than ever before.

Ask your wife (or significant other) to develop her own list of dreams (or passions) and values. Your respective dreams (or passions) and values may be quite different. Some activities you may do together, others separately.

Follow your bliss and listen to your inner self, but try to balance feeling and fact. You may not find a "Eureka moment," when the perfect path unfolds before you, when you discover your life's dreams (or passions) and values at the very moment when life seems to be winding down. Keep trying. I call it your explorer year (or phase). Free from previous limitations, it's a time to experiment. If not now, when?

Beyond your dreams (or passions) and your values, you need to discover your strengths, motivators, and personality type and then formulate and implement a longevity plan which gives you a sense of purpose—a reason to get out of bed in the morning, something that gives you joy.

2. Identify Your Strengths, Motivators, and Personality Type and Then Formulate and Implement a Longevity Plan

Having thought about and written down your dreams (or passions) and values, if you're going to go about your revitalization in a more structured manner, you need to examine your strengths, motivators, and personality type. You then can pull it all together in a written longevity plan that will enable you to strive to achieve your goals.

You want your powers and facilities to find full expression. If you don't use your strengths and your drivers, your imprisoned forces will be in constant rebellion. They cry out for freedom, for expression. The suppression of your powers will result in irritation and unhappiness.

No two of us are alike. Each of us is endowed with specific, dominant strengths, drivers, and personality types.

Do not let your strengths and drivers lie dormant; exercise your will to bring them into full play. Apply to a task all the powers within you. By ardently cultivating your powers, the greater they will become. You will find within you previously hidden resources. Accomplishment blossoms and time flies by. You will say afterward, "That was a great day."

Discover Your Strengths

You need to identify your strengths and select an activity and find (or carve out) a role that will enable you to use these strengths daily.

In their pioneering book, *Now, Discover Your Strengths,*[1] Marcus Buckingham and Ronald O. Clifton distilled thirty-four themes of human talent that best explain the "broadest possible range of excellent performance."[2] In contrast to knowledge and skills that are learned, strengths are innate. Each strength is consistently replicable. It represents a "consistent near perfect performance in an activity."[3] When you use your strengths, you express yourself powerfully and effortlessly. You feel most alive, highly energized, and joyful.

Buckingham and Clifton maintain (and I agree) that you ought to maximize your strengths and not fix your weaknesses, but rather work around your weaknesses that get in the way of excellent performance. Each of us has a vast number of areas where weaknesses predominate.

Don't waste effort on improving these areas. You'll find it takes far more time and energy to go from incompetence to mediocrity than it takes to improve from first-rate to outstanding, using your strengths.

The Buckingham-Clifton book and *Strengths Finder 2.0*[4] by Tom Rath will help you identify your innate strengths.

The thirty-four strengths and their themes are as follows:

- achiever—seek achievement
- activator—want action
- adaptability—flexible, able to respond to the demands of the moment
- analytical—logical, objective, dispassionate
- arranger—want to figure out the best possible way to get things done by sorting out the variables to come up with best possible configuration
- belief—possessing and orienting one's life around a core set of values, often altruistic
- command—want to take charge and impose your views on others, confrontational
- communication—like to explain and describe
- competition—need to compete and win
- connectedness—want to be part of something larger, a considerate, caring bridge builder
- context—having a passion for the past
- deliberative—careful, identify and assess risks
- developer—want to help others achieve their potential
- discipline—want a predictable, orderly world
- empathy—sense others' emotions
- fairness—treat people the same
- focus—seek a clear destination
- futuristic—fascination with the future and its potential
- harmony—look for areas of agreement and try to hold conflict to a minimum
- ideation—fascination with ideas and connections
- inclusiveness—want to include people and make them feel part of a group
- individualization—intrigued by each person's unique qualities
- input—want to collect things

- intellection—like to think
- learner—love to learn and drawn to the process of learning
- maximizer—seek excellence
- positivity—generous with praise and look for the positive in every person and situation
- relator—pulled toward people you already know
- responsibility—follow through to completion
- restorative—problem solving
- self-assurance—faith in your strengths, abilities, and judgment
- significance—want to be recognized and stand out
- strategic—find the best route through the clutter
- woo—love the challenge of winning over others

For each strength, the Buckingham-Clifton and the Roth books detail the strength's qualities, with quotes from those who consciously use that strength, as well as ideas for how you can use that strength in action and how you can work with others who possess that strength.

Try to assess which of your dominant strengths you want to build on in your retirement. From the thirty-four strengths, the print or online Strength-Finder Profile assessment reveals five of the most dominant themes of talent—your signature themes—and how you can translate them into personal success. The assessment will help you identify the main strengths you can use to revitalize your life.

Building upon and utilizing your strengths will significantly increase your chances of having a successful and productive retirement. As you look at your strengths, ask yourself: do they travel to another field, industry, or the pursuit of a new objective?

DISCERN YOUR MOTIVATORS

Besides finding a calling in which you can express your values and employ your strengths, planning for retirement involves looking at what has served as past motivators for you. You want to feel engaged and challenged. Each of us is given the will, a driving power to apply the means to attain an end in order to actualize our dreams (or passions) and realize our values. For a successful and productive revitalization, you need to discern your motivators.

In their book, *Don't Retire, REWIRE!*,[5] Jeri Sedlar and Rick Miners, suggest thirty different ways you may have been motivated to act in your career and personal life in the past. Your motivators stay with you and remain an important part of your life, enabling you to match your deepest needs with your activities. They show you the sources of your emotional payoff that don't go away. Discovering your motivators forms one of the keys to satisfaction in retirement. By enabling you to make sound choices among activities, organizations, and commitments, implementing these motivators in your longevity plan will dramatically increase your plan's chance of success. These personal motivators, Sedlar and Miners call "drivers."

The thirty drivers in alphabetical order are as follows:

#1 Accomplishments—to have accomplishments
#2 Action—to be "part of the action"
#3 Authority—to be an authority figure
#4 Belonging—to have a sense of belonging
#5 Competition—to be competitive
#6 Creativity—to be creative
#7 Current—to be current or "in"
#8 Experiences—to have new experiences
#9 Friendship—to develop friendships
#10 Fulfillment—to be fulfilled
#11 Global—to have global opportunities
#12 Goals—to have and share goals
#13 Identity—to have an identity
#14 Intellectual Stimulation—to be with intellectually stimulating people
#15 Leadership—to be a leader
#16 Lifelong Learning—to be constantly learning
#17 Making a Difference—to help make the world better
#18 Mentoring—to mentor others
#19 Passion—to pursue a passion
#20 People—to have exposure to people
#21 Power—to wield power
#22 Prestige—to gain prestige
#23 Problem-Solving—to be a problem-solver

#24 Recognition—to be recognized

#25 Self-Esteem—to enhance self-esteem

#26 Skills and Talent—to develop skills and talent

#27 Social—to be connected to others

#28 Structure—to have structure

#29 Value—to give value to others or to be valued

#30 Visibility—to have visibility

Select your five most important drivers from this list and prioritize them. Look over your entire life, both professional and personal. Go through the list three times on different days. Go back and look at your values and strengths. Do your values, strengths, and motivators overlap?

KNOW YOUR PERSONALITY TYPE

Another type of assessment focuses on a personality inventory. The most well known, the Myers-Briggs Type Indicator may yield some valuable information for you. You may discover a mismatch between your dreams (or passions)-values-strengths-motivators and your personality type. For instance, an introvert will likely not achieve success as a salesman, nor will someone who cannot face rejection. Your strengths may be most stimulated in a social context. If so, you won't be happy as an isolated, solitary writer.

If you don't want to consult a professional to administer the Myers-Briggs Type Indicator, you can take the test on your own and get an interpretation of the results at www.mbticomplete.com. If you want a professional to administer and interpret the results, there are directories of career counselors at the websites for: National Board for Certified Counselors (www.nbcc.org) and National Career Development Association (http://associationdatabase.com/aws/NCDA/pt/sp/consumer_find).

Other personality assessments can provide useful information. You may want to try the Enneagram, an ancient Sufi teaching that describes nine primary personality types and their interrelationships. The nine personality types are as follows: Reformer, Helper, Achiever, Individualist, Investigator, Loyalist, Enthusiast, Challenger, and Peacemaker.

Your personality type forms the environment in which you live. A personality inventory, such as the Enneagram, or its most up-to-date version—The Riso-Hudson Enneagram Type Indicator, a personality test with 144 paired statements—helps you become aware of the ways in which your personality channels how you behave. It lets you see whether your instinctive response in a specific situation is in your best interests.

Remember: The various assessments are just a starting point for the difficult self-exploration and evaluation needed for your post-retirement revitalization. Ask yourself: what do I want to be when I grow up? You may find it later than others. It's not easy to navigate the elder passage and find the right mix of purpose and play. In optimizing your abilities and your potential, you want to be involved in activities that not only stir your energy and intellect, but also allow you time to enjoy life and enhance your significant relationships.

Your Longevity Plan

To begin to translate your dreams or passions (your *why*) and your vision (your *what*) into a reality, you need a plan—a step-by-step process—so that you can push forward to use your dreams (or passions), values, strengths, motivators, and personality type in a series of logical steps and events. In my experience, it is imperative to pull everything together in a written plan that will enable you to remain active, with sufficient mental, social, and physical stimulation.

Empowered by your self-discovery, you can begin to write a longevity plan to find and achieve your goals. Your plan may include traditional retirement activities, such as travel or being with your grandchildren, recreational activities, for example, golf, or creative activities, such as painting or singing in a chorus. By being self-directed and specific to you, you want your efforts to proceed with a focus on achieving meaningful goals that bring their own emotional reinforcements.

The process of planning (your *how*) is realistic, hardheaded, concrete, and time driven. A written plan will help you answer these questions: What are your goals? Be specific. Make your goals concrete. Describe them in detail. What are your most important action steps for each goal? What are your timelines for implementing each step and your ultimate goal? Try to keep the steps small so you don't let them overwhelm you.

Remember: a longevity plan is a living, evolving document. It's not etched in stone. You will likely need to reevaluate it frequently, say every three or six months. As an organic document, revise it if you face a new obstacle and add how you will overcome it. Parts of your dream or the stages and steps you have plotted may change.

You may want to create a list of the top things you want to do, such as adventure travel, while you're physically able. As the years pass and you look at and re-examine your list, you likely will see many checkmarks, some items crossed off, and new wishes added.

DETAIL THE BARRIERS

As part of your plan, note what hurdles currently stand between you and the realization of your dreams (or passions). What's the resistance—the obstacles—that causes you to be stuck.

Remember: The obstacles may be there for a reason. They enable you to prove how much you want something.

There are two types of barriers: internal and external. Begin by noting your internal barriers, the internal factors that make it difficult for you to reach your goals and feel good. The internal factors that may keep you from being your best include: fear of success (or failure); procrastination; perfectionism; too little money (or too much debt); emotional depression and hopelessness; substance abuse; anger; stress; low self-esteem; resistance to change; being disorganized; indecisive; laziness; being irresponsible with money; feeling victimized; feeling tired and overwhelmed.

In particular, do you fear taking a risk? Inertia often takes over and you wind up doing nothing. You fail only if you stand still. The doors not entered, the challenges not met, even in retirement, often lead to regrets in one's later years.

Ask yourself: how can I minimize the negative impact of each of these thoughts, beliefs, and habits, these self-generated fears that I can control, more or less. Challenge your negativity.

How realistic are each of these internal barriers? Also, don't use a lack of money as an excuse for not trying to live your dreams (or passions) and your values.

Next, consider your external barriers—the tangible difficulties—that impact you and reduce your effectiveness. These may include: your wife (or significant other) who disapproves and does not support you and your dreams (or passions) or who is resentful or envious; general economic conditions (recession, inflation); your location; your age; your need for education and training; licensing requirements; what others will think of your choice. Some, such as general economic conditions, are basically out of your control. However, for many of these external barriers, ask yourself: how can I change the way these factors reduce my effectiveness and impede attainment of my goals?

Anticipate obstacles, address resistors, and plan ways around them. Eliminate your ungrounded fears.

For each obstacle, whether internal or external, list the steps you will take to overcome it. I always like to tackle the most difficult barriers first. Once you overcome them successfully, the rest are easy to surmount.

Further Thoughts on Your Longevity Planning Process

Without a road map, you lack focus. You'll drift along until your dream seems out of reach. Here are eleven suggestions to guide your planning process:

<u>Write it Down</u>. Commit your tentative plan to paper, rather than relying on a computer or keeping it in your mind. For most of us, the act of writing is more significant than inputting a plan into a computer. Writing makes your dreams (or passions) tangible. Writing sets your goals firmly in your mind. Writing it out will likely make more of an impact.

<u>Prioritize</u>. Avoid being overwhelmed by all the things you wish to accomplish. Split your goals into stages: short-term (up to one year), medium-term (1-3 years), and long-term (more than 3 years). Set timeframes to focus your attention on the steps you need to take now. Put your goals on a timeline so you see how long it should take you to get from here to there.

<u>Start Now</u>. Even if you take small steps to start, take action now. Use a to-do list. But don't compare your progress to someone else's.

Ask yourself: What are the three most essential factors I need to do to achieve my calling? What are the three key limiting factors I need to overcome?

Remember: Don't let your days evaporate into too many responsibilities—whether it be volunteering, classes, or part-time work—many of which you wandered into by accident.

Ask yourself: What do I care about? What's personally satisfying for me? Do I want one or two anchors around which I can orient my week?

Set Deadlines. Create daily, weekly, monthly, and yearly benchmarks to measure your progress. What are the key activities you must complete each week? Strive to produce one measurable result, however small, each weekday, so that you bring your dreams (or passions) into reality.

Learning. List what you know and don't know about reaching your goals. List the ways to obtain the needed knowledge and make key contacts.

Learning, especially if you want or need a type of education or experience to fulfill your dreams (or passions) may enter into the mix. Consider: what new information do you need? What technical skills do you need? In what areas do you need to increase your personal competence? What are your best learning environments? Check out community colleges or look into trade schools where you can get the desired knowledge and skills in months, not years.

Ask For Help. Do you have a person and/or a support group you can turn to if internal barriers and/or external obstacles get in the way of your plans? Find support for your plan with relatives, friends, mentors, spiritual or other groups, or perhaps seek out a coach. Find several people who will give you enthusiastic, positive encouragement. Meet with them regularly to receive nudges, positive reminders. Hopefully, they can tell you the truth with love when it needs to be told. Make new connections through networking sites, such as LinkedIn (www.linkedin.com), or by joining online networking groups, such as ExecuNet (www.execunet.com) and The Financial Executives Networking Group (www.thefeng.org).

Identify potential mentors you know in the field and other effective information sources, such as individuals who have gone through a similar transition. Along the way, contact these individuals. Don't hesitate to ask if you need help. If approached properly, even busy, successful people, whom you do not know personally, will likely offer advice and assistance. Don't be afraid to ask. Be open to asking for help and stating: "I have a problem and I hope you can help me with it."

Devising and implementing a longevity plan is rarely a solitary endeavor. Don't be a loner in your quest. Enlist one or more mentors and supporters who can contribute their expertise and connections. Each of us likes to be asked for advice.

After ordination, I sought out a senior rabbi in my community who provided me with helpful information and subsequently, a steady stream of lifecycle referrals.

Internships and Apprenticeships. If you want to get a taste for a new field apply for a full-time or part-time internship so you can learn the language and the culture, gain new skills, and expand your network. Organizations, both for-profit and nonprofit, often seek unpaid interns, who are ambitious, with experience in other areas. Even as an explorer, you provide added value to an organization. Also, look for formal or informal apprentice programs. In seeking internships and apprenticeships, emphasize that your goal is knowledge, not money. You want a learning experience. Check out Internships (www.internships. com) and Interns Over 40 (www.internsover40.blogspot.com). Try out job sampling. Contact Vocation Vacations (www.vocationvacations. com), which arranges brief—two or three day—internships for people to try out dream jobs.

If you want to open a business, immerse yourself beforehand in the desired undertaking. Cultivate someone who owns a similar establishment. Spend time on the premises. Soak up the surroundings.

After committing your plan to writing, including the knowledge and skills you need to obtain, begin to take the first steps.

Don't Procrastinate. Procrastinators give up one day at a time. They move today's unwanted, often difficult tasks into the future. When the future catches up with them, events generally have passed them by. Time spent worrying about what might go wrong is less efficient than time spent doing something constructive.

Start several years before your formal retirement. Give yourself time to develop a second career, make contacts for a part-time consulting business, or get active in community affairs.

Do your homework. If you want to be a docent at your favorite museum, investigate before you retire. The museum may require a six-month, once-a-week training course before you can serve as a docent.

What is stopping you from completing an item? How will completing an unfinished item get you closer to living your dreams (or passions)? See how its incompleteness uses your mental energy. You want to release your energy to go forward. Confront your excuses.

Don't Be Indecisive. Moving forward despite your fears often takes guts. Acts of courage serve as milestones of persistence. Be willing to decide and move forward. Don't fear bombing or being a laughingstock. What your friends or relatives think of your goals isn't important. Consider, but don't be deterred by others' dire warnings. They may be speaking from their own feelings of insecurity and habitual negativity or from their deep-rooted fears of making any significant changes in their own lives.

Be Self-Reliant. Believe in yourself and your ability to follow through. Set achieving your goals as a top priority. If it isn't something you'll make sacrifices for, you won't continue to plow through when the going gets tough.

Be Disciplined. The force of will represents the ultimate success weapon. Strive to achieve your plan regardless of the length of time it takes.

THE IMPORTANCE OF YOUR FAITH AND YOUR WILLPOWER

You need faith in yourself that draws from the innermost powers within you and brings them into action. Have faith in yourself that whatever you set out to do, you can do, that you are here to achieve it, and that it is your mission in life. But remember once you have established your goals and have the faith to attain them, prepare yourself for arduous efforts and success ultimately will be yours.

Do not be afraid of failure. Fear of failure too often brings failure, at any stage of life. Do not enter your calling with doubt or hesitation, do not let forebodings grip you; otherwise you may doom yourself to failure. Have faith in your success and this faith will help you on your path to achievement. Thoughts become realities. Thoughts of success are essential to the acquisition of success. Think of success, aspire to success, work for success, have faith in your success and it will be yours, ultimately.

Let yourself dream your dreams, perhaps for the first time in your life. With faith in yourself you can rise to the heights of your fondest dream. Your past lack of achieving your goals may have stemmed from a lack of confidence in the strengths and motivators you possess, not because of a deficiency in your powers.

With faith in yourself and in your power to overcome the difficulties that stand in the way of your goals, you can attain your dreams. Filled with zest, you can overcome any transient obstacles—internal or external—in your path. Each barrier overcome only lends greater strength for you to grapple with the other obstacles.

You possess far greater strengths than you may think. You are capable of far greater tasks than those you usually venture on. In your consciousness you possess powers of wisdom and understanding, layers of power that are ready for your service. You are capable of achievement.

Together with confidence, you must put forth constant, unceasing effort. Your efforts serve as the key that unlocks your inner strengths and motivators into action. Every weekday must mark a new effort on your part. Even if you make numerous errors through your efforts, it is far better than no errors at all through passivity, inactivity, and indolence. You can correct errors; however, if you do not make any effort, you will remain stationary. It is within your power to know the joy that accompanies your effort.

Your willpower must sustain your efforts for achievement. Enthusiasm enters into your quest, but enthusiasm alone is insufficient. Efforts supported by your will are strong and long lasting. Do not expend your enthusiasm flitting from one project to another, throwing yourself into something for two weeks or a month, and then ceasing all your efforts on its behalf, turning your efforts into another field, with the same short-lived zeal.

You probably know someone like Warren, age 67. Beyond a period of enthusiasm where he shone, he couldn't follow through in achieving his goals. He first tried working part-time in a hobby store. After several weeks, he became frustrated with the hard work of learning something new. After he dropped out, he went looking again. Because of his desire to help others, he found a volunteer endeavor, as a patient ombudsman in a hospital. After experienced the short-lived "high" of beginning anew, he quit after a month.

You need to combine your enthusiasm, which charges your spirit with hope and courage, with the will to keep your eye on your goals. You need commitment, patience, and perseverance.

When difficulties present themselves, when drudgery enters into the picture, as Warren discovered, enthusiasm is often discouraged. Your will adds the light of constant effort to the flame of enthusiasm. Keep your will steadily engaged until you achieve your goals.

What could go wrong? Think long and hard about what you will do when the worst happens. Although you may not be able to foresee and prepare for every obstacle, the act of imagining them and planning how you'll surmount them, conditions your mind to think beyond the snarls and snares you will encounter.

Remember: Believe that good things will happen and they will, ultimately.

Some Further Thoughts on Longevity Planning

Although it is important to develop and stick to a longevity plan, to stay with something new until you master it and get good at it, even more you need to be an explorer in life, but not a dilettante. It's a trial-and-error process. Learn from your failures, they're tutorials in life.

The process of finding your mission in life isn't a linear process. It takes time. So be patient. You're launching a life phase that may last decades.

Don't be surprised if it takes years—your explorer phase—with many missteps along the way to craft your own active retirement. Some of your ideas may fail. You may be forced to reexamine and rework some of your foundational principles.

Remember: There will be bumps along the road to revitalization. You're embarking on your heart's unique journey. You have the opportunity to rekindle your ambitions and reawaken your enthusiasm. It's rarely a straight line or a steady climb up one ladder. Look at life as a continual process of self-reinvention and self-revitalization. Blaze your own trail. Don't conform to others' expectations. It's a chance to write many new chapters in your life's story.

Remember: Know when to give up and redirect your efforts.

We; however, celebrate people who refuse to throw in the towel. Thomas Edison went through innumerable trials before inventing the incandescent light bulb. "I have not failed," he reportedly said, "I've just found 6,000 ways that won't work." Don't be too embarrassed to admit you might have chosen the wrong path. Accept that it's not a good match for you.

Forget the platitude: "Quitters never win and winners never quit." Substitute instead another motto: "You've gotta know when to hold'em and when to fold'em."

Learn to quit the wrong things at the right time. It's easier said than done to know when it's right to walk away from something and when it's not. Moving from a difficult, if not impossible, goal to one that's more attainable helps your emotional and physical well-being. Conversely, not knowing when to give up can damage your emotional and physical health.

One study followed ninety, physically healthy, female teenagers for one year. Those who could not renounce hard-to-achieve goals, such as academic success or body image, experienced increased levels of the inflammatory molecule C-reactive protein, which is linked to various health problems, such as heart disease, Type 2 diabetes, early aging in adults, and emotional problems, for instance, the formation of depressive symptoms.[6]

The pressure of striving for the unattainable can create undue stress. Striving and the accompanying stressfulness may make people forget to focus on their emotional and physical well-being.

Seniors are generally happier; however, if they find new goals to pursue when they give up other goals. In short, don't abandon previous aims without substituting something new.

Step outside a difficult-to-achieve goal and re-evaluate the situation. Ask knowledgeable others to assess the realistic possibility of attaining your goal. If you pursue an objective that constantly frustrates you, such as weight maintenance, you'll likely be less successful in attaining other life goals.

THE CHALLENGES COUPLES FACE

Couples face special challenges in retirement. In addition to the financial aspects of retirement, discussed in Chapters 9-11, couples need to pay attention to their relationship. Questions abound: when will retirements begin; what it should and should not include; whether and where to travel; where to live?

Invest in your marriage (or relationship) emotionally. I knew a husband who amassed a considerable fortune for his family. His wife kept a beautiful home, which she lovingly remodeled and extensively redecorated over the years. However once the husband retired, they found out that they had grown far apart and didn't have enough in common. The building of their magnificent wealth led to their divorce.

In retirement, relationships and family considerations enter into the equation. The pursuit of your dreams (or passions) may impact your relationship with your wife (or significant other). How will defining and implementing your vision impact her needs and your joint needs for the future? You both need to ask: who are we together? What do we want for ourselves as a couple?

Some questions: Do you want to travel, she to stay home? Do you want to spend, she to save? Do you want to cocoon, she to socialize?

Some couples are out of sync. At retirement, men, focusing more on relationships and interpersonal issues, often say to their wives, "I want to spend time with you now." They may feel rejected when their wives, who are often more focused on the outside world, say "Well, I don't have time for you now." She loves her accomplishments at work, the recognition and camaraderie, and doesn't want to give it up to travel.

What is your vision of retirement and does your wife (or significant other) share it? Don't assume that she shares your dreams (or passions) and your values and wants to pursue the same activities as you do. The interests both of you have developed during your marriage (or a relationship) may not now lead in the same direction.

What if you experience growth in your creative or productive energies, pushing forward eagerly with excitement, but your wife (or significant other) doesn't and digs in her heels (or visa versa) or has other interests? Is your relationship sound and adaptable so that the apparent gap between the two of you can be stimulating, thereby strengthening your emotional connection or will it serve to undermine your emotional ties? Your growth in a new activity may lead your mate to enjoy or at least appreciate it. However, if the two of you view the gap as a threat to your relationship, reactions may grow adversarial and the basis for an enduring, harmonious relationship may be lost. The strains in your relationship may show. One of you may become resentful, jealous, anxious, irritable, angry, depressed, or competitive.

Each of you needs to keep growing and remain interesting. Don't suffocate each other. Don't expect your partner to share every one of your interests. Let her pursue interests that don't appeal to you. Use your time alone to pursue activities that enable you to continue growing and developing and remain an interesting person with new insights.

In your marriage (or relationship), one may need to discover new aspects in relation to the other. Hopefully you can both thrive as individuals and as a couple at the same time. As an expert on aging wrote, "Maintaining the right amount of individuality on the part of both partners fosters a process of creative uncertainty and change that can keep the relationship vital."[7] Strive to be creative by discovering something new and bringing this something new into your relationship. Hopefully, you and your wife (or significant other) can find a new activity that draws on your complementary strengths or one where you can harness your similar strengths to produce a rewarding payoff.

You've heard this so many times: you need to communicate and enter into a dialogue. Talk over your dreams (or passions) and your fears and worries. Be prepared to compromise. You must deal with your own wants, needs, feelings, and interests as well as your mate's.

Talk through what you both expect from each other in terms of household responsibilities and leisure pursuits. Work out how you'll divide the shopping, cooking, and cleaning. If you retire and go golfing all day and your wife continues to work, don't expect a friendly reception when she comes home after a hard day at the office and you ask: "What's for dinner?" You may need to change your attitude to cooking or be prepared to eat out.

How you will spend time together is a big issue. Retirement will generally last much, much longer then you imagine. You may want to take one month off before you retire and see what it's like to be together twenty-four hours every weekday.

If you're both at home, you may literally be tripping over each other. Each of you may need his or her own space. Negotiate your personal space and separate telephone lines, computers, and email addresses.

As is so often the case in marriage, timing plays a role. In the first two years of their retirement, couples may experience a dip in the quality of their marriage (or relationship). Both are adjusting to new routines and roles. It takes time to work out the kinks. For some, it can be difficult if they're both home, all day, every day. It's a gradual process.

Too much togetherness can spell trouble. Wives, who see their recently retired, restless husbands as "underfoot," often vow: "For better or for worse, but never for lunch. Now, get out of the house for lunch, at least, if not to an office somewhere." Spending a lot of time together often gives each more opportunities to get under the other's skin.

You need to work out a new routine and rhythm of being together. Although you and your wife (or significant other) love each other, you may not be able to bear spending weekdays together.

Question: How much time do you want to spend together or apart? Do you want to be joined at the hip engaging in activities jointly; pursuing your own interests separately; or arriving at some middle ground on the togetherness scale in terms of involvement and freedom? Too much togetherness only works if you do things you both enjoy. Also, the togetherness set point may change over time.

For most couples, it's probably better for each of you to develop some of his or her own interests and pursue some activities as a couple. When you're both at home, schedule times when you do things separately, but plan to spend time together so you can get to know each other again.

For two-career couples, the timing of retirement is often key. Both may leave their jobs at the same time or one may continue to work. Marriages may do better if both retire at the same time. If one spouse continues to work after the other has retired, strains may surface. If you continue working and your wife retires, you may think you have a full-time homemaker. Conversely, if your wife continues to work while you retire, she may feel that you do not do enough around the house.

Financial questions enter into the picture for two-career couples. How will you live on one salary when you're used to two, without tapping too much of your nest egg too soon? A staggered retirement often makes sense. Having one income when the other doesn't, helps you ease into retirement. It gives you a chance for a test run of your new budget while you can tweak your plans. It enables one of you to hang onto company benefits and postpone drawing down both of your 401(k) plans. It also helps socially. The working spouse continues to be invited to business-related functions you can both attend.

Finally, there are family factors, more generally. If your grandchildren or elderly parents require your time, consider how they will impact on you and your longevity plan.

A WORD ON RELOCATION

Beyond the scope of this book is where to live when you retire: stay put; live in a maintenance free, active adult retirement community with a lot of recreation facilities; move to a warmer climate; relocate to an urban setting with lots of cultural life; or be closer to family. These decisions come with some type of cost—financial, emotional, or both. Talk it over and be certain you and your wife (or significant other) are on the same page.

You need to consider not only the region, the community, and your residence, but also how the place will have meaning for you. Even if you move to be near your children and grandchildren, find a place where you feel a sense of community and can make new friends. If you move to a new area get involved in local activities and become connected. Ask: "what can I do to help?" By getting involved, you will meet people with similar interests and find a place for yourself in your new locale.

3. STRIVE TO BE PRODUCTIVE BUT SEEK BALANCE IN YOUR LIFE

How will you deal with your newfound freedom and the lack of work-related pressure that you'll likely experience for the first time in many years? How will you fill your time?

Because one's productive activity is never complete, your retirement likely will involve some form of work, learning, or creativity, discussed in this chapter, in addition to traditional leisure-oriented endeavors. As you think about being productive, go back and revisit your values. Do you view your life in terms of your wealth and possessions? Or, are you more interested in finding meaning and purpose to your life? Although you may be well provided for, with no need for further effort, if we measure life in terms of fulfilling one's dreams (or passions), you can never retire, for the world's tasks may need you more and more. Apart from altruism, are you delaying your retirement because your 401(k) has plummeted and a sense that your Social Security benefits alone are too little to live on?

WORK AS A PRODUCTIVE ACTIVITY

As you contemplate work as a productive activity, begin by considering: what are you looking for in a work environment? What is your ideal work situation? What kind of schedule would you be comfortable with? How would the job (or the new career) mesh with your family situation and responsibilities? Do you want time for other parts of your life, such as the pursuit of a hobby, golf, or time with your family?

After years of setting an alarm clock, donning work attire, and arriving at a company desk at 8:30 a.m. for the requisite eight-hour day, five days a week, fifty weeks a year, you may opt to choose when and where you work and how many hours you wish to devote to a task. You may want to take life easier and find the flexibility exhilarating.

Let's consider four categories of work as a productive activity: 1) working for wages; 2) working for a fee; 3) working for one's self as an entrepreneur; and 4) working for free as a volunteer.

Working for wages may not mean continuing your present position. You may want to reduce your hours or responsibilities, so it becomes a part-time or flextime position or seek a directorship on the board of a for-profit or nonprofit entity. You may want to change your career, or consider job-sharing. As baby boomers leave the workforce, even if older workers stay on the job, the need for qualified employees in various fields, such as education and healthcare, may overcome the traditional barrier of age discrimination.

In the face-off for jobs, the young vs. the old, particularly in an economy marked by high unemployment, several factors may make seniors less attractive to hire. Some resist training; others dislike answering to younger bosses, or have poor computer skills.

However, people over 65 don't make worse workers. In the information age, older knowledge workers, as opposed to physical laborers, drawing on their general knowledge, experience, and verbal ability, their "crystallized intelligence," are as productive, if not more productive, than younger workers. They generally make fewer mistakes, have a lower absenteeism record, are more dependable, evidence a stronger work ethic, and are less prone to leave. Drawing on their wisdom they are often more even-tempered and efficient. They typically don't get involved in things that their experience and wisdom tells them aren't worthwhile. In short, they make maturity an asset.

Yet, potential employers may be skeptical about retirement-age workers who indicate a willingness to start over, to take a lower salary and less responsibility. They don't have a track record or a platform.

Plan for your second career before you walk away from your first one. Figure out what really matters to you and put a toe in the water before you leave. Building a new network and devising a strategy to pitch your strengths and motivators may take years, not months, especially in a difficult economic climate. Be realistic. Your salary will likely decrease, even if you work full-time.

Look to your former employers (or similar firms). Network—engage in face-to-face conversations. Reach far and wide, including former bosses, colleagues, clients, family, friends, and neighbors to find out about potential openings. Be persistent and devote time to it.

Consult the following online resources for possible leads if you want to work for wages, particularly on a full-time basis:

- AARP National Employer Team (www.aarp.org/employerteam) lists companies and government agencies committed to recruiting and retaining older workers, with links to their current openings

- Action Without Borders, Inc. (www.idealist.org) lists jobs in nonprofit organizations
- The Bridgespan Group (www.bridgestar.org) is an online job board for those looking for nonprofit senior management jobs after retiring from a job or career in the for-profit world
- CareerBuilder (www.careerbuilder.com) posts job opportunities
- CharityChannel Career Search Online (http://charitychannel. com/careersearch) lists jobs in nonprofit organizations
- Chronicle of Philanthropy (http://philanthropy.com/jobs) provides job listings in philanthropy
- Commongood Careers (www.cgcareers.com) offers socially-oriented job seekers positions in the nonprofit sector
- Community Career Center (www.nonprofitjobs.com) is an "online gathering place" for nonprofit employers and management personnel
- Craigslist (www.craigslist.org), among its classifieds, are job listings
- ExecSearches (www.execsearches.com) is a job board for fund-raising, mid-level, and executive positions in the non-profit, education, healthcare, and government sectors
- Experience Works, Inc. (www.experienceworks.org) helps low-income seniors get the training they need to find jobs in their communities
- Federal Jobs Search (www.federaljobsearch.com) helps job seekers find federal government positions
- Gray Hair Management (www.grayhairmanagement.com) provides job leads and employment coaching for senior professionals
- Indeed (www.indeed.com) is a job search engine
- Jobs 4.0 (www.jobs4point0.com) lists job opportunities for those 40 and over
- Monster.com (www.monster.com) is a job database with a special section, Careers at 50+, for older workers. It also offers a job search site in partnership with AARP (http://jobsearch. aarp.monster.com)

- Nonprofit Oyster (www.nonprofitoyster.com) is an online career center serving the nonprofit sector
- The NonProfit Times (www.nptimes.com/careers.html) lists nonprofit jobs
- Opportunity Knocks (www.opportunityknocks.org) posts nonprofit jobs
- Philanthropy News Digest (www.foundationcenter.org/pnd/jobs/index/html) lists job openings at U.S.-based foundations and nonprofit organizations
- The Phoenix Link (www.thephoenixlink.com) connects experienced executives and technology specialists with full-time management positions
- RetiredBrains (www.retiredbrains.com) connects older workers with employers
- Retirement Jobs (www.retirementjobs.com) lists full-time, flexible jobs, and directorships for those over age 50
- Seniors4Hire (www.seniors4hire.com) is career center for those 50 and older seeking jobs
- Trovix (www.trovix.com) a job-matching site, searches the entire Web, including other job boards and company career sites
- Workforce 50 (www.workforce50.com) serves job seekers 50 and over
- Yahoo! HotJobs (www.hotjobs.yahoo.com) is a job search website
- YourEncore (www.yourencore.com) recruits retired scientists, engineers, and product developers

Working for a fee involves temporary or contract work, for example, as a consultant or working on a project. Working for a fee will likely enable you to balance intense, short-term work demands with your desire for increased free time. You may select short-term projects that you can wrap up in a week or in several half days spread over weeks. Between consulting engagements or projects, you can take time to travel, pursue recreational activities, or spend time with your wife (or significant other) and your grandchildren.

Rather than cycling in and out of work for extended periods, you may want a somewhat longer part-time contract role that will let you understand the time commitment involved. Organizations may be more willing to let people focus on using their experience to become problem solvers and mentors. If so, you may want to start you new career with a contract, initially for one year but renewable thereafter. This arrangement gives both sides the option to see if it's going to work out.

Look to your former employers (or similar firms) for possible temporary or contract work. Again, network. Seek out a mentor who can assist you. Keep up your expertise in your specialty. Familiarize yourself with the latest computer technology and software.

Consult the following online resources for possible leads if you want to work part-time or on a contract or temporary basis:

- Dinosaur Exchange (www.dinosaur-exchange.com) lists short-term positions for seniors
- Elance (www.elance.com) posts work-for-hire positions
- Employment Network for Retired Government Experts (www.enrge.us) posts seasonal, part-time, consulting, and project positions in the private sector for former governmental employees
- Guru.com (www.guru.com) posts freelancers' profiles
- International Executive Service Corps (www.iesc.org) uses paid consultants to promote private enterprises in developing nations
- Kelly Services (www.kellyservices.com) offers temporary positions
- Manpower Inc. (www.manpower.com) lists temporary and contract positions
- The Phoenix Link (www.thephoenixlink.com) connects experienced executives and technology specialists with interim management positions
- Retirement Jobs-Jobs for People Over 50 (www.retirementjobs.com) lists part-time, seasonal, and temporary and consulting opportunities for those age 50 and over
- Sologig.com (www.sologig.com) connects contractors, freelancers, and consultants with employers
- Spherion (www.spherion.com) offers temporary and flexible positions
- YourEncore (www.yourencore.com) lists part-time jobs for retired scientists, engineers and product developers

<u>Working for me</u>, the entrepreneurial model, can take the form of a for-profit business or the more philanthropic, social entrepreneurship model. Studies show that Americans are increasingly becoming entrepreneurs at age 50 or later.

You could start your own business. It's easier than ever to have a home-based enterprise. You don't need to rent space or have a lot of staff. With a computer and the Internet, it is much easier to establish and maintain a national, even a worldwide, enterprise.

Handyman businesses, which cost little to set up, seem to do well. These include installing doors, repairing cabinetry, fixing computers, and dealing with Internet providers.

Wayne, a retired business executive, played the piano for his own pleasure since childhood and wanted for years to become a piano tuner. He took classes, purchased tools, and now has more business than he can cover. When he gets an old piano perfectly tuned, he related, "It's like saving a life."

Max's decision to become an entrepreneur came after a corporate merger. After 35 years of climbing the corporate ladder, becoming a vice president of a major corporation, he found himself jobless at age 61. He dipped into his retirement investments and his 401(k) plan and bought a small hardware store. Instead of the three day workweeks he had hoped for, he spends 50 hours a week stocking shelves, helping customers, running the store, and managing two employees. Fulfilling a lifelong entrepreneurial dream, "It's fun," he stated. "I still like it a lot better than anything I did before."

Following the entrepreneurial model may enable you to fulfill a lifelong dream or let you turn an avocation into a business. At this stage of your life, profit maximization may not be critical.

Bill always enjoyed sail boating. He became the proprietor of a boating supply store. Instead of moping around the house, by creating a new life for himself, he looks forward to each day.

Maybe you've dreamed of owning your own B & B. Scott and Alice live their dream, owning a nine-room B & B overlooking the harbor in Christiansted, St. Croix, U.S. Virgin Islands.

Mark retired from his law practice. After leaving a competitive lifestyle and playing golf daily for several months, he reflected on his desire to help people and receive immediate feedback. He enrolled in a massage school with an intense program, requiring 750 hours of training. After becoming a licensed massage therapist, he felt a renewed sense of focus. He also likes his flexible schedule and the challenge of being (and succeeding) as an entrepreneur.

Beware: It will take longer than you think; cost more than you budgeted; and be more difficult than you contemplated. Be prepared for the financial risk and the grueling hours, particularly in the first couple of years.

Questions: Before you take the plunge as yourself:

1. What is your risk tolerance? Are you comfortable with the uncertainty of struggling to make a payroll?
2. What are your time management skills? Can you motivate yourself to not only work but also stop and pay attention to your family?
3. What is your personality type? If you are an introvert, you will likely have a hard time as a salesman. Are you happy working on your own?
4. How flexible are you? Are you willing to take on menial jobs that large businesses have staffs to carry out?

Social entrepreneurship involves filling gaps in the for-profit economy through innovative efforts designed to improve the quality of life in one's community, region, the nation, or the world. Motivated by altruism, social entrepreneurs are pioneering creative, hopefully effective, scalable solutions to social problems. They see a need for some sort of a service, form an organization, seek financing, and aim for expanding their venture so it can support and perpetuate itself.

Bernard Flynn, who had a well-grounded background in agricultural technology, worked for years as a computer programmer. At age 63, he helped found River Partners, a nonprofit organization, based in Chico, California, that plans and helps carry out thousands of acres of river restoration in California. Flynn indicated his broad purpose: "We need to keep our environment whole, a...concern that wouldn't ordinarily be dealt with by the economy at large." Commenting on what he learned for (and about) himself, he noted, "Involving yourself in...

filling gaps left by our for-profit economy is a transforming experience. Just as important is what is going to happen to you. Forming a new organization in later years with younger people is an asset to personality development, and it transforms the way you look at the world, through the lenses of other people's eyes."[1]

In the field of social entrepreneurship, whether in the area of benevolence or spiritual advancement, for example, one's work is never completed. There exists endless tasks. You can, if you choose, fill your days completely to advancing the welfare of humanity. If you devote yourself as a social entrepreneur (or a volunteer) to this chosen endeavor with the same fervor with which you previously devoted to your work, it is unlikely you will be bored, restless, weak, or feeble.

Consult the following online resources if you want to pursue entrepreneurship:

- Bizstarters.com (www.bizstarters.com) offers coaching and training to those age 50 and over starting a new business
- Entrepreneur.com (www.entrepreneur.com) provides online resources for entrepreneurs
- Service Corps of Retired Executives (SCORE) (www.score. org) offers help from successful business advisors

Working for free connotes volunteering. Some can pursue their dreams (or passions) without worrying about a paycheck or a consulting contract. You may want to give something back to others, your community, your region, the nation, or the world, thereby contributing to the greater good. By becoming a mentor to others, your giving back may serve as one of your key legacies.

Studies show that adults who volunteer live longer, likely as a result of their continued social engagement. For example, one study of 128 volunteers between the ages of 60 and 86, who worked with children in inner city public schools, 15 hours per week, over three or four days, when compared with the control group, had better physical and cognitive health, burned more calories each week, and reported more people in their social networks.[2]

Go back over and reconsider your dreams (or passions) and your values. Volunteer to use your wisdom and your expertise in a cause or an issue you deeply believe in. Take advantage of your strengths and motivators to bring a tangible change in others' lives. Identify a cause or an issue you care about. This takes time and reflection. Then, find an organization you can grow with; one you're comfortable with both the staff and the other volunteers.

Rick had a passion for gardening. On retiring from working as an advertising executive, he became a certified master gardener after studying at a local community college. He volunteers 20 hours a week in his county's master gardener program. He also helps educate teachers about how to start gardening programs at public schools.

Investigate the resources in your community. Check out the listings in the local yellow pages under associations. Visit local nonprofit organizations you are not familiar with, gather brochures and information. Check out websites. Move toward membership and participation in one or more organizations you prefer.

Consider entering into a volunteer activity with someone you care about — your wife (or significant other), an adult child, or a close friend — so that your involvement will enrich a relationship you value.

Consult the following online resources for possible leads to get you started on volunteering:

- AARP (www.aarp.org/makeadifference/volunteer/services) provides a volunteer clearinghouse through its Create the Good network.
- Action Without Borders, Inc. (www.idealist.org) helps people find volunteer opportunities in the nonprofit sector
- Adventure Center (www.adventurecenter.com) offers adventure holidays that include some volunteering
- AmeriCorps (www.americorp.org) provides volunteer opportunities in the U.S. for adults, without any upper age limit, in its AmeriCorps State and National and AmeriCorps VISTA programs. There are four corps designed to address needs in low income communities: an Energy Corps to deal with energy efficiency and conservation; an Education Corps to increase student engagement and achievement; a Healthy Futures Corps to improve healthcare access; and a Veterans Service Corps to enhance services for veterans

- Amizade Ltd. (http://amizade.org) offers volunteer placements connecting individuals with service opportunities around the world
- Civic Ventures (www.civicventures.org) sponsors various programs, including Experience Corps (www.experience corps.org), a national service program engaging those over 55 as tutors and mentors for elementary school children
- Corporation for National and Community Service (www.seniorcorps.gov) sponsors its Senior Corps Program which includes (1) Foster Grandparent Program connecting volunteers 60 and over with children, who are emotionally or physically handicapped, abused or neglected, or in trouble with the law (2) Senior Companion Program bringing together physically able volunteers 60 and over with adults in their community to help with daily living tasks and (3) RSVP, a volunteer network for people age 55 and over matching skills and availability, with service opportunities. There are Encore Fellowships in each state, with as many as ten fellows per state, to help carry out service projects in areas of national need such as education, healthcare, energy, and the environment. The program provides training for the fellows to move into full or part-time service in the nonprofit or governmental sectors.
- Cross-Cultural Solutions, Inc. (www.crossculturalsolutions.org) provides opportunities to travel and volunteer with overseas nonprofit organizations
- Earthwatch Expeditions (www.earthwatch.org/expedition) connects eco-conscious volunteers with scientific field research or conservation projects in fifty or so countries worldwide
- Executive Service Corps Affiliate Network (www.escus.org) offers volunteer opportunities to executives and professionals who have had senior level experience in business, government or nonprofits
- Global Citizens Network (www.globalcitizens.org) sends short-term teams of volunteers to developing communities throughout the world
- Global Service Corps (www.globalservicescorps.org) sponsors various international volunteer programs
- Global Vision International (www.gvi.co.uk) offers volunteer vacations for travelers

- Global Volunteers (www.globalvolunteers.org) coordinates international and domestic volunteer work projects combining service and travel
- Habitat for Humanity International, Inc. (www.habitat. org) sponsors various volunteer programs, including Global Village Program, Disaster Response, International Volunteer Programs, and RV Care-A-Vanners
- Health Volunteers Overseas, Inc. (www.hvousa.org) sends health care professionals overseas to implement educational programs in developing nations
- Impact Online, Inc. (www.volunteermatch.org) links U.S.-based nonprofit organizations and volunteers
- International Executive Service Corps (www.iesc.org) uses volunteer experts to promote private enterprises in developing nations
- National Park Service Volunteers-In-Parks Program (www.nps. gov/volunteer) provides a vehicle through which the National Park Service uses volunteers to provide a range of services
- The Nature Corps (www.naturecorps.org) coordinates volunteers for the stewardship of the U.S. national parks
- Network for Good (www.networkforgood.org) provides volunteer opportunities through its website
- Over 50 and Overseas (www.over50andoverseas.org) helps seniors who want to volunteer overseas
- Pacific Whale Foundation (www.pacificwhale.org) offers research internships to learn about humpback whales
- Peace Corps (www.peacecorps.org) is a U.S. government program placing volunteers, up to age 80, in foreign countries
- Points of Light Institute (www.pointsoflight.org) programs include 1-800-Volunteer.org (www.1-800-Volunteer.org), a website portal volunteer recruitment system, 50+ Volunteering Initiative, Family Strengthening and Neighborhood Transformation, and Seasons of Service
- RetiredBrains (www.retiredbrains.com) provides information on nonprofits looking for senior volunteers
- Senior Corps of Retired Executives (SCORE) (www.score.org) uses retired business owners and executives who offer advice to small businesses

- USA Freedom Corps offers a website (www.volunteer. gov) for Americans to find volunteer service opportunities in their area. Its Volunteers for Prosperity website (www. volunteersforprosperity.gov) helps match skilled volunteers with service opportunities
- Volunteer Consulting Group through its boardnet USA (www. boardnetusa.org) connects nonprofit organizations and those interested in serving on a board of directors
- Volunteer Match (www.volunteermatch.org) pairs volunteers with U.S.-based organizations

Through volunteering, you may realize your dreams (or passions) and values as well as test your strengths and motivators.

Matt, a retired business consultant in his 60s, spent one summer as a volunteer building outhouses in a national park. He discovered a latent talent for carpentry that became a lucrative retirement activity.

You may assume that volunteering will be a fulfilling part of your retirement. However, your volunteer position may turnout to be a dead end, completely unsuited to your strengths, motivators, and personality type. Even if you identify a cause (or issue) that inspires you and an organization with a congruent mission, you need to find a position that meets your needs and offers you a challenge, beyond short-term busywork.

Remember: Make certain the volunteer position suits not only your dreams (or passions) and your values but also your strengths and motivators. Volunteering often entails low level, routine tasks. Particularly in organizations that treat volunteers as interchangeable warm bodies.

Jeff retired after 30 years of increasing managerial responsibilities. He hoped to sidestep the ever-too-burdensome meetings that came with his past positions and spend his time with people in need. For his initial volunteer activity, he found himself dishing-out cafeteria-style meals at a senior center in his hometown. The center needed a warm body to do that job and it was not interested in Jeff's strengths and motivators. Jeff soon left this volunteer position. Dishing out meals failed to be a good match for a corporate vice president who once made major decisions.

To pursue my interests in cultural endeavors and helping others, I volunteered for a year at a local performance venue. I found it boring.

Unfriendly colleagues didn't help. I didn't need to hear concerts for free and I didn't like being out weekday evenings. I moved on.

Do you want something different from your former day job or to stick with what you know? Although you may need to work up the ranks of volunteers, does the initial position feel "right"? Be prepared to handle mundane tasks, at least initially. If something appeals to you, can you deal with starting at the bottom? As a museum docent, are you prepared to wear a uniform?

Ask yourself: What type of rewards do you want? Are you volunteering out of idealism — to do something meaningful, to give back, to make a difference? Or, are your motives more selfish — to acquire a sense of purpose for yourself and build new relationships? Or, a mix of idealism and selfishness? How much are you willing to give in return to obtain the rewards you desire?

Stay flexible about the milieu and the venue. Don't have impossibly high expectations. It will take some time to figure out the right fit for you and to work your way as a volunteer into an organization. Few situations will be perfect fits, especially for former executives, decision-makers, and professionals, who will have little or no authority as volunteers.

Consider the logistics. Do you want to attend board meetings at night or spend hours commuting to what seems to be a wonderful opportunity? Certain positions may require considerable effort and a substantial, long-term time commitment. How much time do you want to give to volunteer activities, each week?

Decide on your ideal volunteer position. Search for your dream organization, the kind of place that will make your life fulfilling, one that needs you. Investigate the organization's unmet needs and find the right person to talk to. Let the entity know your interests and strengths. Offer up the work you love and try to find a good symbiosis. Innovative organizations put volunteers to work where they can be most effective and happiest. Even in this smart type of organization, you probably will find yourself working up the ladder again. The challenge may (or may not) be fulfilling.

Kenny had a passion for photography. He found a local boys and girls club that let him snap candid shots to create a record of the kids' activities. "Because the club saw how much I enjoyed taking pictures," he noted, "it's a perfect fit."

As you formulate your longevity plan and contemplate your productive endeavor, whether for wages, for a fee, as an entrepreneur or a volunteer, how much of a commitment, in terms of time, energy, and money, do you want to make? How much responsibility do you want to take on? Do you want to combine several categories of work simultaneously? You may want to find several activities you find simulating so that, in combination, they become a full-time commitment. Do you want to work part-time 20 hours a week and spend about an equal amount of time doing volunteer endeavors? Or, you may want to move from one category of work to another as your interests and circumstances change.

LEARNING AS A PRODUCTIVE ACTIVITY

For some, productive activity may consist of work in one or more of its various varieties. For others, it may be education and continuing to learn new things. You may have enough financially, but you cannot know enough.

Curiosity provides an exciting existence. When we remain curious, we continue to grow and develop. Think about what has excited you throughout your life. What fields of interest have you never pursued, but now find interesting? What would you like to learn more about, whether a previous pursuit or a new area of interest?

As more and more of us recognize that education is not only for the young, you may seek to gain more knowledge, thereby combining your maturity with a rebirth of wonder. The more you know, the more you realize there's much more to know. Today, a multitude of educational possibilities exist for seniors.

Begin by checking out brick-and-mortar offerings in your area. Investigate community colleges and universities, weekend and evening seminars, lectures, and workshops offered by various organizations as well as art, music, and language schools. Consider innovative schools that cater to the schedules and learning needs of adults. They provide seminar-style introductions to practically any subject. Look into taped and video lectures as well as online programs sponsored by your college's alumni association, a favorite university, or other providers of virtual class work via the web. Check out www.geteducated.com, a website that lists and ranks online schools and courses.

Investigate courses offered in your community by various branches of the Osher Lifelong Learning Institutes (www.usm.main.edu/olli/national). Local OLLIs are staffed by retirees teaching retirees. You may want to share your expertise, find an audience for your ideas, and achieve intellectual stimulation by teaching a course in a local OLLI program.

You may wish to combine travel with education. Your college or university may sponsor educational vacations on campus or on trips all over the world. Also, investigate the educational vacation opportunities offered by:

- American Museum of Natural History Expeditions (www.amnhexpeditions.org) enable travelers to embark on world explorations led by the museum's scientists, educators, and curators
- Archaeological Tours (www.archaeologicaltrs.com) offers tours led by noted archaeological scholars
- Copia: The American Center for Wine, Food & The Arts (www.copia.org) operates a discovery center whose mission is to explore, celebrate, and share the pleasures and benefits of wine
- Earthwatch Institute (www.earthwatch.org) provides short-term volunteer opportunities involving ongoing research by members of the scientific community
- Exploritas (www.exploritas.org), formerly Elderhostel, offers a variety of short-term educational travel programs as does its associated Road Scholar program (www.roadscholar.org)
- Enrichment Voyages (www.semesteratsea.org) are short-term educational, shipboard excursions
- Iowa Summer Writing Festival (continuetolearn.uiowa.edu/iswfest) consists of non-credit, one-week and weekend workshops open to writers
- Le Cordon Bleu (www.lecordonblue.com) offers short courses in the culinary arts at various campuses

- National Guitar Workshop (www.guitarworkshop.com) provides weeklong music workshops for guitarists, bassists, keyboardists, drummers, and vocalists
- National Registration Center for Study Abroad (ww.nrcsa. com) evaluates foreign educational programs in a variety of fields
- Oceanic Society (www.oceanic-society.org) sponsors international natural history journeys, participatory research expeditions, and California whale watching trips
- Shaw Guides (www.shaguides.com) lists thousands of choices for learning vacation and creative career programs worldwide
- Smithsonian Journeys (www.smithsonianjourneys.org) provides education travel experiences

You may want your learning to connect you to the world beyond your locality, your region, and the United States. What interests you? Latin America, China, India? Learn a foreign language. If you are able, visit and get connected.

If you embark on a lifelong learning effort, you need to be clear about what you want to learn. You need not pursue formal education, it can be self-taught. Will your learning be a short- or a long-term duration? Plan a course of study that matches your needs in terms of time and cost. Experiment with different learning techniques and approaches. Any significant learning will be hard work, but keep your sense of humor.

Learn to ask fundamental questions, take a fresh look at things, and live without answers, if none are available. Have fun; take a risk. You don't have to prove anything. Don't worry about failing. There are no grades. It's not about getting good grades or pleasing your parents. It's about you, sparking your core interests, possibly discovering a new dream or passion.

Daily, read selected newspapers, magazines, and books. Watch the television programs you want then turn the set off.

Use the stream of your mind to realize something that will count in your life and in the life of others. Do not waste your mind on extraneous, insignificant outlets.

You need to stimulate your brain and find emotional satisfaction congruent with your values, strengths, drivers, and personality type. Most of us won't get the requisite stimulation from traditional retirement activities, such as playing golf every day.

Mental activity in whatever form that appeals to you is vital to keeping your brain alive and alert. A vigorous mental function both helps facilitate productivity in your later years and strengthens your desire to be active, thereby aiding your physical well-being.

CREATIVITY AS A PRODUCTIVE ACTIVITY

Although an extended discussion of creative expression as a productive activity is beyond the scope of this book, apart from working and learning, people may initiate processes that reduce pessimistic mood states and help them manage stress. Even if you're not comfortable with the arts, don't be intimidated or fear being incompetent. Try a creative activity that resonates with you. It may be a new hobby, such as gardening, a volunteer activity, such as helping others solve problems, or writing your autobiography, as a legacy, whether in the form of a journal, letters to family members, or tape-recording your recollections. You can be a writer simply by writing letters to your children or grandchildren.

There are numerous possibilities. Alex paints. David takes photographs. Joe does woodworking. Todd is writing a family history, beginning in the early nineteenth century, in an effort to pass the family's values on to the next generation.

Creativity in its various forms remains possible in later life. You now have the time. Your post-work days give you the opportunity to explore the creative streak everyone of us has, in some form or another. Unleash your powers of self-expression through a personal creative endeavor that matters to you.

BE FLEXIBLE

Unless being deliberative and/or seeking a focus are among your dominant strengths, keep pursuing your best options, but remember some activities will not work out. Be flexible and admit your mistakes. Accept loose ends. Try to make your life qualitatively better, not quantitatively bigger.

Learn from your disappointments and discouragements. Develop a tolerance for failure, for ambiguity.

Remember: It's been said many times; life is a journey, not a destination. Failure is part of that journey (as are successes), providing helpful signposts for turns in the road.

If your work, learning, or creative endeavor does not make you happy, if you do not put forth, joyously and willingly, your efforts and energies, find something else. If the hours drag at your task, making the day tiresome, and you look forward to the day's end, select another activity, which will bring you joy.

Remember: It's a trial and error process. Experimentation and a willingness to explore are important. It's a time to be a risk taker, an explorer. It's when you can use your personal freedom to try different things.

Although the realization "if not now, when," leads to action, remain flexible and open to trying new things. If you try something and it doesn't work out, move on. Test your dreams (or passions) and your values, but be ready to disengage from what doesn't work. If your dream grows faint, go back, revisit your dream, and update your longevity plan.

I set up my own congregation. The response was underwhelming. Finding it difficult to market to those interested in my approach to Jewish Spirituality, I decided to pursue my ministry in other directions, for example, officiating at lifecycle events. I realized I wanted a flexible schedule and not to be tied down to leading monthly or weekly religious services.

If you find a productive activity you love, obstacles will not deter you. Overcoming difficulties will serve as the zest for life and vital happiness. Your faculties will leap into life and find the utmost expression. The joy experienced in a meaningful, productive activity is among our most blessed experiences.

If you fulfill your initial dream (or passion), embark on another dream (or passion), whether to improve a small part of the world or improve yourself, through self-actualization.

SEEK BALANCE IN YOUR LIFE

Despite my emphasis on productive activity in this part of the book, strive to combine meaningful pursuits — a mix of work, learning, and creativity — with leisure and fun. Only you can arrive at the best mix for you.

In the revitalizing process, set aside time for play—for entertainment, spectator sports, travel, and socializing—and being spontaneous and playful. Discover how to play, laugh, and feel free. Try to meet with those who are more playful and spontaneous than you are. Once a month (or more often) go to a place where you can freely express yourself—your inner child—without fear or embarrassment.

You may want to take a year or two to catch your breath and rest up or pursue pleasure to the utmost. You could take the vacations you've always wanted and spend more time with your grandchildren. Think of it as a sabbatical, but keep your eyes open for something that interests you. When your sabbatical is over, you can turn to a productive activity that allows you to pursue your dreams (or passions).

Similar to one couple I know, you may want to take a multi-year jaunt around the globe to swim with the stingrays off the Cayman Islands, go white-water rafting in Alaska, revel through the streets of Rio de Janeiro during Carnival. Or, go skiing for two months a year on the slopes of Chile or the snows of Whistler, British Columbia.

After a retirement honeymoon of a year or two, you may lack a sense of satisfaction. The more important your career has been to you, the more likely you are to find a void in your life after the novelty of retiring has worn off. You'll probably come to realize that the world increasingly keeps a place for people of experience and maturity. By devoting yourself to something useful, identifying yourself with something helpful, you stand for something vital in human existence. You receive an earthly reward—a long and happier life, perhaps supplementing your retirement funds, helping pay for whatever makes your life comfortable, avoiding dependency on your children.

As you go about finding an enjoyable productive activity, be realistic about what you want to do with your time. Avoid being a super-active, super-senior. Don't over-commit. Don't feel pressure to be more active than you want to be. Eliminate what doesn't matter.

Be engaged with life. Devote yourself to activities you want to do and people you want to be with. Focus on what makes you the happiest.

Whatever you do, it is important to have fun. You want to find joy in your senior years.

Do not retire from responsibility, from achievement. Seek and hold on to your dreams (or passions). Strive to find your purpose in life. Follow your bliss. It's never too late. Be free from convention and less seeking of others' approval. Don't worry about what your relatives or friends think.

Identifying yourself with your dreams (or passions) and values, your energy is brought into action. Your body and mind will claim less weakness and infirmity.

Just as it is a source of joy to give expression to one's productive energies, it is a source of happiness to give expression to one's finer character traits: joyfulness, serenity, loving kindness and forgiveness. We turn to your emotional wellness, our next topic.

II. Emotional Wellness: Develop and Maintain Positive Character Traits

Today, we recognize the power of the mind to positively or negatively transform our body. There is a mind-body connection. Because of the interactions that take place between our thoughts and feelings and our body, the mind is a powerful tool in our physical health and wellness. Our thoughts and feelings may not be everything, but they count and influence our physical health, positively and negatively. Our thoughts and feelings can, of course, be influenced by our physical health. Social factors, such as social support, are also important.

Two studies illustrate the physical and mental health benefits flowing from life's positive psychological aspects. One study of 660 individuals aged 50 and older found a link between longevity and seniors who thought positively about aging. Those with more positive self-perceptions of aging, as measured years earlier, lived on average 7.5 more years than those with less positive self-perceptions of aging.[1]

In another study, researchers followed 1,558 initially non-frail Mexican-Americans in their 60s charting their health over seven years. Those with a positive attitude were less frail; they walked faster and had more energy.[2]

Do not let your advanced years be a sickness of the imagination. Do not begin to identify yourself, in your thoughts, with advanced age. Do not interpret any temporary weakness, any restless day or sleepless night as the approach of old age. The cumulative impact of these suggestions on the body is harmful. The body often follows them with great fidelity. The body weakens under their influence—and one may become decrepit and feeble.

Your emotional health—the state of your mind—is at least as important as your physical health. Having a positive attitude towards life, being joyful and optimistic, conquering stress, and being loving and forgiving will make your life more enjoyable and help extend your years.

I met Luke shortly after he celebrated his ninetieth birthday. In good physical health, mentally sharp with a keen mind and a wonderful sense of humor. During his career as a sales manager, he related to me that negativity festers and sales personnel did not respond well to it, which is why they almost never saw it from him. He tried to get his point across in a calm, easy-going manner. Now retired for more than twenty-five years, he reflected, "We increasingly live in a world where people would rather say 'No' rather than 'Yes'. They love violence instead of calm." Throughout his life, he has chosen to be optimistic. He no longer watches the TV news; he craves optimistic ideas and people. To avoid the infirmities of old age, he reminded me to not say, "I am growing weak; I am growing helpless." Rather say, "Although I am advancing in years, I am advancing in happiness, in calmness and health." He emphasized that repeating these positive words—this affirmation—"would help so that emotional and physical health would not desert you."

He noted his own personal struggle to achieve emotional perfection through character development. He tried to conquer his weaknesses and master the frailties of his disposition. As he put it, "I try to control my emotions. That doesn't mean I'm perfect." He urged, "It's never too late to strive to control yourself." For him, self-mastery represented the key to life mastery.

When you see a weakness in your character, whether negativity, envy, anger or impatience, being unloving or unforgiving, strive to correct it. By achieving your goal, whether optimism, equanimity, loving kindness or forgiveness, you have made a supreme conquest. Even at an advanced age, each of us can build and improve our character thereby contributing not only to the betterment of ourselves and others but also to our longevity.

Strive to repress in yourself what you condemn in others or after saying or doing, you regret. Impel yourself to express in yourself what you consider admirable in others and that in which you delight after it is accomplished. This is not easy. You will struggle with your unwholesome tendencies and your noxious habits. This struggle is made complex because you must deal with the very substance out of which you are made, you must grapple with the very mind out of which your thoughts flow and the heart in which your impulses are born.

4. BOOST YOUR JOYFULNESS AND OPTIMISM

This chapter presents a key personal character trait: joyfulness and optimism. Your mind can be a healer or a slayer. Your beliefs—optimism or pessimism (or even depression)—can become your biology and can tip the balance between health and disease. Techniques to build joyfulness and optimism are set forth. Cheerful spirits and a happy frame of mind can accompany you at all stages of life, even in the most advanced old age.

THE IMPORTANCE OF JOYFULNESS AND OPTIMISM

The world is a place of delight. It is charged with hope. The forces of nature are here to test and strengthen us, but not to destroy us. We crave joy, not misery. Our ambitions, hopes, and efforts point to creating joy for ourselves and for others.

The greater your sense of joy and optimism, the greater your ability to cope with hardships and tragedies, the unexpected setbacks, and the unforeseen hurdles you face.

Embrace joy and hope and always try to bring them into your life. Let joyfulness and optimism be of central importance in your life. Carry a hopeful air and joyful thoughts, and everything within you will be young. You will be more energetic, more creative, more likely to find innovative solutions to the problems you encounter. With an optimistic attitude, you will draw positive things toward you.

Strive to maintain the flow of joy and hope. Clothe all of your thoughts, words, and deeds with joy and hope. Having an optimistic attitude, even in seemingly difficult times, will help draw positive people and things to you.

STRIVE FOR OPTIMISM, NOT PESSIMISM

Optimism is an essential virtue and pessimism is a profound weakness. Optimism builds on faith and confidence about the present and the future; pessimism represents discontent and doubt regarding the present and the future.

A pessimistic viewpoint precludes joyfulness. It clouds one's countenance and dims one's vision. Pessimism deteriorates one's mind, destroying its fine edge. A pessimistic mind cannot think as clearly or judge as accurately.

Pessimism destroys a person's ambition, whatever one's age. It causes one to lose interest in the vital aspects of life. Days move sluggishly and colorlessly. Life soon becomes weariness.

Pessimism often predisposes one to failure. It destroys one's courage and bends one's heart. A pessimist looks for pessimism—on TV, in newspapers, or in others' experiences. Pessimism injures not only the pessimist but also others as well. A pessimist radiates his pessimism to others, permeating the atmosphere with his dejection. Pessimistic individuals bring discomfort to others by injecting negativity and dejection into them. Pessimism makes people unsociable, dampening their relations with others.

Eddie, now 77, was raised by a single mother. He faced a difficult childhood. For the past 50 years; however, he has lived an affluent, physically healthy, comfortable life. However, his persistent pessimism keeps him in a paralysis of negativity. When his out-of-town-children announce they are coming to visit, he welcomes the news, but imagines a plane crash, convinced there will be a disaster during their travel. By the time his adult children arrive, he has put everyone on edge. His children's visits have become fewer and further apart.

Pessimism also weakens one's body and lowers one's vitality. Negative thoughts and feelings can be harmful to your body. Modern research bears out these observations.

Professor Martin E. P. Seligman in his book *Learned Optimism*,[1] concludes, based on clinical experiments with human subjects, that how an individual interprets events occurring in life as well as future expectations—one's explanatory style—impacts on one's physical and psychological well-being. Seligman sees clear psychological and emotional benefits in optimism. People who are upbeat (in other words, who are dispositionally optimistic) or who push themselves to be upbeat (in other words, who have an optimistic explanatory style) enjoy better physical and mental health. Conversely, Seligman concludes, pessimism leads to greater levels of unhappiness and failure. According to Seligman, negative thinkers, those with a pessimistic explanatory style, who tend to explain events in a negative way, have weaker immune systems, encounter more infectious diseases, and after age forty-five face more major health problems than optimistic persons. Pessimists are more likely to suffer the chronic diseases of aging more severely and earlier than necessary, resulting in shorter lives.[2]

Researchers have found that negative feelings, such as the belief that unchanging, personal factors cause bad events, predict poor health, even when subjects' initial physical and mental health were controlled.[3] Negative emotions, such as self-reported symptoms of and depression, influence or cause not only problems with our immune system,[4] but also many serious illnesses and conditions, such as high blood pressure[5] and heart disease.[6]

Researchers have also found that pessimism, marked by tendencies toward self-blame, fatalism, and catastrophizing, is linked to untimely deaths.[7] A negative relationship was described between self-reported life satisfaction and mortality in a 20-year study of 22,461 initially healthy Finnish adults, ages 18 to 64 years old. Dissatisfaction among males was associated with increased mortality, even adjusting for marital status, social class, smoking, alcohol use, and physical activity.[8]

Pessimists are prone to and more likely to suffer from depression than optimists. Negative thinking reinforces itself and can lead a person spiraling down emotionally. Depression is almost as serious a health risk factor as smoking. The effect of a major depression on one's body is substantial. It increases the risk of illness and functional decline and tends to accelerate the impact of physical illnesses and disabilities.

Depression is linked to a higher risk of coronary heart disease, even controlling for smoking and diet. Sufferers are up to five times more likely to have a heart attack, placing it among the most potent cardiovascular risk factors. The risk is directly related to the severity of the depression, with a one-to-two fold increase for minor depression and a three-to-five fold increase for major depression.[9]

Depression also increases the risk of stroke[10] and Type 2 diabetes,[11] the latter is the leading cause of kidney failure, blindness, and leg amputations, among other conditions. In sum, depression is linked to premature, all-cause mortality.[12]

FEAR AND WORRY REPRESENT MANIFESTATIONS OF PESSIMISM

Pessimism often manifests itself in various forms of anxiety, a sense of some sort of a threat and a perceived inability to predict, control, or obtain the desired results. Fear and worry as more specific expressions of anxiety, in turn, strengthen pessimism's grip. A gloomy state of mind has a pernicious impact on an individual's whole system, often resulting in physical suffering. Conversely, without fear or worry the mind is free; it can think more clearly, plan more accurately, hope, and achieve.

Healthy fear about the here and now keeps one alert and warns about dangers. Unhealthy fear keeps one down; it imprisons one. You get a little cold and experience fear: "What if I get pneumonia?" You experience chest pain, is it a heart attack or heartburn? Your fear may be inappropriate and unhealthy, filling the atmosphere with gloominess and foreboding. It paralyzes one's action, retards one's energies, and holds back one's creative powers.

When fear takes hold of one's being it often destroys one's calmness and peace of mind. One thinks despondent thoughts, becomes hopeless when facing a crisis, and feels lost in the midst of a dilemma.

Many people are enslaved by worry, one of the deadliest foes of the heart, mind, and spirit. As a pernicious influence, worry is very corrosive.

Worry fills one with fear about the future, robbing him of his present enjoyment and pleasure. Worry prevents one from enjoying his current blessings by filling him with cares about the future. Not only will worry destroy one's joy, it will also contribute to the ruination of mental and bodily health.

Take financial worry. Although you're financially comfortable, you worry about running out of money if you live too long—the dreaded longevity risk. Or, in a sour economy, even if you are wealthy, you become anxious about your spending.

Worry destroys the mind in which it dwells. It consumes one's mental powers. Worry checks one's flow of vitality. It disturbs and retards the stream of one's thoughts, it perplexes one's mind, and it blinds one's reason. Worry distorts one's power of judgment and one's point of view so that nothing is seen in its true perspective. An individual becomes incapable of concentration, clear thinking, or logical reasoning. Events may prove unfavorable, but usually not as unfavorable as the worrier pictures them. As a result of worrying, one becomes easily discouraged; he falls into the grasp of pessimism.

The more one worries, the more one's mind seeks out the causes for worry. Even if causes do not exist, one's mind may imagine one or more causes in order to sustain the habit of worrying.

The mind will magnify things. A worrier typically exaggerates little things many fold. Worry twists and perverts every small incident in life into a gigantic misfortune, into a harbinger of suffering. Worry makes momentous the insignificant.

Worry also impacts negatively on one's body. It disturbs one's rest, making one sleepless and physically exhausted. A worrier tires quickly. Leading to high blood pressure and increasing the risk of coronary heart disease, chronic worrying often shortens human life. In one study, compared with men reporting the lowest levels of worry, men with the highest levels were about 2.5 times more at risk for a nonfatal heart attack. Men with even moderate levels of worry were also at an elevated risk.[13]

Conversely, optimism helps cast out fear and worry, which are among our bitterest foes, undermining our physical vitality, sapping our mental vigor, and shortening our earthly days. Filled with joy, we can close the gates of our hearts against these deadly enemies.

THE PHYSICAL HEALTH BENEFITS OF OPTIMISM

Optimism, particularly an optimistic explanatory style, leads to numerous health benefits. Because optimism increases the tendency to embrace healthy lifestyle choices, such as weight management and exercise, it is associated with lower blood pressure,[14] the reduced incidence of coronary heart disease,[15] protection against stroke,[16] lower mortality,[17] and in general, healthier aging,[18] as well as a variety of health relevant, positive biological processes, such as reduced heart rate, that may be particularly important in old age, when the accumulation of risk factors leads to an increased likelihood of chronic diseases.[19]

In one study, 2,282 Mexican-Americans from the southwestern United States, aged 65 or older, were given a battery of demographic and emotional tests, then tracked for two years. Emotional well-being predicted who lived and died, as well as disability. Those with a positive mood were half as likely to die and half as likely to be disabled in performing the activities of daily living, after controlling for a number of factors, including age, income, education, weight, major chronic conditions, functional status, smoking, and drinking.[20]

Optimism is associated with longevity. A cohort of 839 healthy patients at a mean age of 35 underwent a personality inventory screening between 1962 and 1965. Over the next thirty years, the patients initially classified as having an optimistic explanation for life events had a 50 percent lower risk of mortality (early death) and were generally healthier, both physically and mentally, than the pessimists. The optimists self-reported fewer limitations due to health, fewer problems with work or other daily activities as a result of physical health, less pain, and fewer limitations due to pain. They felt more energetic most of the time, performed social activities with less interference from physical or emotional problems, and had fewer problems with work or other daily activities as a result of their emotional state.[21]

TECHNIQUES FOR ENHANCING YOUR JOYFULNESS AND OPTIMISM

It is not hard to be joyful and optimistic when things are going well and the future looks bright. It is much more difficult when something unexpected happens, when things go wrong, when illness strikes or calamity is at hand, when the future seems to hold no promise. Through meditation and learning to cultivate optimism you can turn lemons into lemonade, and not make molehills into mountains.

MEDITATE FOR JOYFULNESS AND OPTIMISM

Meditation can help you attain and maintain your joyfulness and optimism. Meditation is taking the time to be still, to find a path of silent awareness. Wide-awake, yet physically relaxed, meditation calms the body and the mind.

Use the following as a meditation or visualization twice a day, in the morning and evening, for fifteen minutes. Be patient. You can train your mind to recall moments of joyfulness, thereby dispelling negative or pessimistic thoughts. Through visualization, what you can imagine can often become reality. The power of the mind becomes a powerful tool for transformation.

Joyfulness Meditation or Visualization

Introduction: Create a warm, welcoming atmosphere, an environment of serenity and spaciousness for the journey within. Lower the lights in your room. Close your eyes, sit quietly, calm and relax your body, breathe in and out normally, feeling where the breath flows in and out of your body. Adjust your breaths so that the in and out breaths are the same length, thereby bringing about a relaxation of your body and an alertness of your mind.

Choose a word, a phrase, a melody, an event, or a person that evokes for you joyfulness. Repeat the word, the phrase, the melody, the event, or the person.

Or, visualize a moment of past joy, an event or a person, and reflect on the joyfulness you attained.

Concluding Instructions: Come back to the here and now. Take your time to ease yourself back. Slowly bring awareness back into your body. Feel yourself back in the room and open your eyes.

SUGGESTIONS FOR CULTIVATING JOYFULNESS AND OPTIMISM: THE POWER OF YOUR MIND

Although pessimism and depression we see all-to-often may result from disease or biochemical factors, such as disturbances in brain chemistry, learn to cultivate joyfulness and optimism. Cultivate your joyfulness and bring it to fruition through constant development and expression. Substitute positive life forces for negative ones. You are what you think. Because of the power of the mind, your way of thinking—positive or negative—creates the world you see. You need to maintain a positive "can do" attitude. Consider two different approaches: first, forcing an optimistic attitude and second, learning to reframe situations optimistically.

FORCING AN OPTIMISTIC ATTITUDE: THE POWER OF POSITIVE THINKING

Always give full expression to your power for joy in every place and in every situation in your life. Identify yourself with an optimistic, lighthearted state of mind. Cultivate the habits that make for joy. Embrace the habits of optimism. Think, speak, and act cheerfully. Strive to keep your mind in a joyful state. See life as offering hope and adventure.

It's not too late to select an optimistic outlook on life and make it your habit. Optimism is one of the best habits to foster. Do not let your spirit droop. Do not let external circumstances adversely affect your spirit. Rather, make joy your habit. Animated by the will to be cheerful, your facility for joy soon flourishes. Tell yourself positive things.

Regardless of the weather or other external circumstances, start each day by saying out loud: "What a beautiful day!" When you wake up, it can be a good day or a bad day. Say out aloud: "It's going to be a good day." Begin each day anew; start afresh. By resolving to live this day in a good and joyful manner, you will come to see that day as glorious and precious. Your lips will train your mind. Your affirmation of the beautiful will make your mind feel the glory and the majesty of the world. Visualize your world in bright, harmonious, pleasing colors.

Learn to smile even in the face of seeming calamity. Your smile will carry you through the day, filling you with renewed energy and bringing you hope. Force your lips to smile for a short time period each day even if your heart is heavy. Smile mechanically in the beginning, and gradually your smile will become genuine, emanating from the depths of your heart. You will discover that the posture of your facial muscles can lead to beneficial changes in your mood, thereby triggering positive feelings and emotions.

Through your efforts to make your lips smile, you remove the layer of darkness that surrounds you, allowing light to filter through. You stimulate your inner power of cheerfulness. Soon your heart, your mind, and your spirit will smile.

Find an occasion, a recreation, or a person who can elicit from you joyous, hearty laughter. Laughter will help the clouds of despair to disappear. Laugh and your fears will lose their hold; your worries their grasp; pessimism will not approach you.

Laughing provides some of the same benefits as exercising. It helps you relax. Laughing is good for your body and your mind.

In *An Anatomy of an Illness as Perceived by the Patient*,[22] Norman Cousins described the therapeutic value of humor. He laughed himself back to health, after suffering from a normally fatal disease of the connective tissue.

Keep your sense of humor. Through humor you recognize life's realities, but humor protects you against life's sorrows and anxieties, fear about the present, and worry about the future. Through humor you can see situations in a new way, by reframing them as less threatening and thus fostering a positive perspective on challenging circumstances.

Take yourself away from a difficult situation. Distract yourself from your troubles. Do something pleasurable, something you enjoy. Refill your mind with cheerful thoughts and recharge your heart with hopeful feelings.

Do not listen to or identify with pessimistic thoughts or people or read about or watch tragic events on TV. Rather, read cheerful books and magazines; listen to upbeat music and radio programs; watch hopeful videos, movies and TV shows; and be in the company of optimistic people.

Be selective in the people with whom you associate. Avoid any situation or anyone who interferes with your hopeful, optimistic outlook on life. Do not identify with gloomy people or environs. Seek out aspects of life as well as people who will charge you with joyful influences. Always seek the company of cheerful individuals. Surround yourself with optimistic people; avoid pessimists.

If you suffer reverses in your relationships or in your aspirations for revitalization, water your heart, mind, and spirits with fresh hopes. New dreams will bloom bearing the fruits of success.

Do not let setbacks, which slow your momentum, foil your pursuit of your goals. Wait in joy for things to change. Regroup quickly and be flexible in finding new ways to move forward. Continue to persevere; do not despair. You may need to alter the means of how you go about achieving an objective. Find alternative paths to reach your goal. Always put your setbacks into proper perspective. Step back. Do not let the temporary obstacles you face mushroom into major disasters. Avoid blaming yourself (or others) if things go slowly, for example, in implementing your longevity plan.

Remind yourself of your inner strengths, valuable talents, and good points. Put them to work for you.

Remember: the power of your mind. Replace your negative, self-limiting thoughts with positive, empowering ones:

- Learning how to be hopeful represents a means to joyfulness.
- Expect good things to happen.
- Do not dwell on disappointment.

- Strive to create a positive environment.
- Do not associate with negative people.
- Develop a self-talk that is life affirming.
- Look for goodness in yourself and in others.

Rather than seeing life and your future in pessimistic terms, strive to interpret life and read your future in optimistic terms. Face the present and approach the future with hope, not despondency, and thus escape the clutches of fear and worry. Instead of thinking what you have lost, think of what you have; instead of thinking what you cannot have, think of what is in your power to have. With hope in your potential you can face every situation, every difficulty, every calamity and emerge without the anguish of spirit. With hope, obstacles are removed and barriers are destroyed.

Things will change if you believe they will. To a large degree, the power is within you. Choose life; choose joy.

LEARN THE SKILLS OF OPTIMISM

For most of us, the power of positive thinking is sufficient. You can force yourself to be cheerful, thereby overcoming the hardships of disappointment. Others, however, need to learn the skills of optimism, changing thought patterns and mental habits. They need to learn to turn their habitual pessimism into optimism. They need to replace their pessimistic explanatory style with an optimistic explanatory style.

You can learn the coping skills of optimism to change the way you think about misfortune and help fight anxiety and depression. Your thoughts create your feelings, good or bad. Learning optimism helps you if you are discouraged, especially a chronically negative person. You can learn to stop negative, unrealistic, or distorted thought processes and achieve better emotional heath. If you feel empowered, assume credit for your triumphs, expect good things to happen, learn to challenge negative beliefs, and perceive events as susceptible to your influence, then you can grow with hope and optimism. An optimist sees misfortune as temporary, controllable, solvable, and rooted in circumstances.

Conversely, if one understands good events as temporary and fortuitous, believes that others control his destiny, and attributes his successes to others' doing or to luck, then he grows pessimistic and helpless. A pessimist sees a defeat as permanent, insolvable, catastrophic evidence of personal failing or ineptitude.

Learned optimism focuses on the power of non-negative thinking, by controlling your attitude to people or events. Optimism can be learned as a coping skill; you can unlearn a negative outlook on life, characterized by self-defeating thoughts and irrational beliefs.

Malcolm, age 92, is a retired engineer. When I asked him what's his secret to longevity, he quickly replied: "For over 60 years, I've followed a simple formula. When something bothers me and I can do something about it, I do it promptly. If I can't do anything about, I put it out of my mind." He gave me the following, rather pungent analogy: "After you use a toilet, you flush it. If you don't, you know the smell you'll get after three days."

As you experience frustration, rejection, failure, or setbacks, you need to differentiate situations that are changeable from those you simply cannot alter. Do not waste your time and energy worrying over something beyond your control.

In situations that are changeable, focus on what you can do to affect change. Where change is possible, try to transform things. When facing a difficult situation, one that is within your power to change, commit yourself to finding a solution, not to hiding your head in denial or just complaining. Do not become hopeless or helpless. Learn to problem solve, not just complain or see yourself as a victim.

Where you cannot change a situation, learn to accept and cope with your emotions and reactions. By altering how you interpret a situation, you can learn to turn a negative event into something positive. Make the best of a challenging situation by viewing it in a positive light or growing from it.

Take a specific, but minor situation. Suppose a colleague at your volunteer endeavor does not say "Hello" and avoids making eye contact with you. You could interpret this negative behavior as "unfriendliness." However, your colleague might have been preoccupied with other thoughts and meant nothing unfriendly to you.

You need to dispute your interpretation of "adversity." Ask yourself whether your negative thoughts are in fact accurate, whether your irrational beliefs are in fact correct. Some negative thoughts are constructive and can help you make meaningful adjustments. However, if your negative thoughts and beliefs are distortions, challenge and replace them with realistic appraisals. Argue with yourself about thoughts and beliefs flowing from what you perceive as an adversity. Are your conclusions logical? Is an alternative conclusion more logical? Change how you interpret a situation or another person and shift your feelings and your conduct. Do not misinterpret data or lose your perspective. Separate facts from assumptions.

In situations that are in fact adverse and not changeable, because they are beyond your power to control, do not obsess about the negative.

Remember: "This too will pass."

Beyond separating changeable and unchangeable situations, interpret every facet of your existence with optimism. See life's traumas as challenges, not threats. Shift how you assess the meaning of day-to-day events. Seek to foster a joy that puts a positive interpretation on everything in your life. Remind yourself of your past triumphs. Make and implement a plan to achieve a more favorable outcome. Set modest, immediate, and achievable goals as part of your longevity plan.

Each day, take one negative thought and look at its bright side. Focus on one event you responded to with distress and reframe it so that the good you now see nullifies the distress you experienced.

People can learn to be hopeful and optimistic or helpless and pessimistic. Learn to reframe events and situations in order to find the good, rather than the negative. Once you identify your negative thought patterns and irrational beliefs, you can engage in cognitive restructuring thereby finding a positive approach to life, more generally. Replace your negative, self-limiting thoughts with positive, empowering ones.

DEALING WITH DEPRESSION

What if you find yourself depressed—past the threshold of sadness or the "blues" of everyday life? For older adults losing a partner puts them at an elevated risk of spirit crushing, emotional pain and depression. However, at any age, emotionally healthy people bounce back from their grief and, in about a year; find new sources of support and pleasure.

Ben, age 65, retired four years ago. For the first three years, various activities filled his weekdays, lunches with old work buddies and golf several times a week.

Gradually; however, his connections to his former colleagues became attenuated and his favorite golfing friend died. When he looked in the mirror, he saw he was changing—getting old. For the past year or so, he increasingly spent much of his day engaged in two activities: watching cable news programs for hours and walking miles each day. When home, he drank heavily. Friends no longer meant anything.

Ben and his wife had previously entertained two or three times a week. Eventually, Ben, sullen, irascible and drunk, lashed out at guests, who, in turn, felt unwelcome. No longer did Ben and his wife entertain at home.

Then, Ben's wife and his two children gently confronted him with the unpleasant truth—he's depressed.

Depression is a depressed mood or loss of interest or pleasure in most things important to a sufferer that has persisted most of the time for at least two weeks with at least four other symptoms. These other symptoms include: 1) sleep disturbance, sleeping too much or too little; 2) appetite disturbance, eating too much or too little; 3) loss of energy; 4) feelings of worthlessness or excessive guilt; 5) difficulty concentrating or indecisiveness.[23]

In other words, depression is not mere sadness: rather it's apathy, irritability, difficulty in concentrating, or indecisiveness. Although the classic symptoms of depression include hopelessness and fatigue, many men feel and behave differently. The following chronic behaviors may be possible warning signs of depression: anger, hostility, impatience, anxiety, sarcasm, argumentativeness, frustration, or defiance.

Besides its adverse impact on one's physical health, as noted earlier in this chapter, depression also impairs one's behavior, leading to an overuse of alcohol, not watching one's diet, not exercising or not taking medications, because one does not care. Ben self-medicated with alcohol. There's also a major impact on one's wife, one's children and grandchildren. If one is depressed and irritable, he doesn't want to see his grandchildren and have much fun with them. Ben withdrew from his loved ones and from life itself.

Ben finally realized he had to do something. His physician evaluated whether his emotional plight stemmed from genetic or other medical conditions. Depression tends to run in families and is more common in individuals who have undergone a serious trauma. This did not apply to Ben. He also did not suffer from neurological disorders, such as Parkinson's disease, or organic disorders, such as the flu, brain cancer, anemia, or blood poisoning.

Taking the popular tack, Ben's physician treated him through medication to deal with biochemical causes of his depression. Ben began to smile and appreciate his family for the first time in more than a year.

If you're depressed, consult your physician to lift the clouds. With the right anti-depressant medication, even if the dose is imperfect, within two weeks most patients and their families should notice that something is better.

Many get better through therapy, specifically, cognitive behavioral therapy, in a group or individual setting, designed to make them more self-aware about their patterns of thought and better able to deal with things by teaching them to switch to healthier thought patterns. Look to intense, short-term cognitive behavioral therapy rather than traditional talk psychotherapy to put depression in the past. It will help you examine, challenge, and confront your current emotions and the thoughts behind them as well as learn new interpretations and alternative actions to embark upon.

OTHER STRATEGIES TO ENHANCE YOUR JOYFULNESS AND OPTIMISM

In addition to forcing an optimistic attitude, reframing events, and treating depression, five practical techniques can enhance your joyfulness and optimism.

- Visualize your primary goal (or goals) in life and what it (or they) means (or mean) to you. Revisit your longevity plan. Ask yourself why you initially established an objective (or objectives) and to what extent it (or they) still matter to you. This will help you overcome short-term crises.
- If life becomes overwhelming because a task or an obligation seems too burdensome, take constructive action. Break it into smaller, more manageable parts. Approach different parts one at a time.
- Each evening before you go to sleep, write down what has been bothering you during the day. Keep paper and pen near your bed and during the night write down your fears and

your worries, if you cannot do so before going to sleep. In the morning, you will be more ready to deal with what you have written down. Make and implement a plan to solve the problem. Take specific action and formulate steps to remedy a defined problem. By making a concrete plan, you take the problem out of the zone of apprehension and bring it into the area of remediation.

- Let go of the past. Uproot the past from your heart; banish it from your mind. Forget the failures or the emotional hurts of the past that may have brought humiliation or fear, a tendency to unhappiness, a disposition toward doubt, or a susceptibility to despair. Yes, these failures and hurts, as well as your attendant suffering, were obstacles you encountered. These failures and hurts represented stepping-stones that you were able to overcome on your way to higher reaches.

  If you erred in the past, revisit the situation and determine how to set it right. Offer an apology, express your sincere forgiveness, then drop the matter and do not give it further thought. Let go of the past and move on. Do not wallow in the past.

  Each day before you go to sleep, evaluate your day's activities. If there is anything you regret, especially in your interactions with others, do not let it fester. Determine to offer an apology. Think of how you will speak or act differently in a similar situation or with that person in the future. Then, let go of the day.

- Engage in the lifestyle changes discussed in Chapter 7. Don't smoke. Practice weight management. Exercise regularly.

Joy and optimism is as good for seniors as it is for youth. Naturally, the joys of advanced age differ from the joys of youth. The enjoyments of age are more tender, more spiritual, more in harmony with the wisdom of maturity. Seniors gain enjoyment from reflecting on an inspiring landscape, observing children at play, absorbing the thoughts of great minds. Carpe diem: seize the day and enjoy life to the fullest.

5. Enhance Your Serenity

This chapter presents another key character trait: serenity. Techniques to build equanimity are presented. The importance of maintaining a sustained, active engagement with life through social relationships is developed.

The Importance of Serenity

Peace of mind is essential to personal fulfillment and accomplishment. Lasting achievements that really count in your quest to realize your dreams (or passions) and build on your strengths and motivators are produced when your inner life is peaceful and harmonious.

One does his best work, learns the most, best expresses his creative powers when his inner life is peaceful and his reason and judgment are free to act. When one is serene, one can best express his mental powers. One's thoughts come more readily. One's concentration is at its best. One's powers of memory are heightened. Sound ideas come more quickly and more abundantly. Errors of judgment diminish. One produces his best thoughts and forms his clearest plans. One is able to see and solve the most difficult problems when his inner life is possessed of harmony and a sense of inner peace.

Peace of mind is requisite to personal happiness. When one is serene, one is ruled by his wiser self. When one is calm, his mental balance enables him to receive and accept whatever happens to him.

When one is peaceful, one expresses the best of oneself. One feels the wonder of life. One's best qualities, one's better self and one's best ethical tendencies and virtues assert themselves when he is calm. Joyfulness and optimism flourish on a serene background, a mentally peaceful atmosphere. The wellsprings of loving kindness and forgiveness open up.

A calm mental state enables an individual to better face and solve the challenges life holds for him. One does not feel lost in the face of a crisis; one does not become hopeless when confronted with a dilemma. A tranquil nature better preserves one's physical and emotional well-being.

In contrast, if the mind is in a chaotic, disturbed condition, joyfulness cannot penetrate it. The mental fogginess accompanying stress often includes problems with memory, concentration, multitasking, and setting priorities. There may be an inability to focus on anything with any depth or complexity and difficulty analyzing anything beyond simple questions.

Restless people render those with whom they come in contact restless as well. If your thoughts, words and deeds are agitated, you transmit streams of unease and disturbance to others.

In short, as my mother often reminded me: "When you have tranquility, you have everything; when you lack tranquility, you have nothing."

Although your mind is free from immaturity, strive to keep it free from turmoil, free from stress, anger, and envy.

STRESS IN OUR DAILY LIVES

As you reflect back over the past week, you'll realize that you experienced stress at some point. The subject of stress in our daily lives almost needs no introduction. Reflect on the following: After last month's shopping binge, the credit card bills arrive and you must face paying them. You are about to undergo a painful medical procedure. The supermarket checkout line you pick turns out to be the slowest. Your stock portfolio is tanking. Stress bears down on us relentlessly and intensely. Stressful events happen continuously: traffic jams, incompetent service personnel, tardy friends. Having nothing meaningful to do for long time periods is stressful. You face the increased likelihood of multiple major stressors, such as whether to institutionalize your wife who has Alzheimer's and your being forced to stop driving because of your own physical problems, occurring simultaneously.

Stress is a part of life. Without some measure of stress, most of us would feel bored, stagnant, purposeless. But it's how you perceive stressors and react to different types of stress in your life that matters. Good stress can be challenging and stimulating; while chronic bad stress distress often leads to negative consequences.

At any age, most of us cannot bear too much stress, even resulting from the accumulation of minor irritations. Although some thrive on stress and do not experience any adverse mental or physical response, because they possess stress-hardiness, the burden of ever-increasing stressors, wave after wave, overwhelms our coping abilities. "Whoa," you cry out, "I can't take it any more." What is called allostatic load may result when physiological systems remain activated, despite the termination of an external stressor. Simply put, chronic stress affects the way we feel, think, and act.

We become irritable and impatient during the day and sleepless at night. Life lacks fulfillment; it becomes meaningless. We turn listless and withdrawn. Every phase of our existence turns dark and unhappy, resulting in paralyzing anxiety and even depression.

We see less and less hope. We become easily discouraged and lack fortification against the vicissitudes and hardships everyone encounters. We are helpless when confronted with a dilemma or when in the midst of crisis.

We experience trouble in thinking clearly and suffer memory loss. Being stressed-out brings a lack of accuracy, deficiencies in concentration, gaps in attention, diminished powers of judgment, and a tendency to err and make mistakes. Failures of judgment mount. We become forgetful, lack creativity, and experience an inability to make decisions.

We overeat and avoid exercise. We look to alcohol, narcotics, stimulants, or prescription drugs to correct our ailments. However, nothing seems to solve our plight. We are not quite sure how to handle our stress reactions.

Because the mind and the body are linked, stress exacts its toll in physical and mental illness, and even on human life. Stress represents a perception of a physical or psychological threat to one's self and that one's resources are inadequate to cope with that threat. Stress prepares the body to respond to a perceived threat and danger. A stress-triggering incident, even in an inappropriate circumstance, such as a long bank line or a restaurant reservation mix-up, sets in motion a physiological survival mechanism called the "fight or flight" response. You accelerate the production of a cascade of stimulating or exciting hormones, such as adrenalin, which are sent throughout the body. These stress-generated hormones result in the body becoming all charged up, which of course, is useful in emergencies. Our emotions impact on our nervous system, which controls various involuntary functions. As a result, the heart races, blood pressure increases, muscles in arms and legs tighten. When you feel stressed, your breathing accelerates, becoming very short and shallow.

In the modern world, you are often unable to fight off the stress-inducing crises, physically and emotionally. Your tension never gets released. You cannot downshift. Your revved-up mind and body lead to the familiar physical complaints: headaches, backaches, muscle tension, sleeplessness, and stomach problems. These symptoms, in turn, increase your stress levels.

Chronic, unrelieved stress is detrimental to the immune system. One review summarized more than 300 empirical articles describing the negative impact of stress on the human immune system.[1] Chronic stress lowers the levels of protective immune system cells moving throughout the body. The negative psychological effects of chronic stress block or disrupt the normal function of the brain cells that send messages to the immune system.

Because the constant wear and tear of stress depresses the immune system, a connection exists between stress levels and susceptibility to colds and the flu. In one study, researchers found that individuals who experienced severe, chronic (lasting one month or more), stressful life events—such as enduring interpersonal difficulties with family or friends having the greatest influence on risk—were between two and nearly four times more likely to develop colds than those without such experiences.[2]

There's also a relationship between stressful emotions and heart disease. If the fight-or-flight response is strong or persistent enough, the body is unable to compensate, resulting in a risk factor for heart disease. One study that examined the impact of stress in more than 24,000 people, found that stress more than doubled the risk of heart attacks.[3] Stress exacerbates high blood pressure, bringing about arterial aging that often results in cardiovascular disease.[4] Elevated blood pressure forces the heart to work harder; over time chronically elevated blood pressure leads to damaged arteries and plaque formation. If coronary arteries are partly blocked by fatty deposits, the result can be reduced blood flow to the heart depriving it of needed oxygen. If a clot forms that blocks a coronary artery, a heart attack results. Stress can also raise the level of inflammation in the body that has been associated with heart disease by causing the most vulnerable plaques inside arteries to rupture; triggering blood clots that block blood flow.

Stress also makes us more vulnerable to dementia and Alzheimer's disease.[5] In short; stress represents a biological driver of body and brain aging.

By over-straining our energies, the body and the mind become enfeebled. Peace of mind ebbs. As stress increases, we dread each new day with its new burdens, anxieties, and ever more pressing tasks. We are on a treadmill, never quite able to catch up with everything. We find that we lack the energy to enjoy life.

ANGER AND ITS COSTS

Anger, a strong feeling of displeasure and antagonism, rather than a calm, controlled expression of assertiveness in confronting difficult people or solving problems, represents a negative quality into which we can quickly fall. Manifesting anger becomes a habit. Many of us get angry ten to fourteen times a day.[6]

Healthy and unhealthy anger must be distinguished. Think about when you feel angry. What provoked the emotion? Was it a trust that was violated or betrayed, a feeling of frustration or disgust, or being disregarded, ignored or misunderstood? Was your anger sparked by a sense of self-preservation — a desire to protect yourself or preserve what you believe was correct? Or, does your anger have nothing to do with the current situation but rather represents a coping strategy to manage your anxieties and personal insecurities, particularly your core beliefs of unworthiness and helplessness?

Healthy anger can be a necessary response. It can preserve your reasonable needs and convictions. It can be responsible to get angry. It's legitimate, for example, to feel angry because a former friend spoke condescendingly about you to a mutual acquaintance. Conversely, unhealthy, toxic anger that is unreasonable given the situation can work great mental, emotional, and physical harm; it is poison.

Anger, which can manifest itself in quick, dangerous outbursts, aggressive acts, or a long period of stewing, debilitates one's mind and one's sprits. When a person becomes angry, he loses control over normal reason. Anger saps good judgment and clear understanding. Losing oneself in anger often leads to lashing out recklessly.

Unhealthy anger has its interpersonal costs. It makes us irritable and impatient. It often leads to hostility, a cynical, suspicious or resentful attitude toward others, resulting in aggressive behavior and negative social exchanges, which, in turn, lead to more opportunities to experience anger.

Our anger or hostility often creates an atmosphere of bitterness and resentment. It arouses the hostility and contempt of others. Angry words cannot be taken back; the damage often cannot be undone.

An excessive amount of anger further separates quarreling spouses by making them even angrier and more aggressive with each other. Anger can ruin friendships by turning friends into enemies. An angry person has fewer and fewer friends; not many want to associate with one in whose presence they must refrain from expressing their natural selves or any contrary opinion or else risk exposing themselves to uncontrolled wrath.

Reflect on an antagonistic, angry person you know, someone who is aggressive and quick to explode at the most minor excuse for provocation. How do you deal with him or her? Think of how he or she seeks out opportunities for manifesting irascibility, the object of which is to throw off bitterness. You try to stay out of his or her way, don't you? An angry person's antagonism keeps you at a distance. It creates a barrier between people, leading to the angry person's social isolation.

Anger has its physical health costs. People who are quick to anger evoke the "fight-or-flight" response to their detriment. The kindling of anger quickens the pulse, heightens blood pressure, contracts heart muscles, and increases stomach secretions. Anger makes one's face flush, enlarges eyes, tenses muscles, and throws the entire body into a disturbance. With anger a blazing headache may appear, or ailments may develop in the stomach or heart. Physical problems, especially the risk of suffering a heart attack or a stroke, mount with every rage, every expression of aggressive, inflammatory anger. The "hot responders," those who experience increased blood pressure and heart rate, are especially at risk.

Research findings bear out these anecdotal observations. Proneness to anger raises the risk of coronary heart disease.[7] In a classic study over a twenty-five year period of 255 physicians, those with high hostility scores were nearly five times more likely to develop coronary heart disease than were those with low scores.[8] One study of 1,623 heart attack victims found that an angry episode within the previous two hours raised an individual's risk of suffering a heart attack more than two-fold.[9] Another study of 1,305 older men, those reporting higher levels of anger initially had a two- or three-fold increased risk of coronary heart disease over the next seven years.[10] Anger also increases the risk of stroke.[11] In sum, anger, particularly in its chronic, intense, sustained variety, and hostility are not conducive to longevity.[12]

ENVY AND JEALOUSY

Avoid envy, which results in a loss of the finer powers of the mind, spirit, and body. Many are haunted when they see others who possess more, those who have more wealth. They lose their ease at others' abundance. They are also jealous of others' happiness, real or imagined. They often grow miserable at others' joy. They are unable to hear of a neighbor or a friend's achievement.

Envy comes in all shapes and sizes: house envy, wealth envy, relationship envy, fabulous couple envy. We all know of an impressive couple who seems to have it all: money, loving children and grandchildren; and are very much in love, after decades of marriage.

As a result of envy and the accompanying jealousy, some live in an extravagant fashion, putting forth all kinds of pretensions. One's mind does not center itself on life's vital values and goals; it ceases to identify itself with deeper human interests. When one becomes consumed by envy and jealousy, a mix of emotions result: discontent, poor self-image, and resentment.

ATTAINING AND MAINTAINING EQUANIMITY

Stress, anger, and envy, the opposites of equanimity, often result from one's perception or reaction to external factors—they are one's own creation. Each of us is fundamentally calm and serene, but you need to see to it that tranquility expresses itself in all of your life's dealings and activities, through cultivating patience and contentment, meditating, and using various practical techniques.

CULTIVATE PATIENCE

Through patience you can endure the difficulties and unpleasantness that beset you in life with a greater measure of serenity. Patience teaches us to wait for a better future. Have hope for the future, despite setbacks, even hardships.

Remember: the best will come even if it is delayed for a bit.

Patience is extremely essential if you are not to fall under the burden of the obstacles you face daily. Realize that stumbling blocks exist in any undertaking, especially as you strive to revitalize your existence and implement your longevity plan. Face these impediments, however, with patience.

We all know someone like Al, a sweet and caring man. However, patience was not his strongest character trait. Stuck in traffic, Al became impatient and suffered a fatal heart attack.

You need to know when to be patient. Be patient in all the difficulties that life brings. In particular, be patient with others. Others may not think as you think; others may not feel as you feel; others may not do things as you would wish them to be done; others may not have the same strivings as you have. Your impatience with others indicates that you do not really understand them. Be patient with people as long as they are not doing anything illegal, unloving, or untruthful. When you feel agitated, do not unleash your fury by shouting at or interrupting others. Stand back and let the passion of the moment settle before responding impulsively. Slow down and listen. Strive to put yourself in the other person's shoes.

DEVELOP CONTENTMENT

Turn away from envy and jealousy. Rather, strive for contentment, especially with your material possessions. Contentment softens disappointment; it brings forth your finer elements. It keeps you serene; your mind calm; your heart warm; and your spirit sympathetic.

Moderate your expectations. With what you have, cultivate contentment. You have what you need. Be happy with your life, your health, your economic status, and your family and friends. Take delight in a friend's or neighbor's comfort and achievement as you do in your own. Make the happiness of others your goal and enjoy the success of others.

Don't avoid the fabulous couple. Learn from them. Don't beat yourself (or your wife (or significant other)) with the "blame stick." Let the fabulous couple fill you with hope, even at your age, not envy and jealousy.

But do not mistake contentment with the passive acceptance of your attainments—with what you are. Contentment with what you are leads to stagnation. Reach out to achieve your ideals and values, your mission in life, by using your strengths and motivators. Do more, know more, think more, achieve more. Strive to be more loving and forgiving in your interactions with others.

MEDITATE TO ACHIEVE EQUANIMITY

During the day, even before you feel stress, anger, envy, or impatience getting the best of you, you can attain and maintain a sense of calm through meditation. You can transform yourself and create a healthy, serene atmosphere about you. You can reset your mind to its naturally joyful, tranquil state of radiant calm.

You can meditate to manage your stress, anger, or envy as well as restore tranquility in your mind and spirit by inducing a relaxed state of being. Through meditation, you can develop an attitude of detached introspection about yourself and your relationship to the world. There are numerous styles of meditation. There's no one right way. In some types of meditation, practitioners lose themselves, untouched by day-to-day concerns. The goal of other types of meditation seeks to foster an awareness of what is happening moment-to-moment. Because of the mind-body connection, if you relax your mind, your muscles will follow and vice versa.

In his best-selling book *The Relaxation Response,*[13] Herbert Benson, M.D. presented the Relaxation Response, a demystified form of meditation, a turning inward, designed to induce short-term calming and long-term health benefits, including lowering blood pressure, decreasing the heart rate, and strengthening the immune system. Developed as an antidote to the "fight-or-flight" response that is epidemic in our frenetic society, according to Dr. Benson, the point is "...when the mind quiets down, the body follows suit."[14]

What is going on? The Relaxation Response breaks the pattern of everyday thoughts. Giving the brain and the body a respite results in a physiological relaxation. A significant drop in the body's oxygen consumption accompanies a downshifting in metabolism. Blood pressure drops, heart rate decreases, breathing slows and becomes deeper, and muscles relax and require less blood. The more dramatic effects of using the Relaxation Response are cumulative over time.

Six basic steps must be followed: (1) Sit in a comfortable position with your eyes closed. (2) Let your body and your muscles relax, starting with your face and working down to your feet. (3) Become aware of your breath as you breathe in and out through your nose. Breathe slowly. Each time you exhale, repeat a word, a prayer, or a phrase that is meaningful to you. (4) Disregard everyday thoughts that come to your mind. Return to your repetition and your breathing without judgment about how well you are performing the technique. (5) Continue the repetition for fifteen minutes. Once you finish, do not stand immediately but continue to sit quietly, allowing your thoughts to return. Then open your eyes and sit another minute or so before standing up. (6) Practice this technique once or twice daily; morning and early evening are best.

Using the Relaxation Response, you will start and end your day in a more tranquil state. After several months of meditation, protected against excessive stress and anger the reactions of your body will be less affected by everyday life events. The practice of meditation enhances your control over your life and the daily situations you face. Your sense of equanimity as well as joyfulness and optimism will be enhanced.

As an alternative to the Relaxation Response, you may also want to try one of the next two meditations, for fifteen minutes daily, twice a day. Be patient.

Remember: Both the Relaxation Response and the Meditations for Tranquility are exercises emphasizing slow, deep breathing that helps you relax. Breathe from your abdominal (stomach) area, not from your chest area.

MEDITATIONS FOR TRANQUILITY

Introduction: Find a quiet place. Create a warm, welcoming atmosphere, an environment of serenity and spaciousness for the journey within. Lower the lights in the room, close your eyes, sit quietly, and calm and relax your body. Breathe in and out normally, feeling where your breath flows in and out of your body. Adjust your breaths so that the in and out breaths are the same length.

Mindfulness Meditation: Focus your awareness on your breathing. Observe your breath as you inhale and exhale. Continue to remain aware of and observe your breathing. Rest your mind on the calming waves of breathing. If your attention drifts and you are not observing your breath, refocus your attention and return your awareness to your breath. Remain alert and stay focused.

Equanimity Meditation: Reflect on a current, recent, or past event involving you that you found quite emotional, particularly in a negative way; a stress-, anger-, or envy-inducing event.

Why were (and are) you stressed, angry, or envious? Did your stress, anger, or envy arise from a trivial matter? Ask yourself: was this event and the emotions generated of the same magnitude of the death of your parent or your wife (or significant other)? Was (and is) your reaction proportional to the situation?

Strive to build a reservoir or understanding that will help you deal with various turbulent events as mere ripples in your life. A disturbance in a deep lake triggers only minor ripples, not major waves.

Concluding Instructions: Come back to the here and now. Take your time to ease yourself back. Slowly bring awareness into your body. Feel yourself back in the room and open your eyes.

You may want to link the Relaxation Response or other meditation with some form of focused exercise. The sustained, repetitive quality of walking or swimming, for example, helps engender the benefits of Relaxation Response or other meditation. Two elements are key: first, the use of mental device, such as a repeated word, phrase, or prayer and second, assuming a passive attitude, not worrying about how you are performing the technique, but instead putting aside distracting thoughts and returning to your repetition. Through a focused exercise you can reduce your stress, anger, or envy and diminish your negative thoughts.

PRACTICAL TECHNIQUES FOR ATTAINING AND MAINTAINING YOUR EQUANIMITY

Here are twelve practical techniques you can use to attain and maintain your equanimity. *First,* even if you can't (or don't want to) meditate, do inhale deeply, relax and, do diaphragmatic — from your stomach

— breathing. Allow your abdomen to expand and then fall as you exhale.

Second, you can enhance your tranquility by modifying your thoughts. An optimistic explanatory style can play a key role in your capacity to tolerate stressful or anger-inducing events. You can reflect and change how you think about the challenges you face. Strive to reframe events and personal interactions positively. Do not let your emotions jump into the midst of every problem, whether large or small, or your thoughts escalate into the worst possible scenario. Do not let every dilemma, great or tiny, overwhelm your mind. Replace negative, ingrained thought patterns with new, healthier ones. Ask yourself: will this issue (or problem) matter to me tomorrow, in one month, or in a year from now?

Don't automatically conclude that the brusque service provider is out to get you. Ask yourself: Is the threat real? Is the issue really important? Identifying your values and goals will help you focus on what really counts and stop negative reactions about irrelevant events or concerns. The service provider may be having a bad day or not feeling well.

Perhaps no one described the dynamics of serenity better than Reinhold Neibuhr, a twentieth-century Christian theologian: God, give me the grace to accept with serenity the things that cannot be changed, courage to change the things which should be changed, and the wisdom to distinguish the one from the other.

Third, problem solve and try to achieve the difficult balance between: accepting and letting go in some situations and acting and taking control in other circumstances. It's hard to choose the correct strategy at the right time. Sometimes it may be unwise or impossible to act immediately. When you encounter events or people that justifiably provoke anger, take a breather and wait out the commotion. Do not interrupt a tirade; let another wear himself out, then try to mollify him and respond to the core issue. Look for the chance to prod an explosive person to focus on the solution rather than dwelling on the problem.

Fourth, humor may be effective at lessening the threatening nature of stressful or anger-inducing events through positive reframing. We know that humor and laughter are vital assets leading to a drop in stress-related hormones, while boosting the immune system by increasing the body's defenses against viruses and other infections. A hearty laugh lowers blood pressure and decreases the heart rate, reducing the risk of coronary heart disease, thereby contributing to cardio-protection.[15]

Fifth, each evening, review the day's events and the people you have encountered to identify the sources of your stress, anger, envy, or impatience, for example, whether unsettling economic events or interpersonal relationships. Map out for the next day equanimity-inducing practices and accomplishing nagging, unfinished tasks.

Sixth, you may find it helpful to keep a journal detailing your stress, anger, envy, or impatience. Write down the day, time, place, the triggering person or event, the circumstances, and your mood. Writing things down helps get them off your chest. Identify and find a pattern in your emotional responses. Try to understand what was the real emotion — such as shame, guilt, fear, loss, heartbreak, or hurt — behind your stress, anger, envy, or impatience. Getting in touch with your deepest feelings will improve your physical and emotional health.

Seventh, create and use affirmations—a short, positive thought or a saying that asserts something you know is true, even if it isn't in your life yet. Some examples are: "I am cheerful and calm" or, "I would rather be happy than always right." State your affirmation in the present and phrase it as a positive, first person ("I") statement. By describing a quality you wish to develop or something you want to have manifested, affirmations can effectively reframe your negative thoughts and self-talk into a positive message.

Eighth, even now in your advanced years, you need time management skills and the ability to set priorities. Don't overextend yourself. Learn to say "no" when you are asked to do something that overloads your time or diverts you from essential activities. Live your priorities. Understand how you want to live and why. Regain your balance before you get overwhelmed and stressed out.

Once a month reevaluate your longevity plan and the basics in your life. Clean out the superfluous activities. Put off less important activities.

Identify and avoid time-wasters. Pace yourself in scheduling your tasks, allowing time for emergencies and interruptions. Figure out what part of the day you are most productive and do your essential and important tasks then.

Identify someone you know and respect for his or her ability to control the pace and balance of activities. Have breakfast, lunch, or coffee, monthly, to talk about these issues.

Ninth, get enough sleep. Cut back on coffee and alcohol that can interfere with restful sleep. Also, exercise regularly. Exercise has a calming effect on the body, releasing feel-good neurotransmitters (technically, endorphins) and helping reduce excess stress-related hormones. Moderate exercise, such as walking, helps relieve stress and frees your mind to see, if not smell, the roses.

Identify your favorite outdoor experience and arrange on a weekly basis to walk in the park, listen to the birds, feel the sun or the snow. Regularly focus on and engage in what you regard as life's little pleasures. Zone in on something you really enjoy.

Tenth, implement not only physically healthy measures but also financially sound practices. Financial worries exacerbate stress and contribute to envy. To deal with your financial worries, sit quietly and calculate your annual expenses and income. Take 20 percent off the income figure. You'll probably see that you can still afford your lifestyle. You have enough of a cushion to protect you from a troubled economy.

Eleventh, keep a daily gratitude journal. Write down things, events, or people that you appreciate and are grateful for, no matter how simple. Keeping a gratitude journey helps put events and people in perspective. It will help you decrease the impact of stressful, angry, hostile, or envious experiences. By becoming more aware of your gratitude, the more you free yourself from hostile or envious thoughts or stressful or angry reactions.

Twelfth, be more forgiving of yourself and others. Don't hold onto old grudges. Let bygones be bygones.

Attaining and maintaining serenity will help you feel whole in mind, body, and spirit, despite the losses you encounter and the pain and suffering you face. Equanimity represents a key to successful aging.

Because the mind and body are linked, a quiet mind contributes to a healthy body. The health of the body reverberates in emotional well-being. You also need to recognize the importance of social relationships.

MAINTAIN A SUSTAINED, ACTIVE ENGAGEMENT WITH LIFE THROUGH SOCIAL RELATIONSHIPS

Some of the most beneficial protection against the harmful effects of stress, anger, or envy comes from other people. They help us when we're sick by cheering us up and making us feel loved and valued, and listen to us when we need to talk. You need a social network—what I call a "fan club." People with close social and community ties enjoy better physical and emotional health as well as enhanced lifestyle habits.

Research shows the buffering, beneficial effects of good, solid social relationships, which take two forms: social integration and social support.[16] Social isolation, the opposite of social integration, is associated with an increased risk for morbidity and mortality.

In the famous Alameda County, California study, nearly 7,000 adults were followed for almost a decade. Researchers found that socially isolated individuals, those with fewer social and community ties, were more likely to die than those with more extensive contacts, independent of their preexisting physical health, economic status, or health practices. The death rate was more than double among men with the fewest social connections as compared with those having the most social contacts.[17]

More recently, researchers have found that a low level of social engagement directly impacts (and is a precursor for) mortality later in life, even controlling for physical health and age.[18] A ten-year Australian study found that people aged 70 years or more with a large circle of friends were 22 percent less likely to die (at least during the study period) than those with fewer friends.[19] Strong social ties also delay memory loss among those 50 and older.[20]

In other words, more social integration through participation in a broad range of relationships involving the active engagement in various activities with others decreases the risk of morbidity and mortality. Being part of a social network is a predictor of longevity and both better emotional and physical health, including a decreased risk for developing depression, high blood pressure, and heart disease.

Social support rests on one's social network providing various psychological and material resources. A social network supports one emotionally through positive expressions of affection, esteem, and respect. Others care about you (and hopefully you care about them). In addition to emotional sustenance, others can provide useful information and physical support, such as doing or helping with daily tasks or providing transportation to the supermarket and healthcare appointments. The size of your social network, the quality of the relationships you develop within it, and the nature of the support it provides influence your well-being and the quality of your life. The social support provided by a social network will help sustain you in your advanced years. Social connections will provide the psychological and material resources needed to protect and buffer the impact of emotional and physical illnesses.

A study of 752 healthy Swedish men, age fifty, found that those with high numbers of stressors in the year prior to the baseline exam were at a substantially greater risk for mortality during the seven year follow-up period, but that high levels of perceived emotional support ameliorated this effect.[21] Social support helps reduce high-risk behaviors, such as smoking, fosters effective coping strategies, for example, providing a solution to a problem, and encourages less-debilitating appraisals of a threat, for instance, by reducing a problem's perceived importance. Although social support isn't magic, it generally enhances emotional and physical health, for example, by helping reduce the negative impact of stress, anger, or envy.

Even if you're not gregarious, try to develop a web of meaningful social networks. Stay connected with friends and relatives. These networks will not only provide an emotional safety net but also will help keep you mentally stimulated. Avoid being a loner.

Remember: Men who do not have close family or friends are more likely to become ill and less likely to live long lives.

How many people do you have in you inner circle and what kind of support can they give you? With whom can you talk out a problem, gather information, and get a different perspective?

Ask yourself: is there someone who I can talk with about my problems and who will listen to me? Is there someone who trusts me and whom I trust? Is there someone who will always help me, regardless of the situation, so I never feel abandoned?

Your wife (or significant other) provides the first line of solid social and emotional support, often noticing changes that may signal a health problem. Being married is connected to longer life expectancy. A good, stable marriage is a big health protector. A happy marriage serves as the cornerstone for successful aging.

Some find that if they can rely on more than one person for social support they may be better off than if they look to one individual. Besides you're wife (or significant other), whom can you look to for social support? Children, siblings, and cousins may not make the best confidants. You may want to take steps to increase your social ties beyond your immediate family.

Close friends in whom you can confide can help lessen the impact of a major life event that otherwise would accelerate your aging. However, as we age our social worlds often shrink. There isn't the camaraderie of the workplace. Close friends move away or die. While striving to maintain longstanding relationships, try to develop new ones. Look for opportunities to find others with whom you can work in pursuit of a common goal. Strive to cultivate others to become interested and invested in your regard (and you in theirs). Conversely, disassociate from negative social contacts. Avoid individuals that make you stressful or angry.

Participation in group activities that foster meaningful friendships enhances social connectedness. Try to attend at least one social event each week to improve your social support network.

For example, possibly join a religious organization in your community. A socially supportive environment, such as you gain from religious services, has widely acknowledged physical and emotional health advantages. An analysis of 42 studies involving nearly 126,000 people found that those who attended an organized group religious service on a regular basis had a risk adjusted 29 percent lower mortality rate than those who did not. In other words, religious involvement was associated with the lower risk of death, after adjusting for demographic, socioeconomic, and health-related factors.[22]

Consider the physical health benefits. A significant association exists between higher religious attendance and a lower risk for cardiovascular disease.[23] Among adults, age sixty-five and older, researchers found that those who frequently attended religious services had lower blood pressure than those who attended infrequently.[24]

Volunteer to develop new friends and enhance your social integration and your social support network. To increase the odds of staying physically and emotionally healthy, participate in your community, as a way of receiving (and providing) support. Or, get involved in a new pursuit (or hobby) that will give you a way to connect with new people and cultivate new friends.

To overcome your isolation, especially if you're housebound or live alone, try visiting social networking sites, such as Eons.com, an online community for aging baby boomers. Join networks like Facebook and MySpace. Technology can provide a way to make new connection and new friends.

Seek out those who demonstrate the character traits and the lifestyle you wish to make your own. Avoid those who will disrupt the virtues you wish to cultivate.

Remember: Your poor reactions to stress or your unhealthy anger, for example, are not immutable, personality defects. You can change. With your emotional growth, new personal responses are possible, leading to physical and emotional health benefits.

6. Cultivate Your Loving Kindness and Forgiveness

This chapter presents two interpersonal character traits: loving kindness and forgiveness. After discussing the characteristics of each trait, techniques to build these traits, whatever your age, are set forth. The benefits of providing selfless service through volunteering are considered.

The Importance of Loving Kindness

We are here to express love, which draws people together. We are here to be the presence of love, the vehicle through which our lives express even more love in the world. See yourself as ready to give of your abundance of love to others.

Love resides in the depths of each of our hearts. It is intertwined with the roots of our being.

Love is that power that makes for harmony and happiness. Love brings people together; it holds the world together.

Love heals and soothes. It generates new strength through the birth of kind and tender feelings.

Contrast hatred with love. Hatred makes for separation. Hatred divides us one from another, contributing to human misery.

Hatred brings agony. It makes a person angry. It keeps an individual in a state of bitterness and irritability. Hatred destroys the heart in which it dwells, contributing to emotional and physical illness.

In contrast, a loving attitude not only helps bring you joy, it assists in freeing you from anxiety, anger, or hostility, negative feelings that can create emotional and physical problems.

Love implies compassion, warm-heartedness, and kindness. These attributes link us together.

Strengthening Your Love and Compassion For Others

Practice choosing love throughout the day. Be love's instrument, minute-by-minute, day-by-day. Do and speak the good and the beautiful. Express your love through your compassion, warm-heartedness, and kindness in every situation.

Be compassionate and sympathetic. Compassion is a matter of feeling with and for others. By acknowledging and opening your heart to others' pain and suffering, you feel your unity with others.

Compassion also implies a kindly, tender interpretation of others' motives, words, and acts. A sympathetic interpretation of others' deeds and words will show their better nature. The more you look for the finer traits in others, the finer, in turn, generally everyone becomes.

Our heart is the cementing power between humans. Keep your heart warm and open. Give it the opportunity for self-expression. A warm and gentle heart expresses itself in kindness and compassion. A warm and good heart seeks out others on whom to lavish helpfulness and encouragement.

Do not harbor bitterness or hatred in your heart. Do not erect barriers isolating your heart from others. Do not close your heart in judgment, criticism, anger, envy, fear, or worry. When your heart is closed, you are cut off from the flow of love. If the flow of love is blocked, you experience pain.

Kindness is inherent in each of us. It is in the depths of each human heart. Do not let bitterness, anger, or indifference cloud the natural kindness in your heart.

Nothing binds one heart to another heart more closely than acts or words of kindness. Cultivate kindness and bring it into your words and deeds. Kindness reaches the heart and stimulates love.

Begin the day by filling your heart with love, with compassion and kindness for everyone. Let this natural unity between humans assert itself. Do not obstruct its way. Keep as open a heart as possible.

MEDITATE TO ENHANCE YOUR LOVING KINDNESS

Many have found the Loving Kindness Meditation helpful in facilitating compassionate interactions with others. By generating loving kindness towards others you will be able to deal with your negative feelings regarding difficult people or those with whom you have disagreements and plant the seeds of a positive relationship. The Loving Kindness Meditation will open your heart to the love that transforms every experience, even painful ones.

If you know or meet someone to whom your heart does not incline, offer the Loving Kindness Meditation for ten to fifteen minutes daily, to turn your heart to love him or her. Be patient.

LOVING KINDNESS MEDITATION[1]

Introduction: Create a warm, welcoming atmosphere. Lower the lights. Close your eyes, sit quietly, calm and relax your body, breathe in and out normally, feeling where your breath flows into and out of your body. Adjust the breaths so that the in and out breaths are the same length, thereby bringing about both a relaxation of the body and an alertness of the mind.

Recall to mind someone toward whom you feel great gratitude. Let your feelings of love sweep over this person. Then recall a friend toward whom you have feelings of kindness. Let your feelings of love radiate to that person. Next recall a difficult person, someone toward whom you feel anger or hatred, or someone you fear. Ultimately, focus on the person who has hurt you the most. Let love radiate from your heart to this person. To each of these, express the following:

As I wish to be free from danger and achieve safety,
so may you be free from danger and achieve safety.
As I wish to have happiness, so may you have happiness.
As I wish to have good health and be free from physical or mental
pain, so may you have good health and be free from physical
or mental pain.
As I wish inner peace of mind, so may you have inner peace of
mind.

Now pause a moment and feel yourself surrounded by warmth. Allow any anger, hatred, or fear you feel to dissolve into the warmth and patience towards others. Breathe in patience and feel the spaciousness that patience creates within you. Gently open your heart.

Give yourself time. Wish yourself well. Let your heart fill with loving kindness toward yourself. Say to yourself:

May I be: healed; at peace; happy; free from pain and suffering; free
from anger, hatred, and fear; filled with joy and love.

Toward someone from whom you feel great love may you be: healed; at peace; happy; free from pain and suffering; free from anger, hatred, and fear; filled with joy and love.

Let your love expand. Let your loving kindness radiate to all human beings. May they be: healed; at peace; happy; free from pain and suffering; free from anger, hatred, and fear; filled with joy and love.

May all of our hearts open. May we all be healed by the power of love for each other.

Concluding Instructions: Now come back to the here and now. Take time to ease yourself back. Slowly bring your awareness back into your body. Feel yourself back in the room and open your eyes.

PRACTICAL TECHNIQUES TO CULTIVATE LOVING KINDNESS

Manifest loving kindness and compassion each day in your words and in your deeds. When you bring happiness to others, the emotions of kindness and goodness will grow strong until they become the deepest part of your being. Kind words are not lost; kind acts are not forgotten.

Words are very powerful. Use them carefully. Pay attention to what you say about people. During the day do not speak ill of anyone for any reason. Try to minimize (or, hopefully, eliminate) negative talk about others. Avoid passing on anything negative you have heard about another, even if it is true.

If a friend introduces a mutual acquaintance into a conversation with you by way of gossip, try, if possible, to steer the conversation in a different direction rather than asking for more details. Avoid the company of individuals who gain pleasure in disparaging others.

Do not embarrass or put another to shame, especially in public. Do not wrong another with words that cause pain or distress, for instance, by bringing up unpleasant memories, failures, or past misdeeds.

Train your tongue to speak kind words. Speak kindly to people; speak kindly of people. Speak kind words: words that encourage, that bring out the best in others, that inspire others to higher achievements and better conduct, that offer expressions of appreciation — not words that hurt, humiliate, cause anxiety, make life's burdens grow heavier, or keep one's capabilities imprisoned.

Speaking a kind word kindles hope in the despondent, lifts up downtrodden spirits, and transforms enmity to love. A kind word leaves a lasting, positive impression. You will encourage others; you will give them strength; you will gain their respect.

Express your honest, sincere appreciation and gratitude. Overlook weaknesses in others. Do not dwell on others' weaknesses; do not focus on others' faults. Try to see only the good that exists in others. Speak only of the good in others.

Let your deeds demonstrate your loving kindness. Strive to generate love between yourself and others as well as among people. Through your conduct, your compassion, your warm-heartedness, and your kindness, be a helper to all and an enemy to none. Extend love to everyone you touch in any way. Let love's healing power flow through you in every human interaction.

Although there are innumerable possibilities of expressing your loving kindness, let me offer a few concrete suggestions:

- Extend your hospitality to others.
- Bring peace between and among people.
- Do not injure, exploit, or oppress others through your deeds.
- Do not deprive others of anything to which they are entitled.
- Do not withhold from others any of the freedoms you claim for yourself.
- Facilitate others' self-fulfillment by helping them discover and realize their strengths and motivators.
- Through your words and deeds bring out the best and the highest in others, and always strive to encourage and inspire others in their efforts.

In short, let your love for others serve as your priority in every situation. Daily perform small acts of gentleness, patience, and kindness, one building upon another.

Try to be a love finder, not a faultfinder or a critic. Do not focus on what is wrong or lacking in others. Do not look only for shortcomings or see only errors or deficiencies in others. Whenever you engage in faultfinding, whether in its subtle forms like complaining or worrying, or in its more overt forms, such as overtly attacking others or being judgmental or critical, you feel isolated, separated from other humans and from the goodness of life.

People who live life with the sting of criticism, of judgment, or of complaint on their lips are often very lonely. If you only see others' wrong words and deeds, their shortcomings and weaknesses; if you only find fault with others' opinions and judgments; or if you only see others' stupidity, meanness, and vulgarity, you will shut out any space for love.

During the day, ask yourself: are there important people in your life whom you have not told how much you love and value them? Perhaps you have told them, but not recently or sufficiently. If so, call, write a note, or send an e-mail expressing your appreciation to each of them.

Each evening ask yourself: Did you genuinely love others today? Contemplate your missed opportunities for expressing loving kindness and compassion in your speech and conduct. Vow to express your loving kindness and compassion tomorrow.

EXPRESSING YOUR LOVE AND COMPASSION FOR OTHERS THROUGH SELFLESS SERVICE

Keep your heart active with the passing years. Your heart must continue to cherish the emotion of love. In addition to the passion of love fostered in the heart of youth, it is a higher love, a love of humanity, a love of a better and more perfect world. Strive to direct the flow of your love into altruistic channels—to love others, thereby avoiding wallowing in self-absorption and narcissism.

Each day, remember that you live, in part, to love others and benefit humanity. Dedicate part of your daily existence to helping perfect the world through your selfless service to others. Turn outward and identify with, feel, and do for others.

Each day reach out to those around you by being of service to others. Ask yourself: what can I best do for others to help relieve their pain and suffering, to make their life easier, and to aid them in experiencing happiness? Through your service to others, you cheer the depressed, provide hope to the discouraged, lighten some of the burdens of others, comfort those in pain, console the sorrowful, and kindle hope in human hearts.

You can serve others in numerous ways. Acts of loving kindness and compassion need not be on a grand scale. You can assist individuals and organizations with your compassion and concern, your humor, your prayers, your counsel and advice, your talents, or your money. Give of yourself to others through whatever means is appropriate for you. You can make a difference.

Things or money cannot substitute for time. Volunteer your time to open your heart in joy and give hope to people suffering from the pain of loneliness, homelessness, hunger, or sickness.

Be present for others—to listen, to talk, to care for them. In a world in which everyone is jabbering but few are listening, focus on what someone else really needs.

By offering others your genuine, yet humble, help through your love and compassion, you evoke in others the qualities that benefit humanity. As you radiate love, those with whom you come in contact are positively affected.

In making decisions about how to allocate your time and your strengths, reflect on the goals of offering unconditional love and rendering selfless service to others. Each day ask yourself: How much love am I giving others? How much service am I rendering others? Remember that you can give your love and compassion and not be diminished through your gifts of love and compassion.

Ask yourself: What am I here to give to others? What are my special strengths and the unique means of expressing my talents? How can I best help others?

In serving others, however, do not become a self-sacrificing martyr. Finding an appropriate balance is not easy. In striving to perform selfless services, do not neglect your family, your friends, or yourself. Overcommitment leads to burnout. Focus your efforts. There is a time to say, "Enough." Assert, "I'm just stretched too thin to take on another commitment and do a good job." Set boundaries so you don't get sucked in forever. Build in an expiration date. Learn to say: "I've enjoyed being Treasurer for two years, but I don't want to continue indefinitely. I'll just finish my term. Let it be someone else's turn."

BENEFITS PROVIDED BY SELFLESS SERVICE THROUGH VOLUNTEERING

In *The Healing Power of Doing Good*,[2] Allan Luks concluded that people who help others report better health than their peers. Using mind-body research, survey results from 3,300 volunteers, and first hand accounts, Luks demonstrated that helping others improved the volunteers' emotional and physical health.

According to Luks, the release of endorphins occurring when people reach out in service not only relieved pain but also stimulated the pleasurable feelings he described as the "helper's high."[3] Volunteers claimed both short-term and long-term emotional benefits, including a greater sense of calm and optimism as well as a decrease in feelings of depression. Volunteers indicated they experienced relief from various pain symptoms, including chronic headaches and stomachaches; they reported fewer cold and flu symptoms. There was also relief from the symptoms of chronic diseases.[4]

Studies have shown that frequent volunteers experience significantly reduced mortality[5] compared to non-volunteers as well as improved, self-rated physical and mental health.[6] These benefits are not easily explained by differences in demographics or socioeconomic status, or even by prior health or levels of physical activity and exercise.

The benefits of helping strongly correlate to the consistency of the behavior. Long-term emotional and physical benefits occur only when people engage in a regular regime of helping activities over sustained time periods. The frequency of helping is also critical. Weekly helping (about two hours a week, one-to-one) is much better than monthly or one-time volunteer endeavors. It is also important to let go of any expected results and just feel close to and empathize with the person (or those) one is trying to help.

The benefits of helping are greatest among those with higher levels of other psychosocial support, such as religious involvement. One study of 7,527 people more than seventy years old found that frequent volunteering is associated with less mortality risk. The protectiveness of volunteering was significantly greater in fostering longevity among those who frequently attended religious services (or frequently visited with friends).[7]

Through speaking kind words and performing acts of love and compassion, the habit of love will become the deepest part of your being, replacing the habits of fear, worry, anger, envy, criticism, or suspicion. As you fill your heart with love for everyone, implementing your feelings through your words and your conduct, others will respond with love.

Kindness reaches the heart and stimulates love. The more you love, in turn, generally the more you will be loved.

Always give others your love and compassion, but do not expect any reward in return. Sometimes your love and compassion are not reciprocated. Love without any expectation of another's positive response. Your loving kindness ought to be unconditional and selfless.

THE IMPORTANCE OF FORGIVENESS

Loving kindness and forgiveness are interrelated. By forgiving others, you open your heart and rediscover the capacity to love within you. Each of us is here to express unconditional love and forgiveness.

Forgiveness represents love in action. Forgiveness sets us free to love those who have harmed us and build new relationships with old enemies. By letting go of the past, your right to resent and negatively judge a perpetrator, someone you perceive to be blameworthy, you are able to embrace a creative future in which old wounds become the basis for a new beginning.

You experience love by extending forgiveness to others, by accepting others, and by letting go of the past. By forgiving, you invite love to replace a gamut of negative emotions, including hostility, hatred, fear, anger, rejection, humiliation, judgment, blame, disappointment, or resentment toward a transgressor, any of which constrict your heart and narrow your world.

Forgiveness represents a key to cultivating inner peace of mind and to helping achieve better emotional health by reducing negative thoughts and feelings and increasing positive sentiments and perspectives, such as compassion. Forgiveness helps you surmount past, often painful, experiences that otherwise continue to allow the offender to maintain control over you. Forgiveness not only absolves someone else, the perpetrator, it also heals you, the victim. It's for your own good.

FORGIVENESS IS NOT EASY

Forgiveness is often not easy. It is hard to forgive, especially if you have been hurt badly by a major breach of trust and loyalty, a betrayal that tears people apart, particularly where its effects are irreversible, for instance, murder, adultery, incest, child, spousal, or parental abuse, child, spousal, or parental abandonment, discrimination because of race, gender, or age, or alcoholism or substance abuse. The harm caused by people you are close to can be overwhelming. Forgiveness often demands courage and a strong sense of self to overcome the pain you have experienced.

To make the concept of forgiveness more concrete, contemplate an interpersonal problem, situation, interaction, or relationship you currently face (or have encountered in the past). Think of striving to choose forgiveness in the face of being tempted to perceive another's thoughtless deeds and hurtful words as an attack on you and responding with your own counterattack.

We have all experienced this kind of physical or emotional discomfort. We have felt the pain of another's unkind deeds and words. The body grows tense, the mind becomes tight, and the heart closes.

I once had an insecure, incompetent boss promoted way above his administrative ability and interpersonal skills. He constantly played office politics as he made decisions. He had his favorites and I was not one of them.

I felt anger toward him and became embittered. I kept rolling over the boss in my mind, replaying his "offenses" again and again, like a bad motion picture. Although I'm not a violent person, I would spit at the mention of his name.

Eaten up with bitterness and anger, I was amazed at my unforgiving face in a mirror. The ugliness shocked me.

I gradually recognized the price I was paying for my unwillingness to let go of the past. I saw that holding on to my feelings of anger was self-defeating.

Only by forgiving him could I see him in a more positive light. Letting go of the person and his "offenses," I came to feel less anger and accepted the core of him as the same as myself. I gave him the gift of not judging him anymore or holding him in contempt. I acknowledged that I would not (and could not) change or correct him in any way.

I came to realize that holding onto my resentment and bitterness would hurt me much more than my boss, who was not harmed at all. Admitting that my hateful attitude was just as wrong as what he had done to me, through forgiveness, I broke the chain of resentment that bound him to me, enabling me to be free of him.

In forgiving others, you cannot pretend that you are not affected by someone's hurtful conduct or speech. Forgiveness is not permissiveness. It is not an expression of "anything goes." By forgiving, you do not pronounce as acceptable someone's cruelty, thoughtlessness, inhumanity, or dishonesty.

Others utter words or do things that are unkind and unloving, whether intentionally or negligently, out of ignorance or forgetfulness, or even out of fear or insecurity. They may do cruel or violent things. These actions or statements bring suffering not only to the actors or speakers, but also to others — to you. Forgiveness does not mean condoning, accepting, or justifying another's actions or words. Forgiveness does not excuse someone else's behavior. You cannot ignore another's difficult qualities or his (or her) insensitive, hurtful, or unloving acts or words.

Through forgiveness, you can accept people who have disappointed you by not being perfect. You judge others far less severely. You become more accepting of human frailty, more ready to give the benefit of the doubt. You show that you are willing to let go of your focus on another's "guilt" deserving of punishment and of the way you have been looking at a situation, an interpersonal problem, or a relationship, and not hold on to the past. You become less hostile and more openhearted and tolerant.

Do not let your anger and your hate continue to poison you. Do not carry a grudge, seek to punish or take revenge, or blame another. Letting go of your resentment and relinquishing your goal of retribution lifts the weight of hate and anger from your shoulders, easing your pain, and helping you forget how you were wronged. By forgiving, as I did, you release the offender's hold on you.

Benefits of Forgiveness

Through forgiveness, you shift your perspective and see things differently by looking beyond another's actions, behavior, words, or personality. This shift in perception promotes emotional and physical health. By helping dissolve your fears and worries, forgiveness reduces your anxiety, thereby helping restore your inner peace of mind.

Studies indicate that people, without serious mental illness, who forgave reported positive mental health benefits, specifically decreased anxiety and depression.[8]

The festering anger and hostility generated by an unforgiving nature are bad for your physical health. Holding onto perceptions of past transgressions are like other health-endangering stressors. Unforgiveness produces a similar, hyper-aroused stress response.

Chronic unforgiving perpetuates stress far beyond the original stressful incident, heightening one's blood pressure and heart rate. Because unforgiveness is stressful, forgiveness, by helping you let go of your resentment, elevates your immune system, reduces your blood pressure, decreases your heart rate, and may stave off serious illness.[9]

Small scale studies examining physiological responses (more technically, reactivity) during recalled or imagined offenses have found physical health benefits from forgiveness. In one study, recalled experiences of betrayal that were less forgiven were associated with higher cardiovascular reactivity, measured by higher diastolic blood pressure. Forgiveness was associated with lower blood pressure and heart rate.[10] Another study found that forgiveness imagery produced smaller blood pressure and heart rate responses than grudge-holding imagery.[11] Forgiveness may also have a greater impact on the self-rated mental and physical health of older persons than young adults.[12]

Techniques To Build Forgiveness

I wish I could offer a magic approach you could use in forgiving others or asking others for their forgiveness. However, there is no formula to put forgiveness into practice.

Forgiveness begins with self-forgiveness, which involves recognizing both your goodness and imperfections. Overcome any lingering beliefs of your unworthiness, including recollections of the ways you have been unloving or harmful, past mistakes you have made, or your prior misdeeds, resulting in debilitating feelings of shame, guilt, or remorse. Judge yourself less severely. By giving others the right to make mistakes, you become more willing to do that for yourself.

Beyond self-forgiveness, acknowledge your hurt to yourself, recognizing that someone did something harmful to you. Then decide to forgive, seeing another through the eyes of love, not through the eyes of judgment or guilt, using meditation and practical techniques.

MEDITATE TO CULTIVATE FORGIVENESS

Many have found the Forgiveness Meditation helpful in forgiving someone they dislike or hold a grievance toward, someone to whom their heart has been closed, or in asking another they have hurt for his or her forgiveness.

Begin by making a list of those who have offended or hurt you at any time in your life and with whom reconciliation has not occurred. Take time to make the list. Don't worry about the number of names on the list. For each person, write how he or she offended or hurt you, at least as you now see it. Then list those you have offended or hurt.

With the list in hand, use the Forgiveness Meditation for ten to fifteen minutes, once or twice daily. Be patient. Forgiveness is often a lengthy process.

FORGIVENESS MEDITATION[13]

Introduction: Try to create a warm welcoming atmosphere, an environment of serenity and spaciousness for the journey within. Lower the lights in your room. Close your eyes, sit quietly, calm and relax your body by sitting, reclining, or lying down. Breathe in and out normally, feeling where your breath flows into and out of your body. Adjust your breaths so that the in and out breaths are the same length, thereby bringing about both a relaxation of your body and an alertness of your mind.

Feel yourself surrounded by warmth and patience. Allow any anger or hatred you feel toward others to dissolve into warmth and patience. With each breath, breathe in warmth. Feel the warmth nourishing you. Breathe in patience and feel the spaciousness and the opening of your heart that patience creates within you. Allow the warmth and patience to give rise to forgiveness.

Feel your body. Release any tension or tightness you feel inside, caused by anger, fear, or resentment. Let go of the pride that holds on to resentment. Allow the pain of old hurts to fade away.

Forgive yourself for having harmed yourself, not loved yourself, not lived up to your expectations. Say: for every way I have harmed myself, I offer forgiveness.

Reflect on _____, someone who has caused you pain and suffering; someone who has made you angry, hateful, or fearful, intentionally or accidentally; and send him or her forgiveness. Say: I forgive you. Forgive him or her as best you can. Allow the power of forgiveness to grow.

Out of loving kindness, allow the resentment to fade away. Let go of your judgment of another, and replace it with understanding and compassion. Ask that no harm come to _____ because of what he or she has done to you.

For _____, whom you have caused pain and suffering, anger, hatred, or fear, intentionally or accidentally, ask for his or her forgiveness. Say: I ask you for forgiveness. Forgive yourself for anyone's pain and suffering to which you have contributed.

Concluding Instructions: Come back to the here and now. Take time to ease yourself back. Slowly bring your awareness back into your body. Feel yourself back in the room and open your eyes.

Destroy your list with its names and offenses and don't tell any of the people on it what you have done. Once you have given your forgiveness, let it go. You are emotionally free to go on with your life, leaving the baggage behind.

Also, for those you have harmed in the past, consider writing a note of apology requesting his or her forgiveness. Say that you are sorry. You need not send the letter. The important thing is expressing your thoughts in writing.

Practical Techniques To Cultivate Forgiveness

Through a shift in perception, you hopefully will receive a new vision of someone you are forgiving, helping replace the pain, anger, or hatred with an inner peace of mind. But remember that forgiving another means saying "no more" from a calm, quiet place. Do not condone another's hurtful, negative deeds or words.

To heal a damaged relationship, you may want to take the initiative and try to repair a connection that was (and is) important to you. Although quite difficult, forgiveness often means confronting the offender (even if he or she does not seek forgiveness) face-to-face, sharing your issues, making explicit your concerns, and discussing what you see as the transgressor's "shortcomings." Do not use the confrontation as a means of punishment, intimidation, or embarrassment. Before the meeting, gather your thoughts carefully; writing out your thoughts and feelings is often helpful. Enumerate what changes you'd like to see in the relationship and what adjustments you're willing to make as part of a reconciliation.

Hear the other's explanation for his or her behavior, his or her side of things, his or her feelings. Think about his or her vulnerabilities. Develop a degree of empathy for the "offender." See things from his or her viewpoint.

Offer your support and your constructive suggestions for improvement, without judgment, blame, or attack. Speak sincerely from your heart. Taking a nonjudgmental stance, however hard it may be for you, is especially important. Through an honest exchange, share your feelings, lovingly and truthfully, with the other about his or her "shortcomings." Make it a positive sharing, not a destructive attack.

In a relationship based on mutual trust and open communication, you can gently point out another's errors, weaknesses, or mistakes, hopefully without fear of withdrawal, attack, retaliation, defensiveness, or denial.

In a relationship where you take the initiative in forgiving another but the offender has not sought your forgiveness, the reality often departs from the ideal. Be patient. However, the efforts to mend a broken relationship may be shunned. Be prepared for the injuring party's negative, often defensive, reaction, which may culminate in an intense, painful verbal attack on you, in response to your expression of forgiveness. Regardless of the nature of your relationship or another's response to your efforts, honor the injuring party's process of growth and change, however difficult this may be for you. Don't make it your business to force an agreement if it is not forthcoming. Listen, but don't compromise your principles. Hope for the best, but be prepared for the worst, especially a negative reaction.

If you anticipate an ongoing relationship, you must set some boundaries on your future interactions. You will need to learn to say

"No," calmly but firmly, to another's preferences, demands, or behavior. Stand fast. Back up your words with action.

If your heart does not allow you to love someone you have forgiven, try to think of some great goodness concerning him or her, find one good quality, or hope for something good for that person, so that you may come to better perceive his or her inner worth, however difficult it may be. Seeing good in (or for) another often allows you to begin to relate better to him or her.

Sometimes, the pain and betrayal is so great that we cannot face it alone. Forgiveness may require the companionship of a spiritual leader, a therapist, a close friend, or a support group to find the courage and strength to forgive and love again.

BENEFITS OF A LIFE REVIEW

To reach a state of serenity, inner peace of mind, loving kindness and forgiveness, many find a life review helpful to sort out the chaos of the past and to get things whole. A life review, as a regular, ongoing practice, say every five years, beginning on "retirement" or a significant birthday, provides a helpful means of sorting through what has gone before, particularly one's unresolved life experiences and previously unexpressed emotions.

Bruce had always been emotionally distant and short-fused. He was a scientist who had followed in the footsteps of his scientist father and grandfather. He had assumed that his son, Jon, would carry on the family tradition. Jon resisted. He was constantly drawing. At an early age, he loved to go to museums and could admire paintings long before his peers were mature enough for such an activity. Bruce disdained this as a waste of time; Helen, his mother, encouraged Jon as much as possible.

Under pressure from Bruce, Jon took a number of science courses in high school. But when it came time to apply to colleges, Jon rebelled and announced he wanted to pursue art history. Bruce flew into a rage. From her own funds, Helen paid for Jon's undergraduate education. Thereafter, Jon received various fellowships on his way to a doctorate in art history.

Over the years, while Jon became a prominent art historian, Bruce held a grudge and disdained any move toward reconciliation. He never saw Jon and Jon's children.

As preparations were underway for Bruce's seventieth birthday, he began to question his longstanding hostility. Helen triggered his self-examination by asking: "Do you want your legacy to be a decades-long feud with Jon?"

Through a timely life review, where he confronted several unresolved conflicts, including his relationship with his son, Bruce came to feel less angry about Jon's career choice.

When Jon attended Bruce's birthday party, Bruce made a decision. Although he could not make up for the past decades, he wanted to build a relationship with his son going forward. He realized that his ultimate goal for his son was for him to be happy and productive and follow his passion as he had followed his.

Bruce took Jon aside at the birthday party. "Son," he began, "I want you to forgive me for the way I acted about your career. I was wrong. You were right to follow your dream the same way that I followed mine. You found what you are on this earth to do. So few people ever find what they are meant to do with their lives."

Bruce and Jon both cried and hugged for the first time in years. The healing was complete. Forgiveness was extended and welcomed.

Father and son reconciled and began a new, harmonious relationship. The joy Bruce experienced was inexpressible.

A life review is a do-it-yourself informal process. Taking your own inventory, a life review ought to be comprehensive and encompassing. Keep the random bits and pieces flying out of you. The following may serve as a helpful guide:

- Happy moments and sad occasions
- Expressions of gratitude and appreciation for goodness and beauty in life, including the experience of love
- Accomplishments, experiences of growth, and instances of overcoming a limitation or a challenge
- Regrets, grievances, old hurts, unrealized hopes and dreams, undeveloped talents, missed opportunities, failed relationships, and harms inflicted on or by others

- Important people, from both a positive and negative standpoint, in one's life
- Expressions of emotions and feelings as well as previously unrevealed family secrets

You may want to record, orally, in writing, or on audio or videotape, the events and relationships of a lifetime. Express what is in your heart, ask for forgiveness for past hurts and harms to and from others, make apologies, and achieve reconciliation. You'll come out as profoundly human—warts and all. It will help you explore how you became the person you are today.

The life review also assists in questioning and broadly reflecting on the meaning and purpose of your life. It's a summing up. Go over the past, make amends to yourself and others, look at unresolved interpersonal conflicts and strive to resolve them, address your inner demons and wounds. Celebrate moments of joy. Come to terms with your successes and disappointments in life and in your relationships. Look squarely at your life and feel at peace with it. By getting to know yourself, you will likely become more comfortable with yourself.

Do not feel pressured to engage in a life review. Although exploring one's past provides many benefits, it can be discomforting, even emotionally painful. The memories of significant unresolved conflicts may be overwhelming. Feelings of regret, guilt, even despair may surface.

Although a life review may open emotional wounds, it often provides a basis for healing, a wholeness of body, mind, and spirit. Coming to terms with sources of emotional pain, especially long-standing sources that previously were beyond words, can provide relief and sometimes help resolve one or more interpersonal conflicts, thereby promoting forgiveness and an inner peace of mind.

Having the time at this stage in your life, a life review may take the form of a memoir, or some sort of an autobiography. Many find that writing helps when they are trying to make sense of their life. By telling one's own life story, memoir writing represents a very personal journey inward that may lead to self-examination and self-discovery. By getting a meaningful view of oneself and one's life, writing a memoir often helps in figuring things out.

Finally, a life review, whether or not in the form of a memoir, helps illuminate the fresh potential for one's future. It may provide strategies to take one's life in a new, positive direction, in terms of interpersonal relationships and productive activities. You may learn to swat the should-haves or the could-haves from your existence.

In your advanced years, keep your lips smiling and your heart warm and forgiving, time will lose its dreariness. You will discover one of the best periods of your life, a time marked by less of a tendency to judge others harshly or quickly.

Emotional growth and development occur throughout one's lifetime. In your 60s, 70s, and 80s, you can continue to develop positive character traits. Your emotional development can be invigorating. Although each of us differs in our potential as well as our strengths and motivators, such as one's emphasis on creative expression or spirituality, we can continue to grow and develop emotionally. You can become better at adapting to conditions, calmer in the face of life's difficulties, and more loving and forgiving.

III. Physical Wellness: Keep Physically Fit and Mentally Alert

We all want to live a long, healthy life. It's important to take charge and do what we can to enrich and enhance our lives. We want to join the ranks of the oldest of the old in good shape, physically and mentally, until nearly the very end.

Longevity is a waste if the additional years are characterized by chronic illness, frailty and disability, and an increasingly lower quality of life. However, it is never too late to adopt habits that generally lead to a healthy old age, physically and mentally.

In addition to discovering and striving to implement your dreams (or passions) and your values and enhancing your emotional health, successful aging turns on your choices and behaviors with respect to your physical health — your body, considered in Chapter 7, and your brain, discussed in Chapter 8.

7. Improve Your Body Wellness

Stan's father died when he was 56. When Stan was 12, he remembered he wanted to grab the collar of the white dress shirt his father always wore to work and shake him. He told his dad to clean up his act: quit smoking, get some exercise, stop being stressed out from his job. Stan wanted to shake him for the cigarette cough he woke up to every morning. Stan missed him at his wedding, for not being here for him and his wife to share the birth of their children, for leaving Stan's mom a widow. An all-too-often tale of the past generation.

Today we know that despite decades of risky behavior, such as smoking, a lack of exercise, overindulgence in alcohol, improper eating; the choices you make now can decrease your health risks and increase physical and mental functions beyond past levels. If you choose, you can remain physically active and mentally alert for many, many years. Disease and disability need not be inexorable consequences of aging.

Some of the biological characteristics of old age—loss of vigor and health—are disease processes, not the inevitable consequences of living longer. Some chronic, debilitating diseases are preventable. You can live a long, healthy, productive life, succumbing ultimately to the biological declines of old age, not disease.

Rather than becoming decrepit and dependent, you can age well. You can live a longer, healthier life, achieving high-quality, disease-free advanced years, until shortly before your death. You can end your life with a brief period of illness, thereby achieving what is called a compression of morbidity.

Your lifestyle choices and behaviors can counteract physical and mental deterioration. Although genes are important, how you choose to live is probably more important with respect to the health risk factors associated with aging. Sound lifestyle choices and behaviors can help safeguard you at least to some degree against developing any disorder you are genetically predisposed to. It's never too late to change your lifestyle choices and behaviors for the better. Turning over a new leaf can be highly effective.

Successful aging rests on: first, avoiding disease and disability; second, maintaining a high level of physical and mental functioning; and third, continuing to be active and engaged in life, by remaining productive and building strong interpersonal relationships and a large social network. Keep yourself physically and mentally active and in close contact with others.

The absence of disease and disability, of course, makes it easier to maintain high physical and mental functions. In turn, the maintenance of high physical and mental functions promotes an active engagement with life.

To avoid disease and disability, this chapter focuses on prevention and the maintenance of good physical function. Through prudent habits, many men could reach age 90 in good health and die after a relatively brief period of illness. In one's later years it is less a matter of one's genes and more a question of how one chooses to live. With sound, preventive habits you'll live longer and be less likely to develop diseases and disabilities. You can add years to your life and life to your years, keeping you well and able to enjoy life far longer than you might otherwise have.

THE FIVE PILLARS OF GOOD HEALTH

Living past age ninety and at the same time living well, may be more than merely good genes and good luck. Perhaps only 30 percent of the differences in longevity among people can be traced to heredity.

A study of 2,357 men, who were healthy at a mean age of 72 (with a range of 66 to 84 years) when the study began, found that five behaviors not only were associated with living to an advanced age but also with good general health and independent functioning. Compared with the non-survivors, the 970 men in this study who lived to at least age 90 had a healthier lifestyle, experienced a lower incidence of chronic diseases, and were three to five years older at the onset of chronic diseases.[1]

You've heard all of this before, numerous times, but the study found that five specific behaviors are significantly correlated with healthy survival of men to at least age 90. The five modifiable behaviors are:

1.   abstaining from smoking;
2.   avoiding diabetes;
3.   controlling your blood pressure;
4.   watching your weight;
5.   exercising regularly.

Implementation of these five behaviors in early elderly years strongly predicts survival into advanced years with good health and physical functioning. In short, men with healthy habits live longer and better.

Abstain From Smoking. We all know someone from the previous generation who was done-in prematurely by smoking, a significant risk factor for heart disease, stroke, or lung cancer, among other deadly conditions. For example, Ian Fleming, the English author who created the world's best-known spy, James Bond, provides a model of what not to do. Fleming died at age 56 of complications from pleurisy, an inflammation of the membrane enveloping the lungs, after playing a round of golf, when he had a heavy cold. The real culprits were years of chain-smoking four packs of cigarettes a day and a fondness for alcohol.

The longevity study found that smokers had double the risk of death before age 90 compared to nonsmokers.[2] Not smoking thus represents the first step to effectively compress morbidity, thereby remaining free of disease and disability until shortly before death.

The benefits of stopping smoking are substantial, regardless of your age. After quitting smoking, the risk of coronary heart disease plummets within months. After not smoking for three to five years, the risk of coronary heart disease is indistinguishable from those who never smoked.

Avoid Diabetes. In the longevity study, men with diabetes increased their risk of death before age 90 by 86 percent.[3] It is the leading cause of kidney failure, blindness, and leg amputations. Thickening of the walls of the small blood vessels, as a result of diabetes, can lead to complications involving the kidneys or the eyes. The premature buildup of plaque in diabetics' arteries (atherosclerosis), making arterial walls inelastic and thick, and decreasing blood flow, can result in a heart attack, stroke, or the loss of circulation in the legs. Diabetes can triple the risk for heart attack and stroke. In addition to a host of physical problems, Type 2 diabetes also increases the risk of depression as well as the risk of dementia and Alzheimer's disease.

Diabetes is a disorder of metabolism, namely, the way one's body uses digested food for energy. Most of the food one eats is broken down into glucose, the form of sugar in the blood. Glucose serves as the main source of fuel for the body.

After one digests food, glucose passes into the bloodstream where cells use it for energy. For glucose to get into cells, insulin must be present. Insulin is a hormone produced by the pancreas, a large gland behind the stomach.

When a non-diabetic eats, the pancreas automatically produces the correct amount of insulin to move glucose from the blood to the cells. In someone with diabetes, the pancreas produces little or no insulin or the cells fail to respond appropriately to the insulin that is produced. As glucose builds up in the body, it overflows into the urine and then passes out of the body. The bottom line: as a result of diabetes, a disorder of blood sugar regulation, the body loses its main fuel source, although the blood contains large amounts of glucose.

There are two types of diabetes: Type 1 and Type 2. Type 1 diabetes is an autoimmune disease that results when the body's system for fighting infection—the immune system—turns against a part of the body. Specifically, the immune system attacks and destroys the insulin-producing cells in the pancreas. As a result, the pancreas produces little or no insulin. As noted above, insulin enables sugar to cross from the bloodstream into the cells, where it is used as energy. With diabetes, the body cannot use blood sugar as energy.

About 90 to 95 percent of those with diabetes have Type 2. With Type 2 diabetes, the pancreas produces enough insulin, at first, but the body cannot use the insulin effectively (technically, there's insulin resistance). After several years, insulin production decreases as a result of the pancreatic cells wearing out, producing the same result as Type 1 diabetes. Glucose builds up in the blood, creating a sort of super-sugary fluid, and the body cannot effectively use its main fuel source.

More than 23 percent of all people in the United States over 60 suffer from Type 2 diabetes. The risk of Type 2 diabetes increases if a family member has had the disease, if one is obese or sedentary, or a member of certain ethnic groups (black or Hispanic), and as one ages. About 80 percent of people with Type 2 diabetes are overweight, especially with an accumulation of fat around the waist. Abdominal fat is dangerous because it secretes hormones and other things that counter the action of insulin. In other words, abdominal obesity often results in insulin resistance.

The best protection against Type 2 diabetes: lose weight; stay active and exercise regularly; and keep your blood pressure under control. You can't change your age, family history, or ethnicity. However, you can control obesity and a lack of physical activity. Follow the weight management suggestions discussed in this chapter. In brief, avoid saturated fats and transfats, red and processed meats, and sugar-sweetened beverages and desserts. Cut down on carbohydrates. Eat whole grains rather than refined grains. Have a diet rich in fruits and vegetables.

Regular exercise helps maintain a healthy weight. It curbs the risk of diabetes by: helping the body use insulin and process glucose; increasing the body's sensitivity to insulin, thereby lowering blood sugar levels and the need for insulin; and decreasing one's tendency to eat for reasons apart from hunger.

About three-quarters of those with Type 2 diabetes also have high blood pressure, which increases the risk of cardiovascular and kidney diseases. Watch your blood pressure.

Losing weight, exercising regularly, monitoring blood pressure form the tools for preventing (or controlling) Type 2 diabetes along with oral medication or insulin (or both) to control blood glucose levels. Get a yearly blood or urine test to check for high levels of sugar that may signal trouble is brewing. A blood or urine test may indicate a developing problem with blood sugar metabolism, which, if not controlled, may lead to Type 2 diabetes.

Control Your Blood Pressure. In the longevity study, those with high blood pressure had a 28 percent higher risk of death before age 90.[4] Thus, treating high blood pressure—hypertension—reduces the overall risk of death.

Blood pressure is the push of blood against the walls of one's arteries. Blood pressure depends on: how forcefully your heart pumps your blood and the amount of resistance in your arteries to the blood flow. Blood pressure is recorded as two numbers. Systolic pressure is the pressure against your artery walls as your heart beats. Diastolic pressure is the pressure against your artery walls as your heart relaxes between beats. Your physician will use both numbers to determine if your blood pressure is too high.

As many as two-thirds of people 60 and older in the United States have elevated blood pressure that requires treatment, with about the same percentages for men and women. It is a sign that the heart is working harder than it should thereby increasing the risk of heart attack and congestive heart failure. One's risk of suffering these complications, among others, is proportional to one's blood pressure level.

High blood pressure speeds the development of arterial hardening, creating more strain on arteries and contributing to the build up of plaque, a fatty substance, in the arteries, a condition known as atherosclerosis. As a result of high blood pressure and/or atherosclerosis, the clogged arteries cannot carry as much blood and thus reduce the supply of oxygen and other nutrients to the body's organs and tissues. The heart responds by working harder and pumping more blood, sometimes stressing the heart, a muscle, to the point that it becomes inefficient, unable to pump hard enough.

Coronary diseases develop when the arteries that nourish the heart encounter the buildup of plaque. For example, the continued plaque buildup, particularly of small, unstable plaques, limits blood flow and creates clots that block narrowed arteries, causing a heart attack, the blockage of oxygen-rich blood to a section of the heart muscle. Impaired cerebral blood flow starves the brain of oxygen, resulting in a stroke, a brain attack, which may cause partial paralysis, among other impairments. In addition to heart attack and stroke, untreated or inadequately treated hypertension can lead to kidney failure and Type 2 diabetes.

Certain uncontrollable risk factors play a role in determining your blood pressure. In addition to age, race (black, but not Hispanic) and family history play a role.

Other risk factors can be controlled, such as stress, smoking, weight, and physical activity level. Weight loss and regular exercise, topics considered later in this chapter as well as stress management and tobacco avoidance can help lower elevated blood pressure or maintain a sound blood pressure level. Blood pressure is often decreased by diets rich in fruits and vegetables, whole grains, nuts, legumes, seeds and high in nonfat dairy products, fish, and chicken.

Many will also need medication to normalize their pressure. Consult your physician. Today, more than ninety percent of patients experience few, if any, side effects from blood pressure medications. There are substantial benefits: reducing the risk of heart attack, stroke, and Type 2 diabetes. Aggressive treatment of hypertension is also useful for Type 2 diabetics who otherwise face an increased risk of a number of diseases and debilitating conditions.

Practice Weight Management. Strive to maintain your normal weight. The longevity study found that obese men had a 44 percent higher risk of death before age 90 compared to non-obese males.[5] Obesity refers to having an abnormally high proportion of body fat; overweight refers to a condition marked by a somewhat lower proportion of body fat than obesity.

Today, physicians use your body mass index (BMI), an index of weight adjusted for your height, to screen for obesity and overweight. Your BMI equals your weight in pounds multiplied by 703, with the result divided by your height in inches and that result then divided by your height in inches once more. It is easier with the metric system. You calculate your BMI by dividing your weight in kilograms by your height in meters squared. Someone is obese with a BMI of 30 or greater, overweight with a BMI of 25-29.

Obesity has dire consequences for the elderly. It can lead to a staggering array of aliments — heart disease, stroke, high blood pressure, diabetes, and certain cancers.

About 69.1 percent of all persons in the United States age 65 and over are obese or overweight, with 72.2 percent of all males in that age bracket versus 66.7 percent of all females. In total, 29.7 percent of those 65 and over are obese, 28.7 percent of all males in that age bracket; 39.4 percent of those 65 and over are overweight, 43.5 percent of all males in that age bracket. These are distressing statistics.

Obese 90 year olds and centenarians are extremely rare. Keeping a trim waistline is a requirement if you want to live to advanced years. Before beginning any weight reduction effort, however, have a thorough physical examination to be sure that no organic cause exists for obesity or overweight.

Even a moderate weight loss is beneficial. A 10 percent weight loss can decrease bad cholesterol levels (LDL or low-density lipoprotein) and reduce blood pressure. LDL carries cholesterol through the blood stream and deposits it where it's needed for cell rebuilding. Any unused cholesterol is left in the artery walls where it may begin to rupture, setting the stage for life-threatening clots. Surprisingly, the longevity study failed to confirm other studies that found that high bad cholesterol levels are associated with earlier death.

Try to achieve a healthier eating pattern by consuming lots of:

- fruits (particularly blueberries and strawberries) and vegetables (especially bright-colored vegetables, such as carrots, and one of my least favorite veggies, broccoli). It doesn't make much difference nutritionally, whether you eat them fresh, frozen, canned (without sugar or sodium, of course), or dried. Try for at least five servings of fruits and vegetables, daily.
- nuts, seeds, and legumes (almonds, peanuts, walnuts, sunflower seeds, kidney beans, lentils). Try for a handful five times a week.
- whole grains (cereals and breads).
- non-fat and low-fat dairy products (skim or 1% milk, non-fat or low-fat yogurt, nonfat cheese). Try for two to three servings daily.
- fish (especially salmon, mahi-mahi, catfish, and flounder). Eating fish at least three times a week will increase good cholesterol and reduce both bad cholesterol and blood pressure. It also seems to protect against abnormal heart rhythms and decrease the risk of blood clots. Oils in most fish produce these benefits or take an omega-3 (fish oil) supplement daily.

What to avoid:

- saturated fats, found in butter, cheese, and red meat, and transfats, the latter are formed when unsaturated vegetable oils are hardened (more technically, hydrogenated) and act in the body like saturated fats. Saturated and transfats raise the levels of harmful cholesterol and lower the levels of protective cholesterol. These fats may impair arterial flexibility and promote resistance to insulin, thereby increasing the risk of Type 2 diabetes. Avoid foods cooked in lard and shortening. For a spread, select a margarine that is transfat free. Cook with liquid fats, such as olive oil, instead of butter or margarine.
- red meat.

- fast, processed, and preserved foods.
- fried fish and chicken. Remove the skin from poultry.
- refined carbohydrates (sugars and white, low-fiber starches).

I'm not a fanatic about what I eat, just three reasonable meals a day, never, ever skipping a meal. In particular, don't skip breakfast and try to divide your calories evenly for breakfast, lunch, and dinner, say 700 calories per meal (though I prefer a bigger lunch and a lighter dinner), and eat snacks in mid-morning and mid-afternoon to tide you over to the next meal. Healthy snacks include nuts, seeds, and popcorn. Energy bars can do the trick, but beware of those with too much sugar and too high in fat and calories. Reduce your salt intake by avoiding canned foods and cured meats.

Another key is everything in moderation—fat, proteins, and carbohydrates—as well as reasonable portions. In addition to avoiding harmful foods, strive to be moderate with your food. Do not eat to satisfy your palate but to nourish your body. Do not intake more food than required for your sustenance. Do not eat merely for the sake of gratifying your sense of taste. Overloading your digestive system with excessive quantities of food will prove injurious to your body. Take smaller bites and chew more slowly, wait between bites and between courses. Also, consume alcohol in moderation.

Practice portion control. When you eat out at restaurants, select health-conscious menus and choices. Share large portions of entrees and to-die-for desserts.

Fat, like real estate, is all about location. Avoid carrying your extra baggage in the belly (an apple-shaped physique) where the excess contributes to heart disease, stroke, high blood pressure, Type 2 diabetes, and numerous cancers, including colon cancer. Belly fat cells may be the worst because of their proximity to major organs. These visceral fat cells spew forth noxious chemicals called cytokines that stoke chronic inflammation throughout the body, constrict blood vessels, damage artery walls, and may even trigger other processes that damage brain cells.

Men with a waist of 40 inches or more at the abdomen's widest part are at the greatest risk. In a massive study of 359,387 men and women, normal-weight male participants with waists measuring about

40 inches or more were twice as likely to die as those with waists of 34 inches or less.[6]

As a test of your visceral fat, your physician may calculate your waist-to-hip ratio by dividing the circumference of your waist at the navel by the circumference of your hips at their widest point. A healthy ratio for men is .90 to .95. In short, it's not just your weight, but where you carry your weight.

People cannot generally choose where their fat is stored. That's determined basically by heredity, hormones, and aging. Men tend to deposit more fat in the gut than women.

Even so, to some extent, belly fat represents a modifiable risk factor. You can shed this type of fat by dieting and exercise. Again, avoid saturated and transfats as well as processed foods, especially those high in sugars and refined carbohydrates.

Regularly engage in two types of exercise — aerobic exercise and resistance exercise — discussed in this chapter. Aerobic exercise, such as walking or swimming, is often particularly effective in reducing belly fat. Being aerobically fit changes the metabolic activity of cells. By metabolizing sugars and refined carbohydrates and thus making the body less insulin-resistant, less belly fat accumulates and existing fat is burnt more quickly. Because muscle is efficient at burning fat, adding muscle through resistance training helps get rid of midriff fat. Finally, chill out. If you're under stress, the body releases adrenalin and other hormones, such as cortisol. An elevated level of cortisol may increase the accumulation of belly fat.

Aside from direct genetic manipulation, calorie restriction—eating less—is the only strategy known to extend life consistently in a variety of animal species. In the 1930s, researchers stumbled on a single way to slow the biological forces of aging. Cutting the normal calorie intake by 30 percent boosted animals' lifespans by 20 to 40 percent. In almost every instance, the animal subjects on low-calorie diets proved to be longer-lived and more resistant to age-related ailments. Instead of becoming ill, many of the animal subjects simply died of old age.

Evidence suggests that calorie restriction slows human aging. When you slow aging you push a host of diseases—cancer, heart disease, Type 2 diabetes, and Alzheimer's—to more advanced years. If the response of people to food restriction is similar to that in laboratory animals, the maximum human life span could reach 140 years, with an increase in the average life span to 120 years. Furthermore, a smaller percentage of the aging population would experience chronic, debilitating diseases prior to death.

Although calorie restriction's machinery in humans remains unclear, when people cut calories and lose weight, the body tries to compensate by slowing its metabolic rate and diminishing reactions that release or provide energy. Slowing the metabolic rate represents a defensive mechanism to fight weight loss. It was likely preserved by human evolution because it saved people from starving to death when food was scarce.

In the first rigorous test of calorie restriction in men and women, who were overweight, but not obese, one group of participants reduced their calories by 25 percent and another, decreased their calories by 12.5 percent and engaged in a structured exercise program to burn off another 12.5 percent of their calorie intake. In this small, pilot study, calorie restriction led to a decrease in insulin levels and body temperature, both of which are considered signs of longevity. The two groups of participants also had fewer signs of the chromosomal damage typically associated with aging.[7]

Another small study of calorie restriction showed that people on a strict diet of between 1,400 to 2,000 nutritionally-balanced calories a day for three to fifteen years had younger hearts than normal-weight individuals on a typical American diet of 2,000 to 3,000 daily calories. Although the study is not conclusive, the calorie-restricted hearts were more elastic and beat in a way that made them resemble the hearts of much younger people.[8] An earlier study had found that long-term calorie restriction had a powerful protective effect against hardening of the arteries (atherosclerosis) in humans.[9] In sum, although calorie restriction causes beneficial metabolic, hormonal, and inflammatory risk changes, the exact amount of calorie intake associated with optimal human health and maximum longevity is presently not known.[10]

A key difficulty is that serious calorie restriction, reducing daily caloric intake by as much as 40 percent, while maintaining the recommended daily allowances of essential nutrients, makes most people miserable in the process of attempting it. Think of it: Have you ever tried to go without food for even one day? Most of us can't even function at the end of the day. Few of us are likely to stick to a calorie-restricted diet over a long period. Also, calorie restriction often results in fatigue and a loss of one's sex drive.

Without going on a severe calorie restriction diet, you can take some simple, but effective, steps. Shun processed foods with empty calories. Eat high-fiber foods to curb hunger and replace calorie-dense foods with nutritionally-dense foods. Low-calorie eats, such as kale, blueberries, flax seeds, and tofu, may help you tack on a few more years. In short, overhaul your diet to improve the quality of the calories you eat.

Watch for the development of potent drugs that mimic the effects of calorie restriction and its significant increase in lifespan, but without the need to reduce drastically the daily intake of food. It may be possible that resveratrol, a natural substance found in red wine, can mimic many of the metabolic effects of a calorie-restricted diet.

Another solution is regular exercise. Contrary to what you may think, exercise does not make one so hungry that he eats more than he used to. Exercise will diminish the tendency to turn to food for emotional satisfaction.

Engage In Regular Exercise. Physical activity serves as a key to remaining healthy, successful aging. Physical fitness may also serve as an antidote to mental deterioration.

Exercise cuts the risk of death. In the longevity study those who exercised reduced their risk of death by 20 to 30 percent,[11] depending on how often and how vigorously they worked out, compared with men who never exercised. Physical inactivity increases the risk of developing many chronic conditions, including heart disease, Type 2 diabetes, and certain cancers, as well as the functional losses and disabilities that accompany aging.

Many of us have a hard time thinking about exercising and implementing a regular exercise program. There are, of course, exceptions.

Burt, age 81, related that his physician told him that swimming every other day would help keep his "ticker" going. He swims religiously.

Vic, a physician in his early 70s, still sees patients four days a week. Swimming every other day helps him stay physically and mentally sharp and reduces the risks posed by the onset of Type 2 diabetes. He walks from his home to the subway and then to his office. He also works out and lifts weights regularly. I marvel at his determination to maintain his physical fitness. He stated, "Exercise makes me feel stronger and better."

Staying active delays moderate and severe physical changes. Even if you've been sedentary, it's never too late to get off the couch and to start moving more. You likely have more time to exercise and fewer excuses. Even if you've never exercised before, nearly all of us are capable, in one way or another, of becoming more physically fit. Set goals that are reachable, beginning with small steps. Start with lifestyle exercises, such as taking the stairs, doing moderate yard work, or even walking the dog. Start slowly and gradually build your ability and strength. Although medical clearance is not necessary, consult your physician if you have a known or suspect a possible problem. Strive to stay in shape by maintaining your physical activity, but don't overdo it.

Very little exercise makes a big impact on your health. In one study of 3,206 men and women over the age of 65, men who exercised at least once a week were 40 percent less likely to die during the 12-year study period than those who were physically inactive. However, for those physically active more frequently, the reduction in all-cause mortality risk was about the same as for those physically active once a week.[12]

Many health and well-being improvements exist for seniors who take up exercise. It's never too late to start and receive these benefits:

- Heart disease and stroke—Physical activity can cut in half the risk of developing heart disease or suffering a stroke. Exercise helps reduce the risk of these vascular diseases: by lowering stress levels and blood pressure; raising the level of protective, good cholesterol that removes cholesterol from blood vessels and helps to excrete it; reducing the risk of blood clots that might clog blood vessels; and helping maintain (or reduce) body weight.
- Cancer—Exercise lowers the risk of developing colon cancer seemingly by increasing the rate at which body wastes and cancer-causing substances they may contain pass through the colon.
- Diabetes—Older people who are physically active are less likely to develop Type 2 diabetes than those who are sedentary.

Physical activity increases the sensitivity of cells to insulin, thereby lowering blood sugar levels and the need for insulin.

Exercise helps reduce belly fat, which is implicated in Type 2 diabetes, high blood pressure, and cardiovascular diseases. It aids in maintaining normal body weight or fostering weight loss, especially when combined with a moderate reduction in calories. Exercise helps in losing fat and gaining muscle, making it easier to maintain weight loss because muscle tissue burns more calories than fat tissue does. Vigorous exercise also serves as an appetite suppressant, thereby delaying the return of hunger. In short, exercise, more generally, physical activity, forms a key to successful aging.

Three types of physical activity are recommended: aerobic; resistance; flexibility and balance. You can benefit from moderate aerobic (cardiovascular) exercise—30 minutes at least 3 to 5 times a week. Exercise of moderate intensity, which can be as slow as a 20-minute mile, has most of the benefits of more strenuous workouts. What's important is moving about, swimming in the pool instead of just lounging beside it. You need not become a "jock" to obtain many of the rewards of regular activity.

Try to break into a sweat and perform 30 minutes or more of moderate physical activity on most, preferably nearly all, days. In particular, try to raise your heart rate through a vigorous, but low-impact activity, such as swimming. Cardiovascular exercise strengthens your heart and makes your blood vessels more elastic by forcing them to dilate.

A brisk walk after a meal or a walk to a restaurant can help you get some exercise, but do not make it too demanding initially. Your exercise routine must satisfy your head. It ought to stimulate your mind, not lead to boredom or frustration.

If you don't like walking outdoors, especially in the winter, try mall walking, walk on a treadmill, or use an exercise bike. Spend time on a rowing machine or a stair climber.

In short, try not to be completely sedentary in retirement. Regular exercise, programmed into daily life, just like eating and sleeping, comes close to serving as a fountain of youth, but don't overdo it. If your workout leaves you totally exhausted, you're probably doing too much.

We often overlook the benefits of resistance (strength) training (anaerobic exercise). As we age, we gain body fat at a faster rate, our muscles start to atrophy, our bones become more porous, raising the risk of osteoporosis — the weakening of bones — and other bone disorders. Men's abdomens develop a dangerous layer of fat that's associated with heart disease, stroke, high blood pressure, Type 2 diabetes, and numerous cancers, among other diseases. After age 30, age-related muscle loss sets in and we lose about one percent of our muscle per year.

Three days a week, on non-consecutive days, of resistance training of major muscles keeps them in shape. Lift free weights, use weight machines at a gym, or perform strength exercises, such as sit-ups or push-ups, to strengthen and build muscle tissue, especially the muscles in the front and sides of the thighs that support the knees as well as core muscles of the back, buttocks and abdomen that protect the spine and support the entire body. In addition to guarding against age-related loss of muscle tissue, this type of exercise also improves metabolism. Increased muscle mass helps burn calories. Muscle tissue burns more calories than fat tissue does. Muscle strength reduces the stress on joints and bones; it enhances stability, and reduces the risk of falling. However, start slowly with the heaviest weights you can lift, say three to five times in succession, and gradually increase the weights you use as your strength increases.

Also, add flexibility and balance exercises to your routine. Improving one's balance and reducing the risk of falling is important in promoting longevity. Do some gentle stretching to prevent stiffness and maintain joint mobility. To assure continued mobility, stretch your arms and legs for 10 minutes each day. Strive to improve your balance by daily standing on one foot and then on the other. Hold the pose on one foot for up to ten seconds and repeat it 10 to 15 times before switching to the other foot and doing the same. When starting out, do the balance exercise near a chair so you can steady yourself if you need to.

With regular exercise, your weight will decrease, your heart will be more at peace, your energy level will be higher, and your mind will be clearer.

THE PROSTATE QUANDARY

Getting older for most men encounters an inevitable aspect. The prostate, a walnut-sized gland, is bound to cause some trouble. The prostate, which makes a portion of the fluid that carries sperm during ejaculation, enlarges for almost all men as they age. Prostate enlargement affects at least 70 percent of men over age 50. But prostate enlargement may not be prostate cancer.

Older men face new challenges explored by novelists chronicling the psyche and sexual habits of American men. Their heroes face losses they endure and surmount.

In Philip Roth's *Exit Ghost*, the hero is incontinent and impotent after prostate surgery, "a taunted old man dying to be whole again." As Roth's hero puts it, he's a despairing old man "with a spigot of wrinkled flesh where once he'd had the fully functioning sexual organ, complete with bladder sphincter control of a robust adult male" between his legs. His loss of vigor is permanent. On meeting a young, beautiful woman "rousing the virility in me again, the virility of mind and spirit and desire and intention...and have a woman again and feeling the pleasure of one's power again. It's all called back—the virile man called back to life!" But Roth's hero warns the reader: "There is no virility. There is only the brevity of expectations."[13]

Roth's hero strives to make his old age rich and rewarding. He dedicates himself to work, to his life's purpose, to meaningful activity, in his case, to writing, where he can use his storehouse of experience and his increasing powers of imagination.

PROSTATE STRATEGIES

Men at age 50 and older, especially African-Americans and those with a family history of the disease, ought to have their prostate checked on a regular basis. This includes a prostate-specific antigen (PSA), test a simple blood test, and a digital-rectal exam to test for abnormalities. The PSA test measures the protein produced by the prostate in the blood. The larger a prostate, the more PSA is produced. When cancer is present, the PSA level rises. However, the test has a high false positive rate. In about half of men with an abnormal PSA, the results will normalize in one to four years without any treatment. The test may not reliably indicate how much cancer someone has or how serious it may be. A study of 76,693 men, who were each followed for at least 7 years, failed to produce convincing evidence that PSA testing significantly reduced the chance of dying from prostate cancer.[14] Screening found more prostate cancer, but did not decrease the risk of dying from the disease. Most men who test positive get some form of treatment, but treatment has risks that sometimes far outweigh the benefits, including erectile dysfunction and incontinence.

In addition to a PSA test, your physician may ask: do you experience a twinge or difficulty when urinating; a weak or interrupting urine flow; or getting up more frequently at night to urinate? The prostate gland surrounds the urethra, the tube carrying urine for elimination from the bladder through the penis. When the prostate enlarges it can press against the urethra and impede the flow of urine.

Know your PSA number. For unknown reasons, PSA levels often fluctuate by as much as 30 percent and can rise for reasons apart from prostate cancer. For all its imperfections, it's a marker. More importantly, monitor the change in your PSA number from year-to-year.

Being told you have an elevated and especially a rising PSA (technically, PSA velocity) and that you might have cancer leads into a system of complex diagnostic tests to ascertain whether it is so. You must make some choices about what, if anything, to do.

Appointments lead to more appointments, Internet research to more research. Each medical specialty has its own favored approach.

As a marker of tumor size, a high PSA reading suggests that the tumor is large, and a large tumor may extend outside the prostate to other body parts and begin metastasizing.

If you test positive for prostate cancer, you're poked and prodded. A needle biopsy of the prostate is done and sometimes of the nearby lymph nodes. Some find a biopsy to be a minor discomfort; others experience debilitating pain and in rare cases serious complications. If a tumor is detected, pathologists "grade" two pieces of tissue and rate them on a scale to determine the cancer's aggressiveness. Physicians may do other tests, including CAT scans and MRIs, to see if the cancer has spread beyond the prostate. Don't be afraid of asking dumb questions or that a physician may think you're a difficult patient. Don't stop until you have clarity on the location, extent, and aggressiveness of the cancer.

Even before deciding on what type of treatment to pursue, get more than one physician's opinion about the diagnostic laboratory work—the test results.

There are two basic types of treatment:

- surgery, which can remove the prostate (radical prostatectomy) or minimally invasive laparoscopic (often robot-assisted) surgery, using a laparoscope, a slender tube that enables a surgeon to see inside the body. The minimally invasive route reduces pain, recovery time, and blood loss; most patients go home the next day. Minimally invasive surgery may, however, raise the risk of incontinence and erectile dysfunction compared to more extensive operations.
- radiation, including inserting rice-size radioactive pellets (brachytherapy) in the prostate or external radiation.

There are also hormone treatments to block production of testosterone that fuels the cancer cells.

A mix of treatments may be prescribed. Or, you may opt for watchful waiting—monitoring the slow-growing cancer's progress—before taking any specific action, unless and until the tumor enlarges to a point where treatment to check its growth becomes clearly advisable.

Apart from watchful waiting, you pour over the Internet and try to decide among some not very appealing treatment alternatives. You'll discover that the survival rates for the mainstream treatments are all about the same after five years or so. The most invasive, radical prostatectomy, the gold standard of treatments if the cancer is confined to the prostate, may result in potentially chilling side effects, even in the best of hands, such as permanent incontinence or impotence. If you go the surgical removal route, ask for nerve-sparing surgery to reduce the risk of impotence and incontinence. It is now a standard procedure, but make certain. Surgical treatments can also cause urethra, bowel, or bladder problems. Hormone treatments can cause weight gain, loss of muscle tone, osteoporosis, depression, high blood pressure, loss of erectile function, and diminished mental acuity.

Remember: If you have cancer, a surgeon wants to cut it out. Surgeons and urologists have a natural preference for surgery because they know that best (and that's what they do). Remember the adage: "If you have a hammer, everything looks like a nail." There are less invasive procedures. If cancer has metastasized and spread beyond the prostate, external radiation may be called for. External radiation requires no incisions or hospitalization, but you must generally undergo 40 or more treatments over six to eight weeks. Urinary problems and loss of sexual potency often set in gradually following radiation.

After Stewart learned at age 64 that he had prostate cancer, he faced the difficult treatment decision. The timing made the decision even harder. He was asked to make the decision about treatment at the most vulnerable time, when he was in shock following a diagnosis of cancer.

One day, he settled on surgery; the next day, after more research, radiation seemed more promising to him. He quizzed a surgeon, recommended by his primary care physician, about newer treatments, his experience with various procedures, and whether he had a vested interest in a particular technology. He voiced his fears and asked pointed questions: How many patients have you treated this specific way and with what success rate? What will the side effects be like? On a personal level, he liked the surgeon and had confidence in him, because he was fully qualified and successfully performed a large number of similar operations.

Stewart went to a local prostate cancer support group and spoke with men there. They filled him in on the treatment options and their consequences, even more clearly and candidly than his own internist and the surgeon.

Before opting for surgery, he got a second opinion from a radiologist, who specialized in prostate malignancies. He eliminated radiation because he concluded that without surgery he couldn't be sure what was going on unless the lymph nodes were checked. Surgery let him know where he was. Removing the prostate and examining it in a lab enabled him to know that his cancer had not spread beyond his prostate. Also, surgery did not render him incontinent or impotent.

Stewart received support from his wife and his family. Peace of mind mattered. He got the rest of his life in order before embarking on surgery.

As you sift through the alternatives, do you want to take your chances with cancer and do nothing? Once the tumor spreads from the prostate its progress generally cannot be stopped.

However, no consensus exists about the best treatment for prostate cancer. Neither is there a consensus about the risk of reoccurrence with the various alternative treatments. Discuss all your options openly and fully with your physicians. Get a second and a third opinion. Take careful notes when you meet with physicians. Use the Internet to do in-depth research on your own.

Two men with the same diagnosis — cancer that has not spread beyond the prostate — may appropriately choose different treatments depending on their age, general health, expectations, and priorities.

Watchful waiting was the right alternative for Nick, age 73, who was terrified of surgery or radiation and for whom the possibility of incontinence or impotence was unbearable. Also for mild cases, watching and waiting may be the best approach. Tony, age 61, whose brother died from metastic prostate cancer, found it unacceptable not to treat a tumor.

The time between when a tumor is discovered in the prostate and when it is large enough to escape the gland, if it grows at all, may take years. If you are 75 or so years old, you may want to follow a conservative approach—watchful waiting—and do nothing.

Don't worry about a slow-developing cancer that never causes enough symptoms to prompt a closer look. The overwhelming majority of prostate cancers grow so slowly so that men who harbor them will most probably die of something else. Focus on the more rapidly growing forms of prostate cancer that are considered advanced.

If you're doing watchful waiting, exercise regularly, try a stress reduction program, and watch your diet. Increase your intake of fruits and vegetables and reduce the fats.

Remember: at age 85, more than three-quarters of men have evidence of prostate cancer. Many have lived full lives with it for more than ten years. Most prostate cancers never become dangerous even if left alone. They are slow growing and unlikely to result in any symptoms before the end of one's natural life expectancy. Thus, the new guidelines issued by the U.S. Preventive Services Task Force that sets government policy on preventive medicine, recommend stopping PSA testing for men 75 and older without symptoms of prostate cancer, but took no position on screening for younger men. The task force concluded that at age 75 the potential risks of treatment begin to outweigh the benefits, and the disease, if detected, would not meaningfully impact on life expectancy.

There's considerable value in the preventive health practices outlined in this chapter. Take the necessary steps to prevent life-threatening diseases and if discovered, get early treatment while readily reversible.

8. PROMOTE YOUR BRAIN WELLNESS

Mere physical survival does not guarantee a good quality of life. A meaningful life requires a healthy brain.

Misplacing your car keys (or your cell phone), forgetting the name of a friend, or failing to come up with the right word in a conversation brings to mind the dreaded fear of dementia, if not Alzheimer's disease, a debilitating form of dementia. If you've ever watched a friend or a relative slip into dementia or Alzheimer's, you know the horror of observing the deterioration of the brain. Fearful that each slip of memory foretells the advent of our mental decline, we worry about becoming demented or getting Alzheimer's.

When the MetLife Foundation asked some 1,000 Americans which disease they fear getting the most, cancer was in first place, followed by Alzheimer's. Respondents over fifty-five, most dreaded Alzheimer's, even more than cancer.[1] We worry about losing ourselves, forgetting our relatives and closest friends, becoming nearly totally disconnected from the world around us.

Alzheimer's disease is named for the physician who discovered it one century ago. In 1901, the Hospital for the Mentally Ill and Epileptics in Frankfurt, Germany admitted a fifty-one year old female, Auguste D., who caught the attention of Alois Alzheimer, a staff physician. After developing an intense suspicion of her husband, the woman started behaving bizarrely. She hid objects and became lost in her own home; she started crying loudly, thinking that people wanted to murder her.

After Dr. Alzheimer observed Auguste D., he could not place her illness into any known category. Her behavior utterly bewildered him. She was disoriented in time. Sometimes she would protest madly, expressing the fear that he wanted to cut her open. She frequently dragged her bedding around crying out for her husband and daughter in a horrible voice.

Before she died in 1906, lying in bed in a fetal position, incontinent, Dr. Alzheimer completed a limited clinical evaluation of Auguste D. He found she confused lines when she read and repeated separate syllables many times when she wrote. She was unable to grasp some questions and seemed unable to use certain objects.

When Dr. Alzheimer autopsied Auguste's brain, he noted that damage and cell death had shrunk her brain tissue. He found that tangled bundles of fibers (now called neurofibrillary tangles) had formed inside her brain cells and abnormal clumps (now called amyloid plaques) had accumulated and surrounded her brain cells. He also noticed the hardening of the arteries (more technically, atherosclerosis) that fed her brain. To this day, researchers are unable to pinpoint the degree to which tangles, plaques, and atherosclerosis contribute to Alzheimer's disease.

Diagnosis of Alzheimer's is currently made if three symptoms exist. There must be impairments: first, in short-term memory; second, in another aspect of cognition (such as, a language disturbance, a failure to recognize or identify objects despite intact sensory function, or a disturbance in planning or organization (more technically, one's executive functioning)); and third, in social (or daily) functioning, such as dressing, bathing, toileting, or feeding oneself, although one's muscles may still function perfectly.[2]

Alzheimer patients typically show a gradual downward course of mental, physical, and social deterioration, with the first symptoms beginning subtly. Following a progressive, irreversible deterioration of the brain, in its last stages, usually eight to ten years after its early diagnosis, patients become bedridden and incontinent. They stop communicating verbally.

Although Alzheimer's is the most common type of dementia, for Americans age 65 and over, more generally, the symptoms of dementia differ, depending on which part (or parts) of the brain are affected and the stage of the disease. Common symptoms of dementia include: memory loss (age-associated memory impairment); language loss (such as trouble getting words out); difficulty with organization, concentration, reasoning, or judgment; changes in behavior and personality, marked by mood swings, depression, delusions, paranoia, or aggressive behavior.

The loss of memory represents one of the most frightening aspects of aging. Our memories serve as a key element of who we are. Memories represent an integral part of our personalities. As we lose our memories, we lose our grounding and our identity. It is unsettling when your memory begins to fail and you realize its failing.

Philip Roth's hero in *Exit Ghost,* records:

> . . .I had been having a problem remembering any
> number of small things. To address the difficulty, I had

begun to keep, along with my daily calendar, a lined school composition book — the kind with the black-and-white marble covers that has the multiplication tables inside the back— in which to list each day's chores and, in more abbreviated form, to note my phone calls, their content, and the letters I wrote and received. Without the chore book, I could. . . easily forget whom I had spoken to about what as recently as yesterday, or what someone was supposed to be doing for me the following day. I had started accumulating chore books some three years before, when I first realized that a perfectly reliable memory was beginning to fray...[3]

There is a general slowing of cognitive functioning, beginning for most of us in our fifties and sixties. We all experience "senior moments." A degree of memory loss is normal as we get older. Neurotransmitters, the chemicals that allow nerve cells in the brain to communicate among each other, begin to diminish. The brain shrinks, becoming smaller and weighing less. Because the brain's white matter, the fiber tracks connecting the brain's front matter (more technically, the frontal cortex) to its storage areas change, information takes longer to process.

There is some good news, however. Declines in cognitive functioning, these "senior moments," rarely affect all types of cognitive performance, with most of these losses coming late in life. Many older men are not significantly impacted by minor losses of mental ability, such as short-term memory.

Most seniors maintain a good part of their mental sharpness. Although some mental processes slow with aging, many do not. Older people have some reduction in explicit memory, for example, the ability to recall a specific name or a telephone number. Our learned routines, more specifically, our working memory, which we rely on daily, generally shows little decline with age. The aging brain also has a remarkable capacity to make new connections, absorb new information, and acquire new skills.

It's important to put things in perspective. In one's advanced age, the superabundant energy and vigor that characterized youth are diminished, but these attributes typically are no longer needed.

The brain shows different strengths, generally evidencing maturity of thought and experience, deepening qualities of wisdom, judgment, and perspective. Because wisdom generally increases with age, the older brain is generally a wiser brain. There's a great benefit from having been there, done that, and learned from it. Having lived longer and seen more, a senior's mind can quickly perceive what the mind of youth grasps only after much trial and error. Having wisdom, there's no need for excessive energy and vigor. One can more readily exercise good judgment about important matters, especially those that are uncertain in nature. Because the mature mind can more readily detect fallacies in reasoning and shortcomings in analysis, one is likely better at reasoning, problem solving, and decision-making. A widening focus of attention, which makes it more difficult to latch onto one specific fact, such as a name or a telephone number, enables older adults to know more about many situations and the indirect messages of what is going on than younger people. More profound wisdom and judgment result from being able to assimilate data and put it in its proper place. Seniors often can pull back from a situation and take a broader view of the knowledge and context that are involved, see the larger picture and separate the forest and the trees. They may have a greater capacity to accept some uncertainty and suspend quick judgment for a more measured evaluation.

Despite the generally good news, particularly that brain cells can continue to grow and flourish in our 60s, 70s, and 80s and that most of us gain wisdom, judgment, and perspective as we age, the statistics are deeply disturbing. The percentage of people with Alzheimer's doubles every five years after age 65. Alzheimer's is a disease of the old-old. At age 85, about 50 percent of Americans will experience some diagnosable symptoms of Alzheimer's, such as, disturbances in memory, attention, and orientation, changes in personality, language difficulties, with the figure rising to 60 percent for ninety-year olds.

Most of us are anxiety-ridden, particularly when no known cure exists for Alzheimer's. Yet, strategies exist to slow Alzheimer's, among other forms of dementia.

STRATEGIES TO MAINTAIN MENTAL SHARPNESS

The brain has more plasticity than previously thought. We can generate new brain cells and new connections among them. The brain has many chances to overcome the impact of aging.

Mental abilities can be preserved (or even enhanced) as we grow older. Based on evidence of neural plasticity, people are taking matters into their own hands. You too can be proactive, take control of certain areas of your life, and have a better brain.

Kurt, at age 87, is aging gracefully. Although his pace has slowed, he continues to work, travel, and attend cultural events, among other mentally challenging activities. Although, in part, his mental acuity may be genetic, besides mental stimulation, he follows various strategies, emotional, physical, and practical, designed to enhance mental sharpness.

Mental Stimulation. Maintenance of your cognitive abilities requires the continued use of your mind, the continued engagement in complex cognitive activities. If you're not working (as Kurt continues to do), volunteering, pursuing lifelong learning, or engaged in creative activities, you need to find alternative ways to use your cognitive abilities. You need to keep mentally active. A number of studies support this conclusion.

Researchers examined the relationship between leisure activities— six cognitive activities and eleven physical activities—and dementia in 469 people older than age 75. Some five years later, 124 of them had dementia. The study concluded that participation in cognitive leisure activities, reading, writing for pleasure, playing board games, doing crossword puzzles, participating in organized group discussions, and playing musical instruments, but not physical activities, was associated with a reduced risk of dementia, even after adjusting for initial cognitive status, among other variables.[4]

Other studies point to the importance of ongoing cognitive activities. Results from a long-term study of 801 older Catholic clergy suggested that frequent participation in cognitively stimulating activities was linked with a reduced risk of Alzheimer's disease.[5] In another long-term study of 1,772 cognitively healthy elderly individuals age 65 years or older, on average, those who pursued the most leisure activities, particularly those of an intellectual or social nature, such as reading and visiting friends or relatives, had a 38 percent lower risk of developing

Alzheimer's. The more of these activities participants engaged in, the lower the risk, even when baseline cognitive performance, health limitations interfering with the desired leisure activities, cerebrovascular disease, and depression were considered.[6]

Keep your mind in action. Do brain fitness exercises, such as crossword and other puzzles that challenge the brain and may help create more nerve pathways. A clinical trial involving 2,832 older adults concluded that cognitive training, such as identifying patterns on a series of letters or words, helped improve reasoning skills.[7] Games like chess foster spatial orientation and stimulate inductive reasoning.

Do other activities that challenge the brain on many levels, such as learning a new language or playing a new musical instrument. Continue to learn through a lifetime of taking courses and reading.

Spend some of your time on the golden pages of literature. Volumes exist containing immortal thoughts, pages of everlasting significance. Read challenging materials. Do not waste your precious hours on trashy or ephemeral print or electronic materials. Give free reign to your curiosity. Pursue intellectually-oriented avocations, such as history or science. Join a book discussion club. Try computer-based fitter-brain products. One study of 487 adults, aged 65 and older, found that people who trained on brain fitness software for 40 hours during eight weeks significantly improved their memory and attention skills.[8] However, if you get too engrossed in computer games, you may not exercise or engage with others.

Stimulate your brain with novelty. Brushing your teeth with your non-dominant hand generates more brain activity than your usual routine. Practice writing with your non-dominant hand. Start by making large, print letters and don't worry if they're not perfect. The more frustrating the task, the better the mental workout.

Mental stimulation is healthy for human brains. Whatever you do, do not relax your mind; do not give yourself a mental holiday for the rest of your life. Such a holiday is costly; it is injurious to your being. When your mind does not think, it gradually loses the power of thinking. When your mind does not exercise its reasoning, it gradually loses its potency and fluency.

When you exercise your faculties of thought, your brain remains powerful and energetic. When you keep your mind active in constructive directions, when you persist in achievement, when you continue to identify with your dreams (or passions) in life, you help ward off the mental infirmities of advanced age.

The mind grows through knowledge and achievement. Knowledge is what you take in from life; achievement is what you give to life. Achievement contributes to the growth of your mind. It is insufficient merely to assimilate knowledge, you must use and express knowledge through your achievement to give knowledge its true value. Through achievement you bring into play your mind's creative powers, you call reason into action, and your imaginative faculty into expression. Through continued efforts to achieve, whether through work, volunteering, learning, or creative endeavors, your constructive powers assert themselves. Through constant efforts at achievement, your mind maintains its strength and alertness.

Emotionally-oriented Strategies. Besides mental stimulation, by following strategies designed to enhance your emotional and physical health, you help your brain. Lessen your stress levels. Researchers found that a higher level of chronic stress was associated with an increased incidence of mild cognitive impairment.[9]

Cortisol, a stress-generated hormone, depresses the growth of nerve cells and the connections among these cells, thereby eroding brain architecture. Chronic stress can result in rewiring of brain areas and the loss of volume in areas involved in memory, learning, and decision-making, specifically the hippocampus.

A connection likely exists between emotional health and cognitive ability. People who are depressed suffer from a reduced attention span and poor concentration, resulting in impaired performance and a loss of the ability to form new memories, even a lessened ability to retrieve old memories. Depression may injure brain functions,[10] although this link has not been conclusively established.[11] Self-help measures, such as regular exercise and volunteer efforts, may assist in overcoming mild depression. Practical techniques can enhance one's joyfulness and optimism. If these measures fail, seek professional help.

Remain socially connected.[12] Research indicates the more extensive a senior's social network, including family members and neighbors, the better one's brain is likely to work, especially with respect to memory.[13] Strive for strong ties to your relatives, friends, and community. Take classes and volunteer with others. Apart from those suffering from late-stage Alzheimer's, the social support provided by family and friends seems to influence and enhance cognitive function.

Physically-oriented Strategies. High blood pressure, diabetes, obesity, particularly abdominal fat, along with smoking and heavy drinking of alcohol, raise the risk of age-related cognitive decline.

Avoid vascular problems, such as high blood pressure, which impede the circulation of blood to the brain. High blood pressure plays a negative role by stiffening the artery walls, making it easier for fatty plaque deposits to form, increasing the risk of stroke and the resulting brain damage.

Researchers have noted an increased risk of dementia or an accelerated decline in various mental functions resulting from untreated high blood pressure. In a four-year study of 1,373 individuals, 59 to 71 years old, high blood pressure was associated with cognitive decline.[14] Another study of 3,703 Japanese-American men suggested that elevated levels of blood pressure in middle age can increase the risk for late age dementia in men never treated with anti-hypertension medication.[15]

The brain loves oxygen. When a clogged artery or compromised heart cannot deliver enough oxygen-rich blood, the brain chokes. Starving a brain of oxygen results in a stroke, a brain attack. After the nerve cells die, the brain tissue becomes inflamed, initiating the release of toxic chemicals (this process is called more technically, an inflammatory cascade), killing more brain cells and damaging blood vessels. A stroke may cause partial paralysis, impaired vision, loss of speech, or brain impairments (so-called vascular dementia). A series of mini-strokes, clots in the small arteries of the brain, often result in brain function deterioration, leading to some of the symptoms of dementia to emerge. Stroke-free brains can mute the symptoms of dementia and possibly Alzheimer's disease.

Early detection and proper treatment of high blood pressure is essential. Reducing your blood pressure to normal, through meditation, exercise, weight loss, a diet high in fruits and vegetables and low in fat, and, if needed, medication, will help your cognitive functions.

Type 2 diabetes, a risk factor for stroke, increases the odds of poor cognitive function. A study of 6,370 elderly subjects found that Type 2 diabetes almost doubled the risk of dementia.[16]

Weight loss, watching what you eat, regular exercise, and keeping you blood pressure under control, among other strategies, help reduce your risk for Type 2 diabetes.

Watch your weight, as Kurt does, particularly where fat accumulates. Where you carried your weight in middle age (and carry it now) may serve as a strong predictor of dementia.

People with big bellies, even in their 40s, are much more likely to get various forms of dementia in their latter years. The more fat in one's gut in one's early to mid-40s, the greater the chances of becoming forgetful, confused, and suffering from other signs of senility as one ages. A sizeable stomach appears to increase this risk even among those who are not obese or even overweight, by boosting blood pressure and constricting blood flow.

One study of 6,583 men and women in their 40s from 1964 to 1973, measured how far their belly stuck out (sagittal abdominal diameter (SAD)) and then looked at their records an average of 36 years later (1994 to 2006), finding 1,049 dementia cases. Compared with those in the lowest one-fifth in SAD, those in the highest one-fifth were almost three times as likely to have dementia. Even among those of normal weight, as measured by their body mass index, men with a more than 40-inch waist were almost twice as likely to be demented as those with the smallest bellies. The association held after controlling for other variables, such as high blood pressure, diabetes, and high bad cholesterol.[17]

The combination of high blood pressure and obesity seems particularly destructive to cognitive functioning. A follow-up study of 1,449 individuals lasting for decades found a six-fold increase in the risk of dementia and Alzheimer's disease in those who were obese and had high systolic blood pressure and high total cholesterol levels.[18]

In addition to watching your weight, monitor what you eat. A heart-healthy diet, which lessens clogged arteries limiting the brain's supply of oxygen, reduces the risk of dementia and Alzheimer's disease. A study of 1,880 elderly people found that those who adhered most closely to a diet marked by the high consumption of vegetables, legumes, and cereals, served with olive oil, reduced their risk for Alzheimer's by 32 to 40 percent.[19] Eat plenty of fresh fruits and vegetables (blueberries are often recommended to protect the brain) as well as nuts and fish high in Omega-3, such as salmon. In a study from 1993 through 2000 of 815 individuals, aged 65 to 94 years old, initially unaffected by Alzheimer's, found that those who consumed fish once or more per week had a 60 percent less risk of Alzheimer's compared with those who rarely or never ate fish, even adjusted for age and other risk factors.[20]

Regular exercise enhances not only general physical well-being but also brain health. Researchers have found that regular exercise has benefits for cognition[21] and is associated with a delay in the onset of dementia and Alzheimer's disease. One study of 1,740 adults older than 65 without cognitive impairment at the outset showed a one-third less risk of dementia in those who exercised three or more times a week compared with those who exercised fewer than three times a week.[22] Another study recruited 124 sedentary adults between ages 60 and 75, assigning half of them to an aerobic exercise program that met three times a week to walk and the balance to a control group that did anaerobic stretching and toning. Measuring each group's cognitive functioning before and after the six-month program, the study found certain improvements among those who did the walking.[23]

By improving cardiovascular health and preventing heart attack and stroke that can cause brain damage, regular, moderate exercise, even walking thirty minutes a day, helps the brain in a number of ways. Aerobic exercise, such as walking or swimming, increases the flow of blood to the brain, which, in turn, nourishes brain cells and allows them to function more effectively. In another study, six months of aerobic exercise, but not non-aerobic exercise, bought increases in the volume of various brain regions thereby staving off neural decline in aging humans. Aerobic exercise may be an effective means of rolling back age-related losses in brain structure.[24]

Regular exercise helps promote the growth of new neurons—brain cells—in the hippocampus the part of the brain that controls memory, learning, and decision-making. By improving blood flow, exercise increases the availability of energy to neurons in the brain.

In short, exercise is good for the brain. It helps your brain maintain high cognitive function. Find some activity you enjoy and do it regularly, at least every other day. It is never too late to begin regular exercise.

Brian, age 68, walks thirty minutes daily to improve blood flow to his brain, bringing oxygen and other nutrients for sound cognitive functioning, reducing the risk of mini-strokes and clogged blood vessels, boosting neural growth and brain connectivity, thereby improving his memory and concentration. Even leisure activities, such as ballroom dancing, may help avoid dementia. In short, researchers have found a heart-healthy diet and regular exercise together reduce the risk of Alzheimer's disease.[25]

Consult your physician. A host of other treatable physical conditions, such as, substance abuse, thyroid problems, hormone fluctuations, or diseases of the lungs, kidneys, or liver, can cause memory problems, among other dementia symptoms. Treatment of an underlying condition may reduce (or even eliminate) the symptoms of senility.

Get enough sleep. In our deep sleep, we consolidate memory and cement it in the brain. Untreated sleep apnea is often detrimental to memory.

To get enough sleep, avoid stimulants, such as caffeine, don't drink liquids, or eat for at least three hours before bedtime. Avoid exercising, a stimulant, one or two hours before bedtime. Before trying to fall asleep, try to relax for five or ten minutes. Get on a sleep schedule and stick to it. Avoid lengthy daytime napping and reduce the overall level of stress in your life.

Practically-oriented strategies. Try to forget extraneous things and reduce distractions. Minimize your mental clutter. To compensate for memory loss, use a diary or a personal digital assistant. Like Roth's hero, use a notebook to record information, consolidating everything in one place. Keep a readily visible calendar, a list of daily and weekly activities, and make use of Post-It notes. Maintain a regular routine. Work at remembering, for example, by fixing the location of your car in your mind before you leave a parking garage. Use word associations. In sum, prioritize and carefully calibrate the daily loads you give your brain to handle.

Simplify your life. Slow down and focus. Pay attention if you want to remember something in the future.

GENES VERSUS LIFESTYLE CHOICES

Despite the widespread fears of cognitive loss among seniors, even if your genes predispose you to forgetfulness, among other cognitive impairments, you have some degree of control so that your brain maintains a high functional level. However, despite everything, mental stimulation as well as emotionally, physically, and practically-oriented strategies, you may still develop dementia or Alzheimer's. Similar to many diseases, dementia in its various forms results from a complex mix of genetic and environmental factors. Education attainment and previous intellectual activity generally correlate not only with a decreased risk for dementia or Alzheimer's but also with longer lifespans.

People with higher levels of education, including self-education, through travel and reading, may possess a cognitive reserve, which connotes the brain's ability to develop and maintain extra neurons — nerve cells — and the connections among them. Greater intellectual challenges to the brain earlier in life, likely produce more neurons and connections that may be maintained later in life, enabling individuals to remain more cognitively active. They may also be more likely to stay mentally stimulated and more likely to exercise and follow a heart-healthy diet, among other brain-fitness activities.

Unfortunately, there are no guarantees or quick fixes. At present, there is no pill, only a whole variety of things, mental, emotional, physical, and practical, the kitchen sink approach, that may make a difference, even if started later in life, by individuals with various levels of innate intelligence and education. At least, you'll feel empowered by your efforts at healthy living.

CONCLUDING THOUGHTS WITH RESPECT TO PHYSICAL HEALTH

With moderation as your guide to your advancing years, you can retain the full measure of your physical strength and mental vigor throughout your lifetime. Try also to disregard the premature demise of one or both of your parents.

THE IMPORTANCE OF MODERATION

Strive to live a life of regularity and moderation. As your days advance, your life must become more regular and self-restrained. Moderation represents a key character trait that should be practiced at all stages of life, particularly in one's old age.

Moderation is vital to a long life. Strive to eschew excesses of any nature and learn to be the master of your desires, not their slave. Our desires often surpass our actual needs. Strive to satisfy your needs, not your appetites.

Exercise moderation even in the pursuit of pleasure. Avoid pleasures which are neither entertaining nor re-creative, but which create a spell of excitement, drowning out one's senses and rendering one unable to be aware of one's existence, even briefly. Rather seek pleasures that recreate one's body and refresh one's mind, that augment one's joys and optimism, enhance one's peace of mind, and reinvigorate one's physical and mental powers.

However, too much pleasure, even of the wholesome kind, may make the body and the mind sluggish. Excessive pleasure may not elevate one's happiness; rather it may weaken the body's resistance and render the mind unproductive. In short, excessive pleasure may represent an obstacle to a long life.

Disregard Your Parent's Premature Demise

Do not impress it upon your consciousness that because one or both of your parents died at an early age, that your life on earth cannot be long.

You probably know someone who was so convinced that he would die at about the same age his father did, that he lived all of his adult life with this premonition in his mind. He didn't take care of himself, emotionally and physically; he didn't save and invest for the future. He had no idea of living into old age. By the time he weighed 300 pounds and smoked incessantly, he made it happen.

For years, Mickey Mantle, the New York Yankees baseball player, whose father died young from Hodgkin's disease, was plagued by a morbid fear of his own impending, youthful demise. Expressing surprise that he lived to be 63 after years of drinking and carousing, he remarked, "If I knew I was going to live this long, I would've taken better care of myself."[26]

In some cases, the worry is so conscious, as it was with Mantle, that the manner in which they live causes their lives to become self-fulfilling prophecies. Before Mantle succumbed to cancer that spread from his liver to most of his other vital organs, he had problems with alcohol, which ravaged his liver.

Hereditary diseases, such as heart disease or cancer, while linked to obvious physical health risks, are often cause for unnecessarily heightened fears and worries. For instance, most cancers not inherited. Your physician, by asking four or five questions, can calculate your risk of getting the same type of cancer as one or both of your parents experienced, based on various factors, such as race, age, alcohol consumption, and tobacco usage.

Besides fear and worry, guilt may enter into the picture. You ask: am I entitled to live past the time when my father died or have more than he had? This type of exploration can also increase your fears and worries as well as make you lose your power to face life with optimism and serenity, loving kindness and forgiveness.

Put aside your father's demise or that of his generation. Do not in your mind associate weakness with age seventy, infirmity with eighty, helplessness with ninety.

Your body reacts to suggestions given to it by your mind. These thoughts serve as prompting to your body and leave their mark on your physical well-being. Your body receives these suggestions and often harmonizes its condition to these urgings. You weaken your body and shorten your life through your erroneous convictions as to old age and your thoughts of death.

IV. Financial Wellness: Fund Your Longevity Plan In a Stress-Free Manner

Based on average life expectancies, 64.7 percent of today's 65-year old men in the United States will live to age 80, 23.5 percent will live to age 90 or beyond; 75.3 percent of today's 65-year-old women will live to age 80, 37 percent will live into their 90s. For two married 65-year olds, there's a 51.8 percent chance that one will survive to age 90.

These are averages for the general U.S. population. No guarantees exist, of course. However, if you are reasonably affluent and have taken care of your emotional and physical health, you're likely to live longer, especially if longevity runs in your family. In dealing with wealthier, healthier people, insurers figure they may live two years longer than the general population, with the most affluent Americans living four and one half years longer than their peers. In short, don't underestimate how long you (and your wife or significant other) will live. Although none of us will ever achieve immortality, you face the stark possibility that your money could run out before you do.

In light of this worrisome prospect, a longevity strategy based on sound financial planning begins, in Chapter 9, by estimating your future expenses and your projected income. Next, Chapter 10 considers how to invest your nest egg, focusing first on the allocation of investments in your total retirement portfolio and second on asset location, holding investments in accounts where the IRS can do the least damage to them. Chapter 11 deals with how to withdraw money from your nest egg. The financial wellness strategy developed in these chapters can go a long way to removing some of the worries about future uncertainties.

These chapters provide many general financial rules of thumb to consider in meeting your lifestyle needs. Everyone's financial condition, risk tolerance, and tax situation is different. Obviously, consult your financial and tax advisors for your specific situation.

You likely hold a large variety of assets, some taxable (stocks, bonds, CDs) and others tax-advantaged (401(k)s, IRAs). The variety makes it difficult to know how to construct an investment portfolio and when to tap particular assets.

Before constructing your portfolio and tapping your retirement savings by yourself, ask: 1) do I have the interest in doing it myself; 2) do I have the expertise; and 3) do I have the time? If your answer to any of these questions is "no" then you ought to look to a fee-only financial advisor or a mutual fund company to handle the task. Mutual fund firms, such as Fidelity, T. Rowe Price, and Vanguard, are more than happy to manage your retirement assets and help generate a monthly check for you.

9. Estimate Your Future Expenses and Income

The greatest financial worry in retirement is running out of money. Apart from winning the lottery or receiving a substantial inheritance, you've got to make do with what you've got.

You face two specific financial risks. Your investments may earn less than anticipated. This is the market risk. You or your wife (or significant other) may live longer than expected. This is the longevity risk. Also, your spending could be higher than projected because of inflation or greater consumption of goods and services, especially healthcare.

Kevin and Sally, a married couple, soon will face retirement with a $1 million nest egg. They have paid off the mortgage on their home and have two adult, financially independent children. Kevin, age 64, expects to retire in one year. Sally, age 62, left her part-time job several years ago. Out of their $1 million portfolio, they have $200,000 in various taxable mutual funds. The bulk of their retirement portfolio, some $800,000, is in tax deferred 401(k)s and IRAs.

Kevin and Sally are in good health. Both sets of parents lived until their late 70s.

To fund their longevity plan, they need to begin by figuring out their likely retirement expenses and how much income they can generate.

So too, as you begin to formulate your stress-free financial wellness strategy, you need to estimate your annual expenses. You must know what your likely bills will be for each month (and then for each year) for both essential and discretionary items.

Remember: in retirement you only have a finite amount of resources. Don't underestimate your expenses. Don't think you'll cut back on expenses. You may eat out or travel more often than in the past. Or, you may spend more on spoiling your grandchildren. Focus not only on the basics (mortgage (or rent), food, utilities), but also estimate what your dreams might cost and when. Do you want to take a big splurge vacation and when? Do you dream of owning a boat and spending time going from port to port or owning an RV, visiting twenty states, catching spectacular views of the Northern California redwoods, Mount Rushmore in South Dakota's Black Hills, and the endless vistas of the Great Smokey Mountains in Tennessee?

Watch your credit card debt. Don't respond to the financial challenges of retirement by piling expenses on plastic.

ESTIMATING YOUR EXPENSES

To project your future cash flow needs, begin by looking at your annual expenses, assuming you'll no longer work full-time. I realize itemizing expenses is laborious and you'll probably put it off, perhaps due to pride, but you must do it to avoid a financial calamity. You need to know in current dollars how much you need to generate in order to maintain your desired standard of living. Ask yourself: How much money do I need to at least make ends meet? What is the cost of survival? What is the cost of indulgences that bring pleasure into my life? What do I dream of being, doing, or having? What are the costs of doing what I want to do and having what I want to have?

Use the following charts to help you get started:

Annual Expenses
Annual Essential Expenses
Housing - primary and vacation
> (rent, mortgage, insurance, repairs and improvements, real estate taxes, gardening/plowing/house cleaning, condo or co-op fees, or home furnishings)

    _____

Utilities   _____
Food   _____
Personal care   _____
    Transportation
    (car insurance, gas, maintenance, repairs, parking, bus, or subway)   _____
Healthcare
> (Medicare Parts B and D, Medicare co-payments and deductibles, Medigap insurance, other health insurance, expenses not covered by insurance (dental, eye, ear, nonprescription drugs)

    _____

Taxes (federal, state, local)   _____
Life insurance   _____
Long-term care insurance   _____
Clothing   _____
Debts (auto loan, credit cards, other)   _____

Professional dues   _____
Subsidies for parents and children   _____
Pets   _____
Other essential items   _____
Total Annual Essential Expenses   _____
Annual Discretionary Expenses
Travel   _____
Entertainment and recreation (health club and other
memberships, green fees, court rentals)   _____
Education   _____
Hobbies   _____
Books, newspapers, magazines, DVDs, CDs   _____
Computer, video and audio equipment   _____
Jewelry   _____
RV   _____
Boat   _____
Artwork   _____
Collectibles   _____
Charitable contributions   _____
Gifts   _____
Other items not essential to day-to-day living   _____
Total Annual Discretionary Expenses   _____
Total Annual Expenses   _____

You also need to set aside funds for likely major purchases, such as a new car, significant home repairs or improvements, say over the next five years, and your dream expenditures.

Having a budget in retirement isn't always necessary, but listing expenses and their aggregate annual amount is key. However, many find that a written budget not only provides peace of mind but may also help them enjoy their wealth more, by creating a greater freedom to spend.

As you itemize your current expenses, ask yourself: Am I happy with my current spending pattern? Has my spending changed over the years? What do I and my wife (or significant other) want to spend money on now and in the future? What are my wants and fantasy desires? Does my thriftiness take quality out of my life? Am I and my wife (or significant other) on the same page with respect to spending? Do we both balance our financial personalities (spendthrift, penny-pincher, prudent spender) or are our financial personalities in conflict?

To maintain your positive, emotionally healthy relationship, you and your partner need an agreement on basic money matters, including spending patterns. Yet, it is desirable to leave some room for discretionary spending by each of you. Communicate and negotiate your expectations regarding expenditures. If possible, each of you needs some discretionary funds—fun money—for items the other thinks are frivolous.

While planning for the future, you must think hard about your spending habits. You need to find a sound midpoint between living too frugally, which may take quality out of your life, and spending too much and possibly outliving your funds.

You must make an adjustment for future expenses and inflation. After age 80, you'll likely dine out and travel less. However, life expectancy continues to increase. Medical expenses tend to rise with age and to bulge in one's later years. It's difficult now to guestimate your future health care expenses. Will you suffer a chronic disease, such as Type 2 diabetes? Will you face a serious progressive problem, such as Parkinson's disease?

Estimates indicate that an average married couple, with both spouses age 65, will pay $225,000 for medical expenses not covered by Medicare between ages 65 and 80. You may spend more or less, depending on your health, family history, and insurance coverage. Assume the amount of your healthcare expenses will increase as you age.

Remember: In estimating your future expenses, pay particular attention to healthcare expenses which have a history of annual, double-digit increases, far in excess of inflation. For planning purposes, assume that healthcare costs will increase at twice the rate of living expenses generally.

Beware of rising Medicare premiums, Medicare co-payments and deductibles, Medigap insurance premiums, and out-of-pocket expenditures for preventive health care, dental expenses, eye exams, glasses, hearing exams, and hearing aids. Make certain you know what Medicare and your Medigap policies do and do not cover. Make sure your Medicap insurance and your prescription drug coverage meet your needs as cost-effectively as possible. Set aside funds for medical procedures not covered by insurance.

You must consider the impact of inflation on your expenses and the value of your savings. What will a gallon of milk or a dozen eggs cost in thirty years? Most advisors recommend using a 3 to 6 percent inflation factor. To see how inflation will increase your expenses and erode your buying power, select the number of years from the far left hand column in the next table, say twenty years. Follow that row across until you come to what you expect the annual inflation rate will average over the next twenty years, say 4 percent. At the intersection of 20 years and 4 percent, you find 2.19. Multiply that by what you're currently spending. If it's $100,000 annually, you'll need $219,000 in twenty years to maintain your current buying power. Obviously, the impact of inflation depends largely on the nature of your personal expenses, such as your healthcare costs.

Years	3%	4%	5%	6%
5	1.16	1.22	1.28	1.34
10	1.34	1.48	1.63	1.79
15	1.56	1.80	2.08	2.40
20	1.81	2.19	2.65	3.21
25	2.09	2.67	3.39	4.29
30	2.43	3.24	4.32	5.74

Estimating Your Income

Next, identify the income sources that are available to help fund your expenses. You need to identify which income sources will pay for which of your needs and desires. Start with your sources of regular income.

Sources of Regular Annual Income for You and Your Wife (or Significant Other)
Social Security _____
Pensions (traditional defined benefit plans) _____
Annuities _____
Total Annual Regular Income _____

Do you intend to work full-time, part-time, or consult? If so, include the income from these potential sources of regular income.

You must, of course, deduct income taxes (federal, state, local) and, if you work, the tax that is deducted for Social Security and Medicare. For a rough estimate of the tax bite, use the percentage of taxes from your last year's federal and state income tax returns.

Remember: up to 85 percent of your Social Security benefits are taxable and, if you work, you must continue to pay into the Social Security system even if you're drawing benefits.

Total Annual Regular Income (including work-related income) Net of Taxes
      _____

Does the "guaranteed" portion of your income, namely, Social Security benefits, pensions, and annuities cover all (or most) of your projected essential expenses? Will these "guaranteed" income sources also cover all (or most) of your projected discretionary expenses?

Then, review and list your retirement assets.

Retirement Assets Held by You and Your Wife (or Significant Other)
Tax-Advantaged Retirement Accounts
Employment-Related Savings Plans (401(k), 403(b))   _____
Individual Retirement Accounts (Traditional and Roth) _____
Keogh Accounts   _____
Total Tax-Advantaged Retirement Accounts   _____

Other Assets Available for Retirement Held by You and Your Wife (or Significant Other)
Bank Accounts   _____
Money Market Funds   _____
Certificates of Deposit   _____
Treasury Bills   _____
Common Stocks   _____
Bonds   _____
Mutual Funds   _____
Business Interests   _____
Real Estate Investments (net of mortgages)   _____
Vacation Home (net of mortgage)   _____
Life Insurance (cash surrender value)   _____

Collectibles   _____
Gold   _____
Total of Other Assets   _____
Total of All Assets That Could be Used To Generate
Retirement Income   _____

Note your liquid assets that you can easily redeploy, including tax-advantaged retirement assets, including IRAs, 401(k)s, 403(b)s, and Keogh plans. From this list exclude your non-liquid assets, such as your vacation home, other real estate you own, and your business, that cannot readily be converted into cash, say in ninety days.

Total Liquid Assets   _____

Remember: make certain you and your wife (or significant other) know what assets, including retirement accounts, you own. Make a list of the contact information for each of your retirement assets and any passwords.

Then, add up the estimated annual income from all of your assets that could be used to generate retirement income. Begin by looking at your last year's income from these sources. Obviously, low interest rates or a booming stock market may render last year's figure an unreliable guide to the future, but, at least, it's a start. You may want to assume that your long-term returns from stocks (dividends and capital gains) will equal six percent per year and your bond returns will equal four percent.

Estimated Annual Income from Assets Held by You and Your Wife (or Significant Other)
Income from retirement assets   _____
Bank account interest   _____
Money market funds dividends   _____
Certificates of deposit interest   _____
Treasury bills interest   _____
Dividends on common stocks   _____
Interest on bonds   _____
Dividends on mutual funds   _____

Income from business interests   _____
Income from real estate investments   _____
Income from vacation home   _____
Total Projected Annual Income From Retirement Assets   _____

You must, of course, deduct the income taxes (federal, state, local) on your estimated annual income. Use last year's tax brackets. To be cautious, assume that the federal income tax rate on dividends and long-term capital gains will increase in the future.

Total Project Annual Income From Retirement Assets
    Net of Taxes   _____

Finally, add up the projected annual income from both your regular sources and retirement assets.

Protected Total of Annual Income from Regular Sources and Retirement Assets Net of Taxes   _____

Now compare your income and expense figures. Will the projected annual income from your regular sources and your retirement assets cover: your essential expenses your discretionary expenses?

Your needs and desires probably exceed your income. You probably want to do more for your children and grandchildren. If your projected expenses greatly outweigh your projected income, you need to find a way to bridge the gap. Depending on the size of the gap, you may need to delay your retirement, modify your vision of retirement, or downsize (or prioritize) your desires. If the gap is large, you likely ought to consider delaying your retirement from full-time work for a few years or taking a part-time job in retirement. If the gap is small, consider modifying (and reducing) your spending or changing some big expenditures, such as your travel plans.

From my experience, more often than not, at age 65 and beyond, people don't live within their financial means. Typically, they're not overly frugal. Some even engage in profligate spending which may lead to dire financial consequences in their 70s and 80s.

As you review the balance between income and expenses, I realize that cutting spending often necessitates some type of sacrifice, whether in terms of luxury, pleasure, or mere convenience. Cutting back on expenses when you retire is easier said than done. We don't want to make significant reductions.

However, frugality pays big dividends. Restaurant meals and travel are two key areas where spending typically spins out of control. Cut back on status-oriented purchases. Before your buy big-ticket items, ask yourself: Is my spending wasteful or unnecessary? Do I really need it? Can I do without it? How many do I already have? Do I own anything that could substitute for it?

Remember: never shop for entertainment to alleviate loneliness or to dispel boredom. Shopping therapy doesn't work.

CREATE A RESERVE FUND

Most of us will need to create a reserve fund, a financial security blanket. Assuming you have sufficient assets, but are dependent on your investments for part of your income, you need to set aside a portion of your portfolio as a reserve fund. You can then invest the rest for the long-term, a topic discussed in the next chapter.

This reserve ought to cover one to three years of estimated spending, including upcoming essential and discretionary expenses as well as unbudgeted expenses, such as a new car or home repairs.

Gut Check: How much do you feel you need to set aside in a safe reserve fund to deal with the worst financial disaster you believe could happen, for example, an economic depression?

From this fund, you can write a check to cover your expenses not met by your regular income sources, including Social Security benefits, pensions, and annuities. The cash is waiting for you to pay for your groceries and other essentials. Consider some big calamity (or combination of calamities) that could throw your financial plan out of whack, such as huge healthcare bills, an uninsured loss, a steep, prolonged down (bear) market, or rapidly rising, sustained inflation. If possible, strive to follow the advice of cautious financial advisers and keep two years of projected spending in your reserve fund.

To provide an assured source of cash, place the assets in your reserve fund in: a money market mutual fund; a bank certificate of deposit; a bank money market account; or U.S. Treasury bills. A money market fund is a mutual fund that invests in a wide range of short-term securities, debt instruments that typically mature in ninety days or less. It typically pays higher interest rates than a bank savings account and is basically a cash account, with a return that hopefully will keep pace with rate of inflation. While money market funds offered by mutual fund companies, such as Fidelity, Schwab, or Vanguard, don't carry FDIC insurance, they are about as safe as a bank account, because they aim to maintain a constant principal value.

Bank CDs lock up your money until maturity. If you want to withdraw funds early, you'll pay a penalty.

Look at a bank money market account, the banking version of a money market mutual fund. There are no penalties for early withdrawals from a bank money market account and they're federally guaranteed up to specified limits. Also, they are more liquid than bank CDs.

Short-term Treasury securities, such as T-bills, are another safe place for your reserve fund. T-bills are sold by the U.S. Treasury and they mature in months, not years.

Beware: high yielding money market mutual funds may indicate that the fund is invested in riskier securities. If a fund is yielding far more than others and charges similar management fees, you can assume that it is taking on more risk to deliver the added rewards. Funds with the lowest costs have the least need to take on the added risk to deliver a competitive yield.

Beware: Reaching for extra yield in an ultra short-term bond fund that invests in debt securities with extremely short maturities from three months to one year may be perilous. Fund managers may make aggressive bets, for example, on asset-backed securities, among other types of bonds that may backfire. If you put money into an ultra short-term bond fund because its yield is substantially higher than a money market mutual fund be aware of the risk that comes with it. Investigate the type of securities the fund holds.

As you draw down your reserve fund, replenish it with dividends and interest generated by your long-term investment portfolio. If you need more cash, liquidate a portion of the bonds in your investment portfolio to fund your reserve account. With a significant allocation to bonds, it is likely your cash flow needs will not require the sale of stocks at a significant loss in a bear (down) stock market to refill your reserve account. Furthermore, having a sufficient reserve fund means it is very unlikely you will have to sell a part of your long-term investment portfolio at a significant loss. You will be able to ride out any protracted stock market drop.

Before discussing asset allocation in the next chapter, two interrelated topics relating to expenses must be considered: first, how to meet your long-term care needs and second, the continuing-care retirement community option.

Meeting Your Long-Term Care Needs

You and your wife (or significant other) may enjoy many years of good health. But, like Kevin and Sally, you worry that your health or the health of your wife (or significant other) might deteriorate to the point that one (or both) of you might become a resident of a nursing home for an extended period of time. It isn't just the prospect of illness and the regimentation of life in a nursing home, but the real threat of being wiped out financially by the cost of care. You must focus on how you will finance your long-term care needs, whether at home or in a facility. About 70 percent of all individuals age 65 and above, some 58 percent of men age 65 and above (versus 79 percent of women), will require some type of long-term care during their lifetime. Long-term care consists of personal assistance with the essential, routine tasks of life (more technically, the Activities of Daily Living), such as bathing, dressing, getting around the house, or preparing meals, for those who can't perform these tasks because of disabling physical or mental conditions. Family members often will provide much of that assistance at home. But some 43 percent of those 65 and older will spend some time in a nursing home (or other type of facility), with 5 percent staying more than five years. Males at age 65 have a 26 percent chance of spending time in a nursing home; at age 85, there's a 44 percent chance.

As you will discover (or already know from a parent, relative, or friend), long-term care isn't cheap. You must make the possibility of needing long-term care in a facility or at home, but not provided by a family member, part of your longevity strategy.

Medicare won't pay for your long-term care if you suffer from a chronic illness or are fragile (or demented). Medicare provides short-term home health- and nursing-facility care after a hospitalization. Medicare also offers some benefits for the terminally ill with death anticipated within six months, who enter hospice care. Although the rules keep changing, unless you have modest savings, you can forget about transferring assets to your children so that Medicaid will pay for your long-term care in a facility. You won't want to impoverish yourself to get governmental assistance for your long-term care.

Although it's going to happen for many of us, planning for declining health is tough to face. Few of us want to foresee the time we will need long-term care. We put it off. Apart from huge, unanticipated healthcare expenses not covered by some type of insurance, the cost of long-term care is probably the single most catastrophic financial risk you face.

You've probably heard about someone, perhaps a neighbor or a relative, who slowly declined from Parkinson's disease, for example, shaking and trembling. As his illness worsened, he and his wife hired a live-in home health aide. The cost became staggering. Lacking insurance or sufficient assets, in instances I am aware of, some even went broke and had to sell their house to pay for the needed care. This plight generally, but not always, makes such an impression on people that they buy long-term care insurance to shield them from the budget-busting expenses of a prolonged, chronic illness.

Before you go the long-term care insurance route, consider the funding sources available for your long-term care and that of your wife (or significant other). Will you have sufficient income to pay for both your regular expenses and your care? If not, what assets will you liquidate to pay for the needed care? The cost of long-term care is climbing more rapidly than most people's net worth. Assets may decline in a declining (bear) stock market. You may find it difficult, if not impossible to sell your home. How will the liquidation of these assets impact your plans for your loved ones? Quickly you'll see that you can use long-term care insurance to reduce risks and cover losses you cannot (and do not) want to self-insure.

For some the answer is easy. If Alzheimer's runs in your family, buy a long-term care insurance policy sooner than later. The protection provided by insurance is so important.

However, long-term care insurance is pricey and complicated. If your net worth is less than $3 million you need to consider long-term care insurance to insure against the risk that you'll need costly, ongoing care, whether at home or in a facility. Even for estates larger than that, long-term care policies offer peace of mind and enable you to retain assets to fulfill your financial legacy goals, such as an inheritance for your children and/or grandchildren.

Look to long-term care insurance if you want to leave assets, say of $500,000, not including the equity in your home, to your children and grandchildren and don't want to be a financial burden on them. You don't want to risk having long-term care costs eat up your entire estate.

Spouses may differ on the need for long-term care insurance. Paul and Susan are an affluent couple. More than ten years ago, Paul, now 67 years old, purchased a long-term care policy, with inflation protection, to cover about two-thirds of his estimated long-term care expenses. While Susan, his 65 year old wife, who hates to contemplate aging and infirmity, opted to self-insure and put the savings derived from not funding policy premiums in a separate reserve fund, at least that is what she hopes to do.

Shopping For a Long-Term Care Insurance Policy

Buying a long-term care insurance policy isn't easy. Comparison-shopping is difficult. Policies from different carriers are packaged with numerous bells and whistles. The variables will drive you crazy. Insurance agents will give you conflicting advice. Annual premiums are all over the map. Even if you buy a policy, because you'll still wind up paying for a portion of your care, keep a separate reserve fund.

Before you shop for a policy, look for an agent. In talking with several, you'll probably get conflicting advice. Try to find someone who specializes in long-term care planning and insurance, someone you feel comfortable with. Get recommendations from friends. For the names and contact information of agents selling health-oriented insurance products go to the website for the Association of Health Insurance Advisors (www.ahia.net). Even before you meet with several agents, have a phone conversation in which you grill them about their education, background, and experience in this specific field.

Most long-term care policies have the same basic features. If you develop a qualifying impairment, either a cognitive one, such as

Alzheimer's, or can no longer perform a specified number of six activities of daily living, such as bathing, eating, toileting, or dressing, the policy will pay a certain amount for a stay in an assisted-living facility (or a nursing home) or provide for home care. The insurance company makes the decision that you have a qualifying impairment. Because you probably would rather stay at home, if possible, you want the same payments for both home and facility care. Look for a policy that pays for skilled, intermediate, or custodial home care, not just skilled care, such as that provided by registered nurses. Make certain a policy covers dementia and Alzheimer's disease. Cognitive decline can ravage your nest egg as easily as physical problems.

What's tough is figuring out the number of dollars-per-day—the daily benefit—you need for your care. No one knows when you'll need the care and how much it will cost at that point. Start by getting current estimates of nursing home expenses in the area where you likely will receive care.

Beware: if you need long-term care you will face other charges, such as physical therapy, not included in the basic daily benefit the insurance provides.

Insuring the full cost of future care may make the policy premiums too expensive. Look to self-insurance to cover part of the cost or figure using your Social Security benefits.

Next, how many years of care to insure? Generally, select a benefit period from two to five years. Unless you have a family history of chronic illnesses, it makes no sense to pay for lifetime benefits. The average claim on a long-term care policy runs from 22 to 3 years.

One choice, though costly, is key, automatic inflation protection, using compound, not simple, daily rate increases. Inflation compounded over twenty years before you may need the care will be substantial. Also, as the baby boomers age, demand pressures and the resulting costs will likely increase. So, you need inflation protection unless you're initially buying a policy when you're more than 80 years old.

Look also at the waiting (or elimination) period before the coverage kicks in. It's like the deductible on your auto or homeowner's insurance. Once you qualify for benefits, the longer you wait before tapping them, 90 days or 6 months, instead of the standard period of 30 days, the lower the premium.

Comparison shop, but buy from a strong, well-established insurer. If your insurer goes belly up, you could be left with little or no coverage. Several rating services, including A.M. Best, Fitch, Moody's, TheStreet. com Ratings (formerly, Weiss Ratings), analyze the financial strength of insurers, each using a different scale. You can get the ratings from most of these services, free online. Look for an insurer that has at least 15 to 20 years in the business so that it has the experience to gauge what the rates should be.

You must be able to afford the initial premiums without a lifestyle change and continue paying the premiums for an extended period, perhaps three decades. If your personal finances go south and you quit paying the premiums, you will lose the policy and its benefits. You might receive a check for the policy's residual value, depending on the state law where you live, but there is no way you will get anything near a full refund of the premiums paid.

You may want to consider joint spousal coverage. With married couples, the spouses typically take care of each other for as long as possible as they age. Because married people are less likely to file claims than single individuals, insurers offer 20 to 40 percent discounts on the cost of shared long-term care coverage. Under this type of policy, a coverage limit exists that the couple divides between themselves. A risk exists if one spouse exhausts all of the coverage, the other will lack coverage, if needed, in the future.

Hybrid products, policies that offer the benefits associated with an annuity as well as protection against long-term care expenses may meet your needs. Sellers of annuities are packaging long-term care contracts with their products that pay tax-free benefits. An annuity represents a promise by an insurance company to make a stream of payments to someone (the annuitant) at fixed intervals. Funds withdrawn from a hybrid product to pay for long-term care coverage will not be taxable for federal income tax purposes. Consult your tax advisor. However, products combining an annuity with long-term care coverage often involve a one-time, steep premium, typically $100,000, to buy an annuity that will make a stream of specified payments to the annuitant beginning at a future time together with a long-term care rider. In addition to the need to allocate part of the premium to cover the cost of long-term care insurance, this product is complex. A hybrid involves combining an annuity, a complicated investment, with a long-term care contract, a complex insurance policy. Hybrids generally provide various options, including the amount of the daily benefits, the time period for the long-term care payouts, and the degree of the inflation protection. You will need an insurance expert to help you sort through the options if you go the hybrid route.

OTHER STRATEGIES TO FUND LONG-TERM CARE

Rather than self-insuring or buying a long-term care insurance policy, you may want to consider a reverse mortgage or life insurance. A home equity line of credit generated by a reverse mortgage can be a substitute for long-term care insurance. You have the security of having a way to pay for some of your long-term care, without using any income to fund long-term care insurance premiums. If long-term care expenses do not arise, you won't use the line of credit and your home (and its equity) will pass to your loved ones on your death; however, you must pay the fees involved in setting up the reverse mortgage account. Also, there may be insufficient equity in your home to cover the cost of needed long-term care.

Another alternative is to buy life insurance. It is typically less expensive than a similar amount of long-term care insurance and is certain to pay benefits to your loved ones on your demise with the insurance proceeds repaying the funds spent on long-term care. Drawbacks exist. You must be insurable. It won't be feasible to spend the bulk of a family's assets to pay for the care of one spouse (or partner), leaving the other financially strapped until the survivor receives the proceeds from the life insurance policy.

THE CONTINUING-CARE RETIREMENT COMMUNITY OPTION

Dick, age 85, and Joan, age 80, a married couple, recently sold their residence and opted for a continuing-care retirement community (CCRC), while they were both in good health. Knowing that they could remain in the community at one site, whatever changes arose in their health, served as the biggest appeal of a CCRC for Dick and Joan. They entered at the independent living stage and could move to ever-higher care levels, if their health deteriorated, in the same community.

Continuing-care retirement communities typically include: independent living units; assisted living facilities, if you need help with dressing or bathing, among other activities of daily living; and 24-hour nursing home arrangements, if you require skilled nursing care. CCRCs typically provide two meals daily and a host of leisure-oriented activities. The accommodations are relatively spacious and private with on-site medical care. Residents can move from one type of facility to another, when, and if the need arises, all within one campus, thereby providing peace of mind, knowing that they will enjoy healthcare for life. If you have children, there's no worrying about finding a facility in a time of crisis. Also, you will not be a burden to them. If you don't have children, a CCRC ensures that caregivers will be available.

Because various forms of long-term care are part of a CCRC arrangement, living in such a setting might appear to preclude the need for a separate long-term care policy. However, check on whether the CCRC offers nursing home care at the same cost as the usual monthly payment or, more typically, requires the payment of higher, daily rates. If the latter, you will need some type of long-term care coverage, unless you have substantial assets and want to self-insure.

Even if you enter an all-inclusive type of CCRC arrangement and already have long-term care insurance, hold on to your policy for at least one year. If you're happy and know you will stay there, you won't need your policy. However, if you leave after six months and cancel your policy, you must start all over again to prove you're insurable at a higher age.

Many questions exist about moving into a continuing-care retirement community. It's often a complicated decision. Communities vary widely with different ownership models, entrance and monthly fees, healthcare options, and entrance requirements. You need to compare both the housing options and the fee details before making any decision. The entrance fee gives you the right to occupy a residence; the monthly fee covers certain services and access to amenities. If you wait too long to apply and have health problems, you may be denied entry. Investigate who runs the CCRC and how long it has been in the business. Also, do residents participate in significant decision-making, such as meals?

As was the case for Dick and Joan, a CCRC is useful if you have no close relatives in the area and you don't want neighbors and friends to be responsible for you. Husbands often think they have a built-in caregiver in their wives and may want to remain in their own residences. Women often look forward to moving to a CCRC. There's a point in time when they want to have someone come in and do things for them.

Remember: some things are regimented at a CCRC. For example, you must eat at a certain time. The early dinner hour may prove annoying, at least at first. However, you can sit back. A couple can preserve their privacy. You can set aside time to be the couple you want to be.

If you go the CCRC route, you must decide when to make the move. It's an issue you and your wife (or significant other) should revisit every year or so, even if your health is good, as Dick and Joan did for several years, before making the decision. At a certain point, your health will determine whether the CCRC will accept you as a resident and at what level of care.

If you're interested in a specific CCRC, but want to delay making a decision, see if there is a waiting list. Some waiting lists can be very long, as much as several years. Pre-planning may be vital.

As to fees, there are three options. Under the first option (Type A or life care), you will receive care for the rest of your life, without any significant increase in monthly fees, but with a large, non-refundable entrance fee. This approach works for people concerned about funding future, higher care levels. The trade off: the highest entrance and monthly fees of the three options. The risk: you may never need the higher care levels, but you won't require long-term care insurance.

Under the second alternative (Type B or modified care), you will receive a fixed number of "free" days in the higher care levels, but with a monthly fee increase if you need additional care. As a hedge against future, higher care costs, you may want to keep your long-term care coverage.

Finally, under the last option (Type C or fee-for-service), if you need the higher care levels, additional monthly fees are charged that you pay out-of-pocket or with long-term care insurance. The third option has the lowest entrance and initial monthly fees.

With the second or third options, you do not know the cost of care when you move to a higher level and the length of time you will need the higher level of services. However, with either of these options, the entrance fee may be partly or fully refundable, if you move out or die. In general, the greater the portion of the entrance fee that is refundable, the higher the entrance charge. In other words, by paying an entrance fee, you allow the CCRC to invest your money until you need more care. Because you'll lose money by leaving the CCRC, do plenty of research to make certain you'll be happy. Stay overnight; eat meals there; ask residents what they like and what they don't enjoy.

By shifting the risk of future higher medical and care expenses to you, the second or the third option generally is best if you want to take on higher levels of financial risk in order to reduce the entrance and monthly fees. You save money if you never need the extra care.

With good health and longevity in their families, Dick and Joan selected the third option — fee-for-service. Because they have substantial assets, they do not face the risk others may be exposed to: what will happen if they run out of money and need more care?

With the second and third options, unless you have substantial assets, you likely will need long-term care insurance to cover the additional costs associated with assisted living and/or nursing care. Some CCRCs offer discounts on monthly fees for residents with long-term care insurance. In short, you must decide on the level of financial risk you want to take and how much control you want to retain over your money.

Regardless of which option you select, ask: what basic services and amenities, such as, scheduled transportation and planned social, educational, recreational, and wellness activities are included in the monthly fee? Also, who makes the final decision whether a resident needs a higher level of care? Monthly fees invariably go up, even if you don't change the level of care. If you strain to meet your monthly expenses when you enter a CCRC, you'll likely find it even more financially challenging as the rates continually increase. Ask about the history of rate increases and occupancy levels during the past few years.

One final point. As Dick and Joan discovered, coordinating the sale of a residence with entrance into a CCRC can be a challenge. If you must sell by a given date to fund the entrance fee, you may not be able to take advantage of a good market for home sellers. Or, the CCRC may let you pay the entrance fee in installments or when you sell your home.

Once you see the entrance and monthly fees, you'll realize that the decision to enter a CCRC represents a complex, major financial commitment. Be prepared to experience sticker shock when you see the cost of some CCRCs. Be certain you're confident about the company's financial solvency. You must plan to cover the future monthly fees as well as ongoing, regular living and healthcare expenses not covered by the CCRC, such as, phone service and dental care, by the income stream created by your "guaranteed" income sources and your retirement savings. Consult your tax advisor regarding the deductibility of the medically related expenses of the CCRC's entrance fee and monthly fees.

One of the keys to financial success in retirement turns on keeping control of expenses, essential, discretionary, and extraordinary. As one financial expert put it: "...[T]he biggest mistake that I see people of wealth making is a single-minded focus on investment returns with no thought about their spending patterns. At the end of the day expense control plays a larger role in the success of a financial program than the entire array of specific investments."[1] Remember this sound advice.

10. INVEST YOUR NEST EGG

Having estimated your future spending and income, you can turn to investing your nest egg. As you'll see in this chapter, learning to invest isn't that difficult. Before you do anything, take some time and learn some of the basics about investing, whether you're a retiree or a pre-retiree, whether you're well-to-do, financially comfortable, or only have modest savings.

Ted, age 62, had hoped to retire in three years. After the stock market cratered in the fall of 2008, reducing his 401(k) plan and his IRA by about 50 percent, he scuttled his retirement plan. Because he based his retirement date on the size of his portfolio, what he called his 201(k) plan in early March 2009, he had to postpone retirement so he could try to increase his net worth. "I may be 70 before I can retire. I need time to rebuild my retirement assets. I must maintain my health so I can continue working in the meantime," he noted, after watching the stock market collapse, taking its toll on his retirement investments. "It's unnerving." With nest eggs shrinking, housing prices falling, and anxieties about their financial futures growing, in late 2008 and early 2009 many of the oldest baby boomers put the brakes on plans to leave their jobs.

For most of us, our projected "guaranteed" lifetime income sources, such as Social Security and traditional pensions, will not cover our expenses for the rest of our lives, even if we make some modifications to lessen the gap between income and outflow. Apart from creating a reserve fund, you must decide on the asset mix—the asset allocation—for your portfolio, probably your biggest investment decision. Then, you need to determine which account—taxable or tax deferred—is best to hold each investment.

Careful asset allocation is critical. You want a diversified portfolio designed to avoid the worst effects of bear (declining) markets in common stocks and the adverse impact of inflation on bonds. However, there's no one asset allocation strategy that's right for everyone.

SOME INVESTMENT BASICS

I recommend that you construct your investment portfolio using two types of securities: common stock and bonds. You won't be the hit of a cocktail party or Thanksgiving dinner discussing your investment strategy. However, over the long-term, I guarantee, you'll do better than your "hot shot" brother-in-law who pursues day trading or follows a TV investment guru.

Generally speaking, common stocks are riskier than bonds, but offer higher returns, at least over the long haul. Shares of stock represent an ownership interest in a corporation. After a company pays all its expenses for any year, the remainder is available for its shareholders. The firm can retain all of its earnings or a portion can be returned to shareholders as dividends or through share repurchases. The price of a share of stock may increase or decrease in value. With equity ownership, you hope that the value of your shares of stock will exceed the rate of inflation (and hopefully taxes). Generally speaking, over long time periods, the ownership of stock has produced greater returns than the ownership of bonds.

Bonds are debt instruments. By buying a bond, you lend money to a corporation or governmental entity. You receive fixed interest payments as long as you own the bond. By holding a bond to maturity, you will receive the face value of the bond, typically $1,000.

In general, the farther away the maturity date, the higher the interest rate the bond pays. The weaker the company, the greater the risk of default (and thus the lower its credit rating), the higher the interest rate. The safest bonds are those issued by the U.S. Treasury.

If you sell a bond in the market prior to maturity, you may receive more or less than its face value. If interest rates rise (among other factors), the bond will fall in value. Although high quality bonds provide a reliable, future income stream, as a result of inflation, the purchasing power of that income shrinks continually.

ASSET ALLOCATION: DEALING WITH FOUR TYPES OF INVESTMENT RISKS

In making an asset allocation between stocks and bonds, you must find the mix of stocks and bonds that best suits your goals and circumstances. The objective in sound asset allocation focuses on the risks associated with an investment and the desire to minimize the likelihood of unexpected results. There are four types of risks: market, manager, implementation, specific.

With a broadly diversified portfolio, the big risk is *market risk*. This risk focuses on the possibility that share or bond prices will decline in response to market-wide developments, such as a recession or a rise in interest rates. You can't eliminate market risk, but you can decide how much market risk you want to bear. Ask yourself: am I willing to endure the stock market's short-term ups and downs in the hope for more appreciation potential over the long-term?

Ask anyone who endured the stock market declines of 1973-1974, 2000-2002, or 2007-2009, a stock market crash is a huge threat to retirement financial security, trailing only catastrophic medical costs or long-term care expenses. You don't have years to make up for downturns in the stock market.

Just as stock prices rise crazily upward in a bull market, they spiral irrationally downward in a bear market. In the 48 percent catastrophic 1973-1974 decline, the 49 percent collapse in 2000-2002, and the even more chilling 57 percent drop in 2007-2009, stocks just got cheaper and cheaper. These fierce bear markets mauled investors repeatedly.

A 50 percent decline in stock prices plays havoc with financial plans painstakingly devised for one's "golden years." As the result of a significant bear market, especially in the early years of retirement, devoting a substantial part of one's portfolio to stocks could lead to the evaporation of retirement dreams.

You don't want to reassess your retirement plans if the stock market, the bond market, and the real estate market, go south as they all did in 2007-2009. The triple dip whammy was unprecedented since the era of the Great Depression in the 1930s. Wave after wave of bad economic news may lead you to panic unless you have implemented a sound financial plan.

Once you've decided to take on some degree of market risk, you face *manager risk*. Ask yourself: is my goal to capture market returns within a category (such as stocks) or seek outperformance? If you turn the management of your assets over to someone else and if you want outperformance, you must accept manager risk, that is, the possibility that the manager's selection of shares will underperform the stock market generally. Studies indicate that few professional investment managers consistently beat the stock market over the long-term. Apart from transaction costs (the expenses of buying and selling securities), investment managers are often victims of poor stock selection, volatile stock market swings, or an out-of-favor investment style. You will likely come to accept the returns of the stock market as a whole and resist the temptation to try to exceed these returns. This conclusion will lead you to indexing via a mutual fund or an exchange traded fund.

Rather than your trying to pick stocks by yourself, you'll look to a mutual fund or an exchange traded fund to do your investing for you. A mutual fund pools money from investors. An equity mutual fund invests in shares of common stock; a bond mutual fund invests in debt instruments. Some mutual funds invest in both shares of common stock and bonds.

Mutual funds offer a number of advantages over individual stocks and bonds, notably diversification. Owning shares in mutual fund gives you a slice of businesses tailored to your objectives.

Exchange traded funds (ETFs) are a type of mutual fund with shares bought and sold on a stock exchange, at any time during the day, incurring a brokerage commission just like any stock trade. ETFs started out as low-cost, tax-efficient index funds, designed to mimic broad stock market averages, similar to index mutual funds, discussed below, but that trade like shares of stock. With this type of ETF you own a single security that represents a basket of other securities and tracks a broad index, moving with the value of the underlying investments. Newer ETFs have evolved into a niche financial product that focuses on a narrow slice of a broad asset class, such as healthcare or a single country, such as France. More exotic ETFs provide access to more unusual asset classes, such as gold. Most recently have come actively managed ETFs that aim to beat the market with astute stock picks.

For all their advantages, I am not a fan of ETFs, despite their low costs, tax efficiency, and the convenience of trading on a stock exchange throughout the day. With an ETF, you'll be tempted to try to time the stock market's ups-and downs, another impossibility for the average investor. Also, I wouldn't try to bet on ETFs for specific economic sectors, industries, or specific countries. The narrower an ETF's focus (or a mutual fund for that matter), the higher the risk and the accompanying volatility.

An index fund is a type of mutual fund that invests in all (or nearly all) of the stocks or bonds that comprise a specific index, typically, a broad stock market or bond average. In contrast to an actively managed mutual fund which aims to pick stocks, the manager of an index does not buy and sell securities in an attempt to "beat" the index. An index fund merely seeks to track a selected index.

Because most actively managed mutual funds underperform the stock or bond market over the long-term, most experts recommend index mutual funds. These low-cost (in terms of trading expenses and management fees), broad-based offerings ought to form the core of your portfolio. With an index fund, you won't worry about manager risk, that is, an investment manager picking the wrong stocks and badly lagging behind market averages.

If you seek market returns, you face *implementation risk*, namely, the possibility that an index fund's returns will diverge from those of the index it seeks to track. Today, index funds of leading mutual fund complexes capture the returns of their target indexes. Also, because index funds, whether mutual funds or ETFs, trade (buy and sell shares of stock) infrequently, they are highly tax efficient for taxable accounts, a topic considered later in this chapter.

The wide exposure to stock and bond markets provided by index funds removes another investing concern known as *specific risk*. It's the chance of losing money if a company's business implodes. This is the occurrence of one or more unexpected and unwelcome events that can sink a narrowly focused portfolio. With an index fund, you won't fret about your wealth imploding because of a few disastrous stock picks.

Eliminating manager, implementation, and specific risks still leaves you exposed to *market risk*. Diversification between stocks and bonds tempers the adverse impact of market upheavals. Your money is spread between stocks and bonds, investments that, over the long-term, tend not to rise and fall in step with each other, but not always.

Using Index Mutual Funds

To implement a sound asset allocation strategy between stocks and bonds, invest in three low-cost, no-load (no commission), index mutual funds. One index fund to cover U.S. stocks; a second for international stock markets; and a third for the U.S. bond market.

Index investing offers low management expenses and low portfolio turnover. By keeping pace with the market, index funds do an astonishingly good job of beating actively managed portfolios.

* For domestic (U.S.) stocks, there are basically two choices: the Standard's & Poor's 500-stock index, one of the most widely followed stock benchmarks, or the total stock market index, which mimics the Wilshire 5000, a benchmark that tries to encapsulate nearly every tradable, domestic stock. I would recommend using an S & P 500 Index fund, such as the Vanguard 500 Index Fund, which focuses on more established, larger U.S.-based companies, representing a broad spectrum of the American economy. As an alternative, you may want to consider the Vanguard Total Stock Market Index Fund, which tracks nearly all U.S. stocks.

Beware: People construct stock market indexes, such as the S & P 500 Index. Individuals make choices as to which stocks to include in an index, thereby managing the index, at least to some degree. These choices determine the resulting returns. As firms drop out of an index as a result of bankruptcies or mergers, they must be replaced. Sometimes they are replaced by firms in a different industry. Or, a firm may be kept in an index, even if it would fail to meet the current criteria for being added to the index, for example, if it lacks the minimum stock market capitalization, that is, the number of shares outstanding times the price per share.

In the S & P 500 Index, stocks are ranked by stock market capitalization. Companies with a bigger market capitalization comprise a larger percentage of the index. Thus, the biggest market cap stocks comprise the highest percentage of the index. With bigger market cap stocks more prominent, the fifty largest companies in the S & P 500 Index determine most of the returns, with the remaining 450 stocks having little influence on the results from this index. Thus, with an S & P 500 Index fund, you get ultra low expenses (and low turnover rates) and basically the ownership of the 50 largest U.S.-based capitalization stocks, by stock market value.

Recently, other index funds have been created to weigh stocks by some method other than stock market capitalization. Some rank stocks by their dividend payouts or other business fundamentals, such as earnings or book value (a company's assets less its liabilities). A dividend-weighted index, for example, rebalances its composition regularly, typically once a year, to favor stocks that pay the highest dividends. With a dividend-weighted index, investors buy dividend-paying stocks when their prices are low relative to their fundamentals, thereby reducing the presence of "overvalued" stocks, offering the promise of higher returns with lower risks and greater relative safety in down markets, at least in theory.

Beware: Approach with caution any claim to a new paradigm. We don't know for certain how an index with a value-stock basis, such as a dividend-weighted index, will perform over the long-term.

* For foreign stocks, you will want a broad-based index fund of stocks issued by companies based in the major markets of Europe and the Pacific region, such as the Vanguard Developed Markets Index Fund. For an even broader-based index of firms in developed and emerging nations, you could pick the Vanguard Total International Stock Index Fund. I'd stay with the more established companies in the Vanguard Developed Markets Index Fund.

* For a bond fund, select a high-quality corporate and/or federal government bond index fund. The possibilities include the Vanguard Total Bond Market Index Fund, which has an intermediate-term (5 to 10 year) profile or the Vanguard Intermediate-Term Bond Index Fund, which concentrates on bonds with maturities in the 5 to 10 year range, again giving it a targeted intermediate-term focus. The Vanguard Intermediate-Term Bond Index Fund that consists of U.S. Treasuries and investment-grade corporate bonds does not hold mortgage-backed or asset-backed securities, making it less risky in comparison to the Vanguard Total Bond Market Index Fund that holds these securities. I'd go with the safer choice.

An index-type of bond fund will not only generate reliable income but also serve as ballast to make your nest egg generally more stable. However, as we saw in 2008, stocks and bonds can behave badly at the same time. You likely will want to select a bond fund that invests in intermediate-term bonds for their lower price volatility compared with long-term bonds. If you're concerned about rising inflation rates over the long haul, look into a short-term, index bond fund, such as the Vanguard Short-Term Bond Index Fund, which invests in a sample of short-term debt instruments, having maturities between one and five years. The prices of short-term bonds are substantially less sensitive to interest rate changes than are the prices of long-term bonds with maturities of ten years or more.

Remember: not all bond funds are low risk products. Do your homework or retain a fee-only financial advisor. In the 2008-2009 credit crunch and the ensuing financial meltdown, some bond funds contained mortgage-backed securities of dubious value. These funds were certainly not a low risk choice. Avoid bond funds with loads of speculative-grade ("junk") issues.

If you are in a high federal and state income tax bracket, you may want to substitute an actively managed short- or intermediate-term municipal bond fund for a taxable bond fund. Consult your tax advisor. Look for a highly rated single-state fund or a national bond fund, such as the Vanguard Intermediate-Term Tax-Exempt Fund.

Bond Laddering

For your bond (fixed-income) investments, if you don't want to use a bond index fund or an actively managed, short-term bond fund, both of which lack a maturity date and a fixed yield, you may opt to set up a series of laddered bonds, with staggered maturities from one to five years, that will produce income each month, but reduce the market risk resulting from interest rate fluctuations.

If you ladder your bond investments over a 5-year period, you divide the amount to be invested into five equal portions and purchase bonds maturing in each of the next five years. As the bonds mature beginning at the end of the first year, replace them with new five-year bonds.

Through laddering and purchasing a series of bonds periodically you always will have a segment of your fixed-income portfolio coming due annually. Because the laddered bonds mature regularly, you invest part of your capital in the current bond market. If interest rates rise, you will have funds to go into the bond market and buy higher-yielding bonds; however, the balance of your bond portfolio will be tied up in debt securities with lower interest rates (and prices). Conversely, if interest rates fall, you will purchase newer, lower interest rate issues. Because bonds will mature each year, you face less pressure to liquidate shares of stock in your portfolio at fire sale prices if you suddenly need cash. Having a secure income flow from laddered bonds provides confidence to let money invested in stocks continue to ride out a stormy market.

When combined with a reserve fund, laddering will ensure that you will have cash when you need it. You'll be able to outlast a down (bear) stock market without being forced to raid the equity portion of your portfolio and sell stocks when they're down.

If you go the bond ladder route you will likely need to allocate a smaller portion of your capital to your reserve fund. A reserve fund for six months of expenses, for example, reduced further by your guaranteed income sources, not two years of expenses, may be sufficient.

For your laddered portfolio, use U.S. Treasury or high-quality corporate or municipal bonds. Because they are exempt from state income taxes, U.S. Treasury bonds provide a good alternative. In addition to income tax benefits, U.S. Treasury securities are easy to buy and sell, with only modest transaction costs.

Depending on your tax bracket, tax-free bonds may be the best choice. Municipal bonds are exempt from federal income taxes and may be exempt from state and local taxes. Beware of private activity bonds that are subject to the dreaded alternative minimum tax. Consult your tax advisor.

Remember: no-load (no commission) bond funds, offering convenience, professional management, and diversification, provide many advantages. Achieving a similar level of diversification with corporate or municipal bonds using a laddering strategy is a daunting task, even for experienced fixed-income investors, unless you have a substantial portfolio. For a successful laddering strategy, you'll need at least $250,000 to invest in the bond portion of your portfolio to obtain the benefits of diversification, unless you invest solely in U.S. Treasury securities.

Remember: Laddering won't maximize the potential returns from the bond portion of your portfolio or achieve the highest current income. By staggering the maturities and keeping them relatively short, you can protect yourself somewhat from inflation. The shorter term securities will allow you to take advantage of rising rates that generally accompany inflation. Laddering offers better performance in an inflationary environment than allocating all of the debt-oriented portion of your portfolio to one bond maturity date, particularly one thirty years in the future. Laddering will give you exposure to the highest yields available, for the selected periods, while minimizing the risk of capital loss and providing a degree of liquidity.

If you go the laddering route, watch out for bonds having a call date prior to maturity. A call provision gives the issuer the right to cash out the debt instrument on the specified date, when it is to the issuer's benefit to do this because of a decline in interest rates. You may not be able to replace the called bond with one yielding a similar interest rate.

Selecting a Target Asset Allocation

How much risk you can stomach will help you determine your allocation between stocks and bonds. Beyond a gut check, the following four questions will help you find your tolerance for risk, give you a realistic sense of how bumpy the ride is likely to be, and help you figure out your right portfolio mix.

1. Do you want the principal of all of your investments to be risk-free? Yes _____ No _____
2. Do you want your investments to be exposed to a degree of risk to increase the likelihood of higher returns, at least over the long-term? Yes _____ No _____

If your answer to question 1 is Yes and question 2 is No, remember the trade-off offered by bonds, for example, those issued by the U.S. government or high quality corporations: a lower rate of return than if you include some stocks in your portfolio (at least over the long-term) and generally an absence of protection against inflation in return for the assurance of your capital, at least at each bond's maturity. You will lack a source of growth to protect against long-term erosion of your purchasing power. Over the course of twenty or thirty years, inflation will likely wreak havoc with your standard of living. Ask: will I be upset at not keeping pace with inflation or be envious of my relatives or friends whose equity-oriented portfolios substantially increase in value over the long-term?

Allocating part of your portfolio to stocks turns on the assumption that stocks (in other words, equities) will appreciate more than inflation over time so that the real purchasing power of your wealth will increase.

Shares of stock represent claims on assets, buildings, equipment, and patents generating earnings that likely will at least increase with inflation. Thus, stocks offer a superior long-term potential in contrast to fixed-income investments. Because stock prices, at least over the long-term, reflect corporate profit growth, equity investments will likely outpace the rate of inflation over time. Taking some risk by investing in stocks helps your upside possibilities and reduces the risks of running out of money in retirement. There are no guarantees, however.

Shares of stock have not outpaced inflation over shorter time periods. Inflation is only one of many factors that impact stock prices. In the short run, other causes, such as an economic slowdown or investors' attitudes to risk, can predominate. Generally speaking, the longer the time period, the greater the likelihood that equities will outpace inflation. In sum, over the long-term, equities will do a good job in preserving purchasing power and delivering returns in excess of the rate of inflation.

Because inflation will likely eat away at more than half of the return from conventional, long-term (thirty-year) bonds, if you say "Yes" to question 1, you ought to allocate the bond portion of your portfolio to intermediate or short-term bonds (or bond funds). Or, consider allocating a portion of your bond portfolio to a fund made up of inflation-protected bonds. These funds invest, for example, in U.S. Treasury Inflation-Protected Securities (TIPS), the most readily available variety of inflation-linked securities that pay a predetermined yield and adjust the value of a bond's principal for changes in the U.S. consumer price index to preserve its purchasing power. This type of bond protects the money you already have. Among TIPS mutual funds, consider the Vanguard Inflation-Protected Securities Fund. A TIPS mutual fund offers instant diversification and convenience, such as the automatic reinvestment of interest payments. However, even with a no-load (no commission) fund, you face annual expenses and must be comfortable with changes in this type of a fund's net asset value.

Beware: Holders of TIPS bonds pay federal income taxes on both the interest they receive each year and on the increase in the TIPS's principal that annually adjusts to keep pace with inflation. While the income taxes are due each year, the principal increases aren't paid out until a bond matures. TIPS holders must pay the tax bill from another source. Thus, hold TIPS in a tax-advantage retirement account, such as an IRA, discussed later in this chapter.

Beware: TIPS can be more volatile than other U.S. government bonds. Their maturities tend to be longer than conventional Treasuries. Longer-maturity bonds gyrate more in response to interest rate changes.

To deal with the ravages of inflation, you may want to look at other inflation-linked products for the bond portion of your retirement portfolio. You could turn to inflation-linked, five-year corporate bonds that pay a fixed interest rate, say 2 percent, plus the year-over-year change in the U.S. consumer price index. The market for these bonds is relatively small if you want to sell them before maturity and you face the risk of the corporation issuing the bonds defaulting on the interest payments or going into bankruptcy. If you go this route, stick with high-quality corporate bonds.

3.   Do you want part of your portfolio to be invested in international (non-U.S.) stock markets? Yes _____ No _____

In answering this question, remember that some 60 percent of the world's stock market value currently resides in companies located outside the United States and that more than three-quarters of the world's economic activity takes place beyond the United States.

Up until 2008, it was believed that diversification—spreading the risk—would help total portfolio performance. If U.S. stocks fell, foreign shares would rise. Thus, by spreading your money around and not putting all of your eggs in one basket, you could reduce the chances of being hurt financially if one market sector takes a big hit, at least that's the theory. However, U.S. and overseas markets may move together during severe downturns, such as in the fall of 2008, when gloom spread around the globe. Thus, you may feel that stock markets worldwide are linked today in the age of globalization.

Apart from the benefits (or risks) of diversification through international stock markets, many leading U.S. firms derive a considerable portion of their revenues from overseas activities, thereby providing exposure to the global economy. You may have a bias toward investing in U.S. companies that are household names, ones you hear about in the news.

4. What is an acceptable level of downside risk in light of your long-term return expectations? In other words, how much short-term risk can you bear? Specifically, in a twelve month period, what percentage loss for the investments in your portfolio (both stocks and bonds) could you tolerate before you sold some or all of your shares of common stock? 20%____ 10%____ zero ____.

Before answering this all-important question, ponder that in some cases you may be unable to recover financially from a stock market drop. A 20 percent or more drop in your total portfolio (both stocks and bonds) could be devastating to someone already retired, perhaps forcing him back into the workforce. What if the stock market declined by more than 50 percent, as it did in 2007-2009? How would it impact on your lifestyle? Would you need to go back to work? If you can't stomach a 20 percent decline in the total value of your investments, you ought to reduce the percentage of your portfolio allocated to stocks.

In the stock market crash of 2008, you probably saw many of your friends and relatives, whatever their age, wringing their hands, worrying themselves into bad health. Hitting the panic button, some ran out and sold every stock they owned. The risks associated with a portfolio too heavily weighted to equities was too much to bear. Fearful of another Great Depression and worried about a complete financial collapse, some wanted to stuff their money under the mattress.

In the gloom of October 2008, worry about losing even more money, led Ernie to switch from stocks to bank CDs. The severe stock market drop turned Ernie, previously a buy-and-hold, long-term investor, into a short-term market timer. In the brutal September-October 2008 stock market decline, where he saw half of his retirement savings vanish, he simply didn't have the stomach to tolerate two consecutive down years (let alone the possibility of more). He indicated, "I just didn't have any staying power. I couldn't watch any more of my money going away." Filled with memories of his grandparents' struggles during the Great Depression, he was especially sensitive to losing money. Because of his desire not to make any future mistakes, he chose not to invest in stocks in the future. He vowed never to buy another share of stock as long as he lives.

You likely know several people like Ernie who, in October 2008, sold their portfolio of stocks. They basically said: "I can't take it anymore. I can't sleep. I can't deal with it."

If you sell everything, like Ernie, and get out of the stock market after a plunge and think it's going even lower, chances are that you may sell at the lowest point, the worst possible time. By not investing in stocks, Ernie could no longer gain the opportunity to profit from equities over the long-term. He risked missing out on the historically higher average returns generated by stocks once they recover. He also took on the risk of continued inflation. The after-tax income generated by his bank CDs will likely purchase less and less in the future.

Remember: Periods of stock market turmoil generally are not good times to make significant changes to your investment portfolio. You face the risk that emotions will drive your investment decisions.

You need an investment plan, one in which your asset allocations match your risk levels. Have a plan and stick to it even in a stock market slump. Try to keep your emotions out of the process.

Stock market downturns happen all the time. Expect a drop of 25 percent every 10 or 15 years. Declines of 50 percent seem to occur every thirty years or so. A dose of humility is in order. Don't be overconfident about your chances for investment success.

If you have an appropriate financial plan, one that takes into account your sensitivity to the risk of stock market declines, one that does not result in your stomach doing flip-flops each day, the best strategy is to do nothing. Stick with allocating part of your portfolio to stocks to generate long-term appreciation that stays ahead of inflation. Although stocks are volatile in the short-run, the purchasing power of bonds erodes over time. That's a risky bet over extended lifespans.

Returning to the list of four questions, if your answer to question 4 is zero, reconsider questions 1 and 2.

If you select a 20 percent portfolio drop question 4 as bearable, this points to a medium risk portfolio allocation; a 10 percent choice, a low risk allocation.

Remember: Manage your investment wealth with an eye toward your emotional well-being. The bottom line: reduce the percentage of your portfolio allocated to stocks.

PUTTING IT ALL TOGETHER

Most retirees (or soon-to-be retirees) will fall in the low or medium risk category. If you are in the low risk category (and could only withstand a 10 percent drop in the value of your total portfolio in any year), I recommend the following asset allocation:

- 14 percent to an S & P 500 or total U.S. stock market index fund;
- 6 percent to a total international stock market index fund;
- 80 percent to a U.S. bond market index fund.
- If you don't want any international stock market exposure, put 20 percent into a domestic (U.S.) index fund.

If you are in the medium risk category (and could withstand a 20 percent drop in the value of your total portfolio in any year), I recommend the following asset allocation:

- 28 percent to an S & P 500 or total U.S. stock market index fund;
- 12 percent to a total international stock index fund;
- 60 percent to a U.S. bond market index fund.
- If you don't want any international stock market exposure, put 40 percent into a domestic (U.S.) index fund.

Select a leading mutual fund complex that offers low-cost index funds in the proportion that gives you the asset allocation you want. These include Vanguard (www.vanguard.com), Fidelity (www.fidelity. com), or Charles Schwab (www.schwab.com). Using index funds avoids the high, ongoing management expenses charged by many actively managed mutual funds, thereby bolstering your returns. Also, by not constantly trading, you also reduce transaction fees and taxes.

Generally speaking, the bond part of your portfolio provides safety, lessening the volatility of your investments, while giving you some income. As noted earlier in this chapter, the longer a bond's maturity, the more a bond will drop in price as interest rates rise. Because studies show there's little difference in the historical returns between long-term and intermediate-term (or short-term) bonds, you're better off with intermediate-term or (short-term) fixed-income securities.

Beware: In the Panic of 2008, unprecedented circumstances led to a rout of the corporate bond market. The safe haven came under attack. Despite the general expectation that bonds would rise in value when interest rates declined, buffering a portfolio's returns in a bear stock market, the global credit crisis shattered these assumptions. Benefiting from investors' flight to the highest quality assets, only bonds issued by the U.S. Treasury or backed by the U.S. government held their value. Intermediate- and short-term corporate bonds, a core holding for portfolio balancing, fell in value. The prices of many municipal bonds went down. In a once-in-a-century occurrence, investors abandoned all types of bonds, except for U.S. Treasuries.

Your asset allocation will likely shift over time. You'll want to pare your stock holdings, as you get older, so that you have more of your portfolio in bonds. In your 80s, your remaining life expectancy (and that of your wife or significant other) may not allow the stock portion of your portfolio sufficient time to recover from a severe market downturn.

Those in the low risk category likely will want to reduce their equity holdings, by, say, 1 percent every two years, so that at age 80, they divide their portfolio: 10 percent to stocks and 90 percent to bonds. Those in the medium risk category will likely want to be 20 percent in stocks and 80 percent in bonds by age 80.

From decades of personal experience, don't take too much risk with your retirement investments. Err on the side of caution and you'll sleep better at night and have lower stress levels.

The more common problem is being too aggressive. Tim, a 75 year-old widower, keeps nearly all of his multi-million dollar portfolio in equities. Seemingly, he can stomach the risks that go with a complete commitment to long-term growth. However, he needs to realize he has enough to meet his goals of a worry-free retirement without running out of money and having money left over to leave to his loved ones. Although he has enjoyed favorable, long-term investment results over four decades, he doesn't need more and more money.

If you haven't saved enough to support the lifestyle to which you've become accustomed, don't try to play catch up by investing too aggressively. As a result of the uncertainty and your worries, what usually happens is that you can't sleep at night. As Randy noted, "You lie awake. You can't get it off your mind. What's going to happen to my savings, all the things we've save for?"

TARGET-DATE MUTUAL FUNDS

If you find the investing process too complicated and bewildering, you may find comfort in target-date mutual funds, offered by many mutual fund complexes. Basically, a target-date fund shifts its asset mix as you age, thereby reducing the exposure to stocks. It goes from an aggressive, stock-heavy portfolio to a more conservative bond-oriented investment mix the closer you get to the selected retirement date. Target-date funds now include funds for those in retirement, which grow ever more conservative in their asset allocation. Once you retire, they're a convenient way to stay invested partially in shares of stock while drawing steady income from bonds. In short, by using a target-date fund that makes all the investment decisions for you, you'll stay invested in stocks in tough times and be less likely to chase a hot investment that may flame out.

If you want to go the target-date route, strive to keep your investing costs low. Carefully watch your investment expenses, such as management and other fees. Higher fees do not indicate better management or lead to enhanced performance.

Target-date funds offered by mutual fund complexes differ in their stock-bond asset mixes. You must compare their asset allocation strategies. Because a target fund is a fund-of-funds, they can consist of index funds (for example, used by Vanguard) or actively managed funds (for example, used by T. Rowe Price).

THE NEED TO REBALANCE YOUR PORTFOLIO

Once you select and implement your target asset allocation between stocks and bonds, you must rebalance your portfolio periodically and sell positions that have done well and buy those that have underperformed. Over time, your stock and bond funds will increase or decrease in value. Rebalancing means getting your investments back in line with your target asset allocations. If you don't rebalance, you can end up with a portfolio that's quite different from (and potentially far more risky than) the one you started with. You may be reluctant to trim an investment that's done well lately, particularly your stock funds, but cutting back will lock in profits on investments that are up and help insulate yourself from outsized losses. Rebalancing forces you to do what is emotionally uncomfortable, but generally financially productive.

In rebalancing don't overdo it. Constant tinkering is unnecessary. Examine your portfolio, once a year, perhaps when you do your year-end tax planning or at tax time. Make changes and rebalance if the allocation veers five or more percentage points from your target allocation.

Although rebalancing will lead to more consistent returns, keep in mind you may incur tax costs when you rebalance investments in your taxable accounts. So, rebalance investments in these accounts only when necessary. To minimize tax consequences, you can just rebalance within your tax-advantaged accounts. In a stock market downturn, you could sell some investments in a taxable account at a loss, offsetting your capital gains to lower your tax bill. Consult your tax advisor.

Beyond deciding how you want to allocate your investments, you need to consider where to place your retirement assets. Your wealth will last longer if you manage your assets to minimize your taxes.

SELECTING THE TYPE OF ACCOUNT IN WHICH TO HOLD YOUR ASSETS

The account in which you hold an asset is important. There are two types of accounts: tax-deferred retirement accounts and taxable accounts. A good mix of tax-deferred and taxable accounts will make it easier to manage your tax burden.

In deciding where to place your assets between these two types of accounts, one key factor is the difference between the federal ordinary income tax rate and the long-term capital gains rate. The greater the difference between your ordinary income tax rate and the long-term capital gains rate, the more important the correct allocation of assets between your taxable accounts and your tax-deferred accounts. Also, the lower the difference in the rates of return on various investments, the more important the correct tax allocation becomes. In other words, if stocks earn only a few percentage points more than bonds, tax allocation becomes crucial.

Significant benefits exist to holding long-term capital gain assets, such as stocks, outside of tax-deferred accounts, such as 401(k)s and traditional IRAs. When held in a taxable account, the gains from the sale of stocks and other capital gain assets held for more than one year are taxed at the preferential long-term capital gain rates. Also, apart from long-term gain distributions from stock mutual funds, taxes on gains are deferred until these investments are sold. If a capital gain asset declines value, you can sell it, with the loss offsetting your capital gains for the year and up to $3,000 of ordinary income. Consult your tax advisor for details.

Putting tax efficient assets—specifically shares of common stock or stock index mutual funds—in a taxable account will generally earn higher returns than if these assets are placed in a tax-deferred account depending on the tax rate imposed on dividends and long-term distributions from stock mutual funds. Strive to minimize trades each year in your taxable account, but sell investments with paper losses to offset gains for the year, including long-term mutual fund distributions.

If capital gain assets are held in a traditional IRA or a 401(k), no taxes exist on the gains from these assets while held in the account. Thus, if trades are made, taxes on the gains are deferred. However, when gains are distributed from a deductible traditional IRA or a 401(k), they are taxed as ordinary income for federal income tax purposes, subject to an exception for nondeductible IRA contribution withdrawals. The higher your ordinary income tax rate, the greater the benefit from holding capital gain assets outside of tax-deferred accounts, in other words, in your taxable account.

If you trade equity mutual funds or exchange traded funds frequently in a taxable account, which I don't recommend, the short-term (one year or less) gains are taxed at ordinary income tax rates. Thus, if you hold tax inefficient investments, such as bonds, bond mutual funds (particularly those that own high-yield ("junk") bonds), and most real estate investment trusts that generally generate ordinary income, you likely will benefit from holding these assets in a tax-deferred retirement account. This strategy will enable the dividends, interest, and gains to compound tax-free before being subject to taxation. Consult your tax advisor.

Most investors want to follow a tax-efficient strategy. This means holding stocks and other growth investments in a taxable account. These assets should be held for more than one year before being sold. Also, favor tax efficient mutual funds that make small distributions from the sale of shares in most years. This points to actively managed mutual funds having low turnover rates and making relatively small, long-term gain distributions as well as index mutual funds and exchange traded funds. Your taxable account ought to hold the following assets: non-income producing real estate (raw land), high-yielding stocks, and equity mutual funds that pay dividends.

Beware: Putting these tax-advantaged investments in your tax-deferred account, you convert capital gains into ordinary income. Distributions from a traditional IRA or a 401(k) are taxed as ordinary income.

Note: If you have a substantial nest egg, you can put assets, apart from stocks and bonds, into your IRA. If your IRA custodian is amenable, your IRA can hold real estate, privately-issued company stock, and mortgages. However, the Internal Revenue Code prohibits all types of IRAs from owning life insurance and collectibles, such as art, stamps, coins, or gems. Your tax advisor can fill you in on the details pertaining to collectibles as well as the tax consequences of an IRA earning unrelated business taxable income, for example, from publicly traded master limited partnerships, and the prohibited transaction (self-dealing) rules.

Once you decide how to invest your nest egg, eventually you will need to focus on how to crack open your nest egg.

11. CRACK OPEN YOUR NEST EGG

Leaving aside your "guaranteed" lifetime income sources, such as Social Security and a traditional defined benefit pension, you must decide which of your assets to tap and when. You need a plan to keep the checks coming to you for a retirement that could last 30 or 40 years.

Most of us begin dipping into our retirement savings when we first "retire" at 62 (when people can first file for Social Security benefits) or 65 to 67, the age Social Security considers your "normal retirement age," depending on your birth year. As appealing as retirement at age 62 may sound, it could put a considerable strain on your savings, leading you to remain in the workforce.

If you look ahead to living to age 90 or 95, and even have a big enough portfolio to savor this phase of your life, from the modestly moneyed to the really rich, you can't take your financial future for granted. Over the decades, you will likely face periods of roaring inflation and a volatile stock market marked by several consecutive down years with portfolios clobbered by prolonged downturns.

In the early part of your retirement, a massive stock market slump can wreak havoc on your nest egg by causing serious long-term damage. If your $1 million nest egg invested entirely in stocks slides by 15 percent in the first year of retirement, you need an outsized return of 18 percent in the next year to get even. To recoup your losses and end up with a modest 5 percent return, you need your investments to soar 23.5 percent. The bigger the downturn, the more your equity investments must work in subsequent years to get you even or slightly ahead. Also, when you are closer to financially depleting your principal in your 80s and 90s, a big crack in your nest egg can cause outsized problems.

You need to be careful if you look to your portfolio of stocks and bonds, whether in taxable and/or tax deferred accounts, to fund your retirement. Rotten stock or bond markets can rip apart the best plans.

You now face the deaccumulation phase. Brace yourself for withdrawal angst. If you're no longer working for pay or a fee, or you don't own a business, you'll probably need to draw on your investments to fund part of your expenses. Once you have a realistic picture of your expenses and income from your overall portfolio, a systematic withdrawal plan can provide an income stream through automatic, periodic drawdowns from your portfolio. Spending dividends and interest feels like a paycheck. Selling assets to generate funds seems like a depletion of hard earned capital. However, today most of us can't live by the old adage: "Don't touch the principal."

Beware: Don't overestimate how much you can withdraw from your nest egg. You want to avoid a withdrawal schedule that depletes your nest egg too rapidly. Conversely, if you fear running out of money you may live more frugally than required. You don't want to spend your "golden years" scrimping and find yourself at age 92 with a massive portfolio but few fond memories. Most of us won't face that problem.

You don't want to be like George and Ann, a married couple, who expected a financially comfortable retirement. Five years after George retired, Ann stated, "We didn't realize how much everything would cost. We're seeing our investments go down and the cost of living go up, forcing us to spend about 10 percent of our retirement investments (including dividends, interest, and principal) each year." Because they underestimated their expenses in retirement, Ann continued, "Our savings are going out just too fast for us." They were worried that if they didn't make some changes they might outlive the income from their assets; they might run out of money before they ran out of life. They quickly made a cost cutting move. Rather than replace their second car, they decided that one auto was enough. For them, giving up a second car didn't indicate downward mobility, but the beginning of fiscal sanity.

Typically, you'll face longevity risk, namely, that you will outlive your money. How long you will need stream of income requires a guestimate. For most of us, first check on your normal life expectancy, and then add or subtract years based on your health and family history.

Most of us underestimate our life expectancy. Many base their assumption about life expectancy on family history. Although this may be an effective method, it overlooks the continued advances in medical treatment. You may expect to live to age 75 because your grandfather lived to that age. But, if you were born in 1955, you can probably expect to live far longer than your grandfather who was born in 1905.

Remember: You have a 50 percent chance of outliving your current life expectancy. The good news is that you could live to a ripe old age, but the bad news is you must finance it.

Couples typically use their joint life expectancy. To be conservative, if your wife (or significant other) is much younger than you, use her longer life expectancy. Using this approach means your money must be stretched over more years.

Rather than embracing a simple rule of thumb, such as basing your spending needs in retirement, for example, on an amount equal to 80 percent of your pre-retirement, after-tax income (including salaries, dividends and interest), work the numbers. As with George and Ann, you may find that your financial needs in retirement will equal or exceed your spending during your working years. As a new retiree, likely in good health, you may want to travel more or fix up your house. Consider your desires for far-flung travel, home renovations, a new car, healthcare expenses, long-term care insurance, golf club membership, or help paying for your grandkids' education. If you haven't tallied up your expenses and income, you ought to before deciding how to crack open your nest egg.

SELECTING A WITHDRAWAL RATE

Determining a realistic withdrawal rate from your retirement nest egg, including both your taxable accounts and your tax-deferred accounts, as well as your dividends and interest, represents a perplexing question. Although most of us would like to take out more, say 6 to 7 percent per year, as a general rule of thumb financial planners recommend using a 4 percent withdrawal rate, including dividends and interest. However, a one size—one approach—does not fit everyone.

Example: Lee's retirement savings (taxable and tax advantaged) total $1 million. With a 4 percent rate of withdrawal, he could withdraw $40,000 in the first year. Many planners would advise increasing the amount he could withdraw by, for example, 3 percent each year to keep pace with inflation so that in the second year with a $1 million portfolio Lee would withdraw $41,200.

In the early years of retirement, say the first five years, you may want to skip the annual adjustments for inflation and keep the withdrawal amounts steady, pulling out 4 percent of your portfolio's value at the end of each previous year. Assuming 40 percent of your nest egg remains in equities, thereby helping your savings keep pace with inflation, with a fixed 4 percent withdrawal rate, your nest egg has a good chance of providing you (and your wife or significant other) a substantial income stream for as long you both live.

Beware: You probably will owe income taxes on the amounts you withdraw, so you can't spend the entire sum. Also, if you spend dividends, interest payments, and distributions from mutual funds, these sums count toward the amount withdrawn.

First Warning: By following a fixed percentage of withdrawals from your portfolio, even if the stock market is falling, the money taken out and spent is gone for good. During a bear (down) market, more shares of stock must be sold to maintain the same income stream. It will not be there when the market begins to rise, and the future growth of your nest egg generated by the stock portion of your portfolio will be based on the smaller asset figure. This is called reverse dollar averaging: the risk of having to sell holdings when the stock market is declining to meet spending needs. When you withdraw money from your equity investments on a regular basis, with variable returns from one year to the next, you will generally receive a lower effective return over the years. By withdrawing a fixed dollar amount regularly, you will sell more shares when the stock market is low and fewer shares when it is high. The bottom line: your money will run out sooner with variable investment returns than with constant returns.

Assuming you have a balanced portfolio of stocks and bonds as well as a reserve fund, avoid withdrawals from the fluctuating part of your investments, your equities. Begin by withdrawing only from your reserve fund. If the stock market suffers a severe, multi-year decline, turn to the bond portion of your portfolio to replenish your reserve fund. By liquidating some bond funds and postponing the sale of stock funds in a down market, you can refill your reserve fund and ride out a protracted stock market drop.

Second warning: Whatever withdrawal rate you select, remember that the amount withdrawn from your portfolio could fluctuate markedly. Getting an increase in income depends on good portfolio performance. If your total portfolio declines in value, you must slash your spending to cushion the blow. However, by not pulling out a fixed dollar amount, you won't run out of money because you've limited your withdrawals to a percentage of your remaining portfolio, your bear market balance. Thus, if your $1 million nest egg in year one is worth $800,000 in year two, with a 4 percent withdrawal rate, you'd withdraw $32,000. The downside is that few of us look at our spending patterns in this manner. It's very, very difficult to cut back. No more shopping sprees, no cruises, and fewer restaurant meals. Most of us want to maintain the same lifestyle year-after-year by spending dollars adjusted for inflation, not a percentage of our retirement portfolio. You want to avoid an unpleasant roller coaster ride in your standard of living, but may be forced to make fewer big-ticket purchases.

You need to exercise care in selecting a withdrawal percentage. Recognizing that 4 percent may be too low a percentage, particularly for more affluent retirees, resulting in unnecessary scrimping, you may use a 5 percent withdrawal rate in your early years of retirement if you're prepared to use a lower rate later in life.

Your health and family history enter into the equation. For example, if you are in poor health and your parents died before their peers, you could opt for a higher rate of withdrawal, at least initially. However, you must also consider the life expectancy of your wife (or significant other).

There are other factors to consider. Do you see your nest egg maintaining its size as you age or getting bigger, for example, through a substantial inheritance? Do you want to spend all of your assets, pay for your grandchildren's education, or leave some money to your children or to charity?

Rather than withdrawing a fixed percentage of a portfolio's value (with or without an adjustment for inflation), there are at least three other approaches (aren't you glad you're thinking about this topic). *First*, as a new retiree, you may want to consider a flexible approach in deciding how much to withdraw each year. Begin by using the discipline of a low, say 3 or 4 percent, drawdown rate, based on your portfolio's value each year, to help you get used to managing your spending for the first five years when you're no longer working. During this five-year period, don't automatically step up your withdrawals along with inflation. Rather, let your investment performance determine the amount of your withdrawals, based on the fixed percentage rate you selected. By limiting yourself to withdrawing a fixed percent of your portfolio, you won't run out of money. However, the income generated by the portfolio may not keep pace with inflation. Monitor your spending and make adjustments.

You may be forced to trim spending by postponing some travel or eating more meals at home if your portfolio plunges. It's an ongoing process. After the initial five years, you can look at your actual expenses, your projected spending needs over the next five years, as well as the value of your portfolio, and consider a somewhat higher withdrawal rate, say 5 percent, at least in some years. At that point, you may want to seize the chance to buy a new car or take a luxury cruise. At the end of the first five years, say when you are 70 or so, and find that your portfolio has grown faster than the rate of inflation, you can reevaluate your situation. However, you must be prepared to slash your withdrawals if you get hit with a horrible stock market decline or your expenses if you encounter rampant inflation.

Second, for the first few years of retirement, a relatively young, wealthy, and healthy retiree may want to spend 7 percent of his total portfolio (taxable and tax-deferred accounts), including dividends and interest, for pent-up demands, such as travel. Thereafter, for most of us, our lifestyle becomes more regular with spending and the required withdrawal rate declining according. Sometime after age 75, spending may decline again. Then, even if you are healthy, you may be less active. In the final spending stage, when you incur significant medical or long-term care expenses, you may be well-insured and other expenses may decline.

Beware: The need for money may not decline with age. Although you may travel less as you age, you will likely need more money for healthcare or because you cannot care for yourself and you need assistance.

Third, you can set your initial spending rate at what you guestimate to be a sustainable level, but be prepared to vary withdrawals and spending based on stock market fluctuations. If a stock market downturn hits and you're already retired, look at your spending. Consider postponing buying a new car, putting off home remodeling, or going on that safari. Ask yourself: can I trim my annual spending by 20 to 30 percent until the stock market rout is over? To avoid having to cut back significantly in down stock markets, resist splurging too much in up markets and maintain an adequate reserve fund.

Whatever you decide to do, in figuring your withdrawal strategy, remember it's a guestimate, but plan on living to age 90, at the least.

Half of all people live beyond their projected life expectancy. In other words, the odds are one in two that your nest egg will need to last longer than you think. Most couples fail to think about their joint life expectancy. If you are married, the chances are good that you or your wife will live to at least 90 and will need a source of income that lasts that long. There's a 51.8 percent chance that one member of a 65-year-old couple will reach age 90 and a 25 percent chance that one will live beyond 95.

Consider the twin impact of inflation and life expectancy. Most of us underestimate the corrosive, long-term impact of inflation. In retirement, you'll be exposed to inflation for a long time. The cost of healthcare, a key expense for retirees, has gone up considerably faster than other expenses. The longer you live, the more inflation corrodes your purchasing power.

Before you begin to tap your nest egg, you need a diversified portfolio consisting of stocks and bonds as well as a reserve fund. This type of portfolio, together with a prudent withdrawal strategy, will likely keep pace with inflation and provide funds to last as long as you (and your wife or significant other) do, assuming you're reasonably affluent.

If your annual retirement living expenses (including income and real estate taxes) equal less than 3 percent of your total assets, you likely will be able to fund your lifestyle using a conservative asset allocation approach. Everyone else should consider annuitizing a portion of his nest egg.

THE ROLE OF ANNUITIES

The plunging stock market in 2008-2009 and the losses on many types of bonds blew a hole in many retirement portfolios. Yields on money market funds and certificates of deposit were very low. Some turned to annuities.

Bill, age 70, was concerned about running out of money during his lifetime. He recognized that his investments in stock and bond index mutual funds could be depleted if he lived a long time. He was particularly concerned about an extended period of poor stock market performance.

Imagine yourself 85 years old, in good health, but in no position to return to full-time work. Assume your portfolio plummets in value and you can't pullout as much money as you expected. Well before age 85, like Bill, you may want to consider an annuity.

With extended life expectancies, running out of money and watching the purchasing power of your income erode are two of the biggest retirement worries. If your nest egg isn't that big to start with, consider taking a portion and putting it into an annuity. This way, despite fluctuations in the stock market, with an annuity and Social Security you can lock-in an assured amount of income to cover at least your essential expenses.

An annuity represents a promise contained in a written contract by an insurance company to pay someone (the annuitant) a stream of payments at fixed intervals for a fixed period, say the annuitant's lifetime. To purchase the contract, an individual pays the insurance company a lump sum amount or makes a series of payments. The payments by the insurance company to the annuitant may start immediately (an immediate annuity) or in the future (a deferred annuity).

The term "annuity" likely conjures up the image of an elderly person receiving a payment each month for the balance of his life. You can't outlive a lifetime annuity with payments keyed to your lifespan.

An annuity can help you guard against running out of income, especially if you have modest savings. To ensure a lifetime income stream, you could carve out say 25 to 50 percent of your total retirement assets and buy an annuity. Obviously, you'll not need an annuity if you've accumulated so much money that you face a minuscule chance of running out of funds. But most of us encounter the longevity risk—the risk of outliving our money.

With this strategy, an annuity (together with Social Security benefits) will provide a secure retirement income floor, but probably not all of your retirement income needs. If you're financially comfortable, you may want your Social Security benefits and annuity payouts to cover your essential monthly living expenses, with funds withdrawn from both your taxable and tax-deferred accounts covering your discretionary expenditures. You can invest the rest of your portfolio for growth and income, with the non-annuity portion of your portfolio helping you maintain your purchasing power after inflation. You can arrange your withdrawal plan to provide the additional income from your portfolio.

Deciding on the right percentage of your portfolio to allocate to an annuity depends on a number of factors: the amount of your assets; your income needs in retirement; your guestimate of how long you're likely to live; how much money you've put aside in a reserve fund. The more you expect to live a long life and worry that you might outlive your assets, the higher the percentage of your portfolio to allocate to an annuity.

All annuities feature tax deferral. In brief, no tax benefit exists in funding an annuity. However, earnings are not taxed while in the annuity account. Taxes are payable as the annuity payouts are made. Part of each payout represents a tax-free return of capital invested. The taxable part of each payout is taxed as ordinary income for federal income tax purposes. Consult your tax advisor for details.

FIXED ANNUITIES

Insurers sell two types of annuities: fixed or variable. Fixed annuities provide guaranteed payments, regardless of stock market fluctuations. They offer safety and solid income, particularly in a time of high stock market volatility and low (or nonexistent) stock market returns. Unlike a bond or bond mutual fund, the principal value of a fixed annuity cannot fall if interest rates rise. The insurer takes the risk of interest rate fluctuations.

Fixed annuities are either immediate or deferred. With a fixed immediate annuity, you make a lump sum cash payment to an insurance company and in return receive payments right away (within no more than one year after the annuity is funded) for life or a specified period of years.

With a fixed deferred annuity, you purchase an annuity with either a single payment or a series of payments, to be invested by an insurer, tax deferred, over time before the payments start to you. Prior to the payout beginning, you're guaranteed a specific interest rate for a certain period of time, typically one to five years. Thereafter, the insurer establishes a renewal interest rate, which could be higher or lower than the initial rate. There's a low minimum guaranteed interest rate.

With a fixed deferred annuity, the fees may be steep, there may be surrender charges (the penalties slapped on investors who want out early), and the products can be complex. Search for an annuity where the surrender charges are minimal. Watch the payout restrictions. You want flexibility and the ability to: withdraw the account as a lump sum; transfer the annuity to another insurer; take periodic withdrawals without a schedule; arrange a payment schedule over a number of years or for your lifetime. In any event, with a deferred annuity, at some time, typically at age 85, you must annuitize the account and convert it into a stream of payments.

PLANNING WITH A FIXED IMMEDIATE ANNUITY

A fixed immediate annuity purchased from a reliable insurance company will provide a guaranteed income stream, typically monthly, for life. The security feature of predictable income makes a fixed annuity appealing. Pick a reputable insurance company to guard against the insurer becoming insolvent and being unable to continue making the payments.

Earning a high yield doesn't mean much if the insurer goes bankrupt. The modest state insurance guarantee funds won't help much. The federal government does not insure annuities. The insurer's financial soundness represents your only guarantee.

Check all four rating agencies: A.M. Best, Fitch, Moody's, TheStreet. com Ratings (formerly Weiss Ratings). Pick an insurer with a top rating from several of the raters. You may divide your purchase among several insurers.

By carving out 25 to 50 percent of your investment portfolio and buying a fixed immediate annuity that pays a lifetime income, you can use that income to supplement your Social Security benefits and a 4 percent withdrawal rate from your remaining portfolio. The annuity's payout will be greater than the interest you could collect by investing in high-quality bond mutual funds. The extra income from each annuity payment you receive consists of interest plus a portion of your principal, prorated over your life expectancy.

If you don't have enough capital to set aside two years of expenses in a reserve fund, consider putting a substantial part of your assets into a fixed immediate annuity. Implementing this strategy in your early 70s will extend the life of your portfolio and reduce the chances of you outliving your assets. Also, if your Social Security benefits and the likely income from your retirement assets don't even cover your essential expenses, you'll probably need to annuitize even more of your savings.

Beware: On your death, your wife (or significant other) or your heirs won't get anything from a fixed immediate annuity unless you buy an annuity with some type of death benefit guarantee. If you're not careful, no one will receive the annuity's principal if you die before your life expectancy.

The solution: select a distribution schedule calling for the payouts to continue for: 1) the greater of your life or a specified period of years (naming, one or more beneficiaries) or 2) the joint life of you and a beneficiary, say, your wife. Most married couples opt for a joint and survivor annuity, with the survivor getting a specified percentage of the initial payout for as long as she lives.

Naturally, there's a trade-off for these protective features, namely, a reduction in the income stream you and your loved ones will receive from the annuity. The more flexibility an annuity contract provides, the more you pay for the protection in terms of a lower payout.

By giving up control over and access to their capital once transferred to an insurance company, many are wary of purchasing a fixed annuity despite its advantages. It's an irrevocable decision. You surrender any claim to your principal in exchange for the payouts. Fixed annuities offer a higher yield than bank certificates of deposit, in part, because annuities are less flexible. To deal with the lack of liquidity, many fixed annuities now allow owners to withdraw up to 10 percent of the account, each year, without incurring any penalty. This provision is called the "free corridor." With a periodic withdrawal feature, you can take some money out when needed.

Shop around for the best deal. Yields on a fixed immediate annuity vary widely, even among top-rated insurers. Check out www. immediateannuities.com or www.AnnuityShopper.com. Avoid buying a fixed immediate annuity when interest rates are at historic lows.

Dealing With The Risk of Inflation

A fixed immediate annuity typically lacks protection against inflation. The payouts are fixed in amount. The yield on the amount you invest is determined by what the insurer expects to earn on its portfolio. Typically, the yield approximates that on intermediate term (5 to 10 year) corporate bonds.

To reduce the risk of losing purchasing power, consider: an inflation-indexed annuity, a variable annuity, or an equity-index annuity. With an *inflation-indexed annuity*, the insurer will make payments for the annuitant's life (or a term of years), but the payments will be adjusted annually to reflect changes in the Consumer Price Index. In the unlikely event the CPI moves down, the payout will not go down. Typically, a limit exists on the percentage adjustment so that the payments will not rise by more than 10 percent in one year. The inflation-indexing feature reduces the initial payments by 20 to 30 percent.

Or, you could select a *variable annuity*, which like a fixed annuity, comes in two flavors: immediate or deferred. You select how the account will be invested among mutual fund-type accounts offered by the insurer, many containing a sizeable portion of stocks. Thus, the value of the annuity and income-payout level fluctuates based on the performance of these investments. Variable annuities offer the promise (but not a guarantee) of an increase in payments, which may help keep pace with inflation. Conversely, if the stock market declines, the payouts will decrease. As with a fixed annuity, taxes on the earnings generated by a variable deferred annuity are postponed until the payouts begin.

To deal with the annuity payouts fluctuating with the investment returns in the annuity accounts, with one type of variable immediate annuity, you can select an assumed investment return (AIR) from several choices offered by the insurer. The higher the AIR you select, the higher the initial payout you will receive. Thereafter, future income payments will vary depending on how the investments you have chosen perform relative to the AIR. If the actual returns exceed the AIR, the payments will rise. However, if the actual returns do not at least equal the AIR, the payments will decline. Thus, if you go the variable immediate annuity route, select a relatively modest AIR, say 5 percent. This reduces the initial payment to you, but makes future reductions less likely.

To guard against a cut back in payouts, if the underlying mutual funds tank, variable annuities with "living benefits" contain various types of investment performance guarantees. For example, one living benefit rider provides the purchaser with monthly income from when he elects benefits to start (after age 59 ½) until he dies, with the benefit amount dependent on his age at the start date. At a minimum, the annuitant will get back his initial investment, the so-called guaranteed minimum benefit base. Many contracts increase the guaranteed minimum benefit base annually to incorporate investment gains; some versions even guarantee an appealing compounded annual growth of the initial investment. However there's no option for a lump sum payout of the guaranteed minimum benefit base. The buyer must take the guaranteed minimum benefit base as a payout over years or the smaller sum in the underlying mutual funds, not the higher guaranteed minimum benefit base. Also, there's a guaranteed lifetime withdrawal benefit under which a buyer can annually withdraw a specific maximum percentage, depending on his age, of his fund account or guaranteed minimum benefit base, whichever is higher. The catch with these living benefits: higher total fees and expenses as well as a complicated product.

There's also a guaranteed death benefit feature with variable deferred annuity. If the owner dies during the annuity's accumulation phase, that is, before the payouts commence, his heirs will get at least the amount of his original investment, even if the portfolio has lost money. This option likewise reduces the amount of the payouts.

Beware: Watch the management fees on the funds selected as well as the mortality and administrative charges on a variable annuity. Search for a low cost product.

Even with a low cost variable deferred annuity you will need the earnings to compound for at least ten years to overcome the expenses, including the mortality and administrative expenses and the management expenses for the funds selected, unless the investments you select generate a high return. If you need an income stream right away, generally you're better off with a fixed immediate annuity.

In the search for a high return if the stock market rises, and a guaranteed minimum yield when shares are flat or fall in value, there's also an *equity-index annuity* (EIA). With an EIA there's no downside risk and you get safety, but watch the viability of the insurer offering the product. You earn a guaranteed minimum return of 1 or 2 percent a year on your investment and if there's a jump in the stock market, as represented by an index, such as the S & P 500 index, you'll receive part of the gain. Although, the insurer guarantees that the EIA will not drop in value, the product is extraordinarily complex.

An EIA uses a stock index return formula. Once you select the index from the options offered by an insurer, some EIA's credit the owner with the full return generated by the index for the year based on a specified return formula; others use a participation on rate, say 75 percent of the return computed using the return formula. Also, with a performance cap a ceiling limit of 7 to 10 percent may exist on any year's return, so that the account earns, for example, 75 percent of the formula's return up to a maximum of 8 percent per year. The account is credited with interest, with the amount of interest based on stock market returns generated by the index, not actual equity investments. Numerous formulas exist for computing the amount of interest. Some formulas do not count dividends paid during the year.

Look at the fees in connection with an EIA. After the insurer calculates the return for a year, it subtracts various fees. The account only receives a net-of-fees return. Check also the surrender charges imposed if an investor withdraws all (or some) of his money before the passage of a specified period (the surrender period). In some EIA contracts, the surrender charges last for the contract's life. With a long lock-up period and high surrender charges, only invest money you won't need during the surrender period. You probably will need to leave the money in the EIA for at least 10 years to obtain the maximum benefits. Even after the expiration of the surrender period, some EIA's will not allow the withdrawal of funds in a lump sum, but require the payout as a stream of payments from the insurer (annuitization) or place a maximum percentage on withdrawals in any year.

Although the return on an EIA in any year can't be less than zero (that's the good news), the returns generated will vary from year to year. In a period of strong stock market gains, you will receive only part of those returns, at a substantial cost in terms of fees and hidden traps.

MORE PLANNING SUGGESTIONS FOR FIXED ANNUITIES

Let's say you like the most straightforward annuity product—a fixed immediate annuity. To gain the advantage of this type of annuity and reduce the disadvantages, consider delaying your purchase until age 70 or even later. The later you buy an annuity, the higher the payout. Also, try to buy an annuity when interest rates are relatively high.

Try laddering your purchases. You could purchase a series of fixed immediate annuities periodically, thereby reducing the chances of buying at an inopportune time when interest rates are low. Rather than sinking 25 percent of your portfolio into an annuity at one time, put a portion into an annuity every year (or two) between ages 70 and 80. Even if interest rates remain the same, because of your higher age, the guaranteed income will increase each year with the purchase of each annuity. Laddering provides flexibility if your circumstances or needs change. For instance, if your health deteriorates, suspend further annuity purchases. Again, consider buying annuities from several insurers to spread your risk.

A fixed immediate annuity can offer longevity protection. Let's assume you think you'll live to age 90 and perhaps even into your 90s. To protect against the back-end risk of outliving your assets, for example, a 65-year old man could, for about $165,000, buy an annuity that provides an annual income of $10,000 until age 85, at which point the annual payments would jump to $50,000 until his death. In contrast, for about $126,000, a 65-year-old man could get fixed annual payments for $10,000 for life. The downside: by purchasing a longevity annuity, you lock in today's projected investment returns based on current interest rates.

If you're relatively well-to-do you may want to consider an advanced life, fixed deferred annuity. The owner, typically age 65, deposits a nonrefundable, lump sum with an insurer. The insurer agrees to begin making payments when the owner turns a specified age, for example, 85. When purchased, the insurer tells the owner the exact amount of the future payments.

With this type of annuity, you could allocate your portfolio into two portions. The first would pay for your expenses to age 85. A small portion of your portfolio would be used to fund an annuity for the post-85 retirement period, if you live that long.

Trade-offs exist. If the annuitant does not live to the payout age, say 85, the insurer keeps the money. To deal with this drawback, insurers offer return of premium options; however, this feature reduces the payouts. An advanced life, fixed deferred annuity also fails to offer inflation protection. Policies are beginning to offer inflation indexing, but, again, at a cost. However, with this safety net in place, you could withdraw a greater percentage of your savings, say 6 percent, than would otherwise be prudent.

OTHER INVESTMENT VEHICLES

Besides annuities, you may want to consider a new category of mutual funds, called income replacement or managed payout funds. Income replacement (also called target distribution) funds generate income for a specific period, liquidating all of their holdings to a zero balance by a certain target date, such as twenty years. Your money plus the investment gains will be returned to you in monthly installments over the fund's life. If all goes well, your payments will rise to keep pace with inflation, but there are no guarantees. As the years pass, the asset allocation of this type of fund shifts more to bonds.

Managed payout funds seek to deliver regular monthly payments while preserving the initial invested assets, for example, for those who want to leave assets to their heirs. With a managed payout fund, you select the payment pattern you want, say an initial, annual distribution rate of 3, 5, or 7 percent of the amount invested. The higher distribution percentage appeals to those who need more income, while the lower distribution percent is for those who can get along on less but want more growth potential. Given the discussion earlier in this chapter, a 5 percent withdrawal rate may be more realistic if you are interested in this product. Once you select an annual distribution rate, the fund does the rest for you without the hassle of figuring out what your withdrawals should be with the goal of preserving your capital indefinitely. Whether this type of fund can sustain the payouts without tapping into your capital depends on its investment results. The income payments may come out of capital and the fund could decline in value. A sharp drop in payouts could occur with a prolonged stock market decline.

Warning: With an income replacement or a managed payout fund, you can't be certain how big the future payments will be. There's no guarantee that either of these investments won't lose value.

Besides the two approaches, these retiree-oriented funds differ on whether they just stick to stocks and bonds or also invest in a broad spectrum of asset classes, including commodities and real estate. Assets with little historical performance correlation to one another may aid returns and help preserve capital; at least that's how the sales pitch goes.

However, neither an income replacement nor a managed payout fund carries a fixed annuity's guarantee of specific payouts. But it's not an irrevocable decision. Unlike a fixed immediate annuity, which ties up principal, these funds provide retirees with access to their money; and with managed payout funds, account balances that can be passed along at one's death (or prior to the target date for an income replacement fund). Both of these funds remove much of the decision-making about how to manage and tap the assets while offering professional investment management.

For tax purposes, distributions from these funds may comprise a combination of income, capital gains, and a tax-free return of capital. If you hold one of these funds in a taxable account, the sale of shares each month to make payments to you generates a capital gain (or loss). Thus, put this type of fund in a tax-deferred traditional IRA or a rollover IRA. If you hold one of these funds in a tax-deferred account, those age 70 ½ and above must consider the impact of these retiree-oriented funds on the required minimum distributions from an IRA, discussed later in this chapter. Consult your tax advisor for details. Also, watch out for expenses.

Remember: If you have a modest lifestyle and substantial savings you'll likely be fine with a portfolio of stock and bond index mutual funds, rather than a product designed to generate a specified level of retirement income. If you're not at the affluent level, you could, of course, use a two-part strategy, with part of your savings going to buy a fixed immediate annuity and investing the remainder in a managed payout fund.

USING YOUR HOME TO GENERATE CAPITAL

You may want to consider selling your house and downsizing to something less expensive. This will cut your monthly expenses and give you cash to invest or put into an annuity.

If you own your residence, the mortgage is fully (or nearly fully) paid off, and are 62 or older, you may want to look into using a reverse mortgage to tap part of your equity without moving and get tax-free income from the loan proceeds. The funds can help with medical bills, home maintenance expenses, property taxes, and serve as a source of cash for new spending on travel and gifts to grandchildren. You can also use a reverse mortgage to buy a home, a topic beyond the scope of this book.

With a reverse mortgage, the lender gives you money using your house as collateral, similar to a regular mortgage, but with no minimum income or credit score required. The amount of the loan is tied to your age (the older you are, the more you can borrow), the value of your house, and existing interest rates. You can receive: a lump sum; monthly payments; a line of credit; or some combination of these three options. You retain ownership of the residence during the reverse mortgage period. There are no monthly repayments to make. The loan typically bears a variable interest rate. The interest compounds as long as the loan is outstanding and is added onto the loan balance, becoming a substantial part of the indebtedness. Death or moving out fixes the term of the loan. When the loan comes due, it is paid by the proceeds from the sale of your house. On the sale of your residence, any equity remaining after repayment of the reverse mortgage (and other mortgages or loans) will be paid to you, if you're alive, on moving out or your heirs on your death. If the sale price is less than the amount due, the lender suffers a loss.

Beware: Taking out a reverse mortgage means less money for your heirs. If you go this route, watch the origination and loan-servicing fees, insurance premiums, and closing costs.

Look to a reverse mortgage beginning in your late 70s, and only if you have exhausted other financial options. It doesn't work if you want to leave all of the equity in your home to your children. Another factor is how long you expect to be in your home. It doesn't make sense to pay the upfront charges if you plan to move within a few years.

For those who qualify for a home equity loan and can make the monthly payments, it's usually the better option rather than a reverse mortgage.

EVERYTHING (WELL MOST EVERYTHING) YOU WANTED TO KNOW ABOUT REQUIRED MINIMUM DISTRIBUTIONS

You're probably aware of the need to take required minimum distributions (RMDs) from your tax-deferred accounts, including traditional IRAs, SEP (Simplified Employee Pension)-IRAs, Simple (Savings Incentive Match Plan) IRAs (mainly for small business owners and self-employed individuals), 401(k)s, 403(b)s (the non-profit world's version of a 401(k)), and Keoghs, at some point in time. RMDs may start to be taken in the year you turn 70 ½, but must be taken beginning no later than April 1 of the following year. For all subsequent years, you must take your RMDs by December 31. RMDs trigger federal income tax consequences discussed briefly in this chapter.

RMDs From IRAs. For purposes of computing your required minimum distributions, you combine all of your deductible and nondeductible traditional IRAs (as well as your SEP-IRAs and Simple IRAs) into one account. If you are required to take withdrawals from inherited IRAs, these IRAs follow a different schedule. Don't include your inherited IRAs (also known as Stretch IRAs) in your calculations. Consult your tax advisor for the rules concerning inherited IRAs.

In your IRA calculations do not include your Roth IRAs or your 401(k), 403(b), or Keogh plans. You are not required to take minimum distributions from your Roth IRAs, although beneficiaries who inherit a Roth IRA must begin RMDs. The RMDs for your 401(k) plans are discussed later in the chapter.

In figuring our RMDs most of us will use Table III, the Uniform Lifetime Table (www.irs.gov, under Forms and Publications).

IRS Publication 590 - Individual Retirement
Arrangements (IRAs), Appendix C. Life Expectancy Tables
Table III
(Uniform Lifetime)
For Use by:
• Unmarried Owners,
• Married Owners Whose Spouses Are Not More Than 10 Years Younger, and
• Married Owners Whose Spouses Are Not the Sole Beneficiaries of their IRAs

Age	Distribution Period	Age	Distribution Period
70	27.4	93	9.6
71	26.5	94	9.1
72	25.6	95	8.6
73	24.7	96	8.1
74	23.8	97	7.6
75	22.9	98	7.1
76	22.0	99	6.7
77	21.2	100	6.3
78	20.3	101	5.9
79	19.5	102	5.5
80	18.7	103	5.2
81	17.9	104	4.9
82	17.1	105	4.5
83	16.3	106	4.2
84	15.5	107	3.9
85	14.8	108	3.7
86	14.1	109	3.4
87	13.4	110	3.1
88	12.7	111	2.9
89	12.0	112	2.6
90	11.4	113	2.4
91	10.8	114	2.1
92	10.2	115 and over	1.9

If you named your wife as the sole beneficiary of your IRA and she is more than 10 years younger than you, use Table II (Joint Life and Last Survivor Expectancy Table) to calculate your joint life expectancy when figuring the required withdrawals. Consult your tax advisor for further details.

Look at the Uniform Lifetime Table, find your age and divide your account balance by the appropriate number. Although this seems confusing, the example below will help make it clear. For purposes of the RMD, finding your age means using the age on the birthday that occurred in the year when you turned 70 ½. If you turned 70 ½ on

June 1, your 71st birthday would be December 1, so you would use 71. However, if you turned 70 ½ on August 1, your 70th birthday was February 1, so you would use 70.

Even though you have until April 1 of the year following the year in which you turn 70 ½ to begin taking the required minimum distributions, you base the withdrawal amount on your account balances as of December 31 of the year before the year in which you turn 70 ½, not December 31 of the year you turn 70 ½.

Example. Greg had $300,000 in a deductible, traditional IRA on December 31 last year. He turned 70 ½ on October 1 this year. He would divide the account balance by 27.4, the life expectancy factor in the Uniform Lifetime Table for age 70, because he turned 70 on April 1 this year, his first distribution year. The age Greg uses is his age on the birthday that occurred in the year when he turned 70 ½, that is, this year. He can take his first RMD at any point during this calendar year. Greg must withdraw at least $10,948.91 from his RMD, by April 1 of the next year. Greg must base the withdrawal amount on his account balance as of December 31 of the year before turning age 70 ½. He can take this first distribution in any way he likes, monthly, quarterly, in a lump sum at the beginning or end of this year. Greg must take out the full amount of his first distribution by April 1 of next year.

In considering when to take the first required minimum distribution, Gregg must keep in mind that two sizable IRA distributions in the next year could bump him into a higher federal income tax bracket, increasing the tax rate on the distributions. Thus, it is generally better to take the first RMD by December 31 of the year in which the owner turns 70 ½; thereby spreading the first two distributions over two tax years.

You do not pay taxes on your total traditional IRA balances that come from nondeductible contributions. Your nondeductible contributions come out proportionally. You divide the total of your nondeductible IRA contributions (more technically, your basis) by the total value of all of your traditional IRAs. You apply that percentage to your distribution amount to figure out how much of your required withdrawal is tax-free.

Example. Frank contributed $30,000 to a nondeductible, traditional IRA. That IRA is now worth $40,000. He also has a separate deductible, traditional IRA with a current value of $60,000. The nondeductible contributions of $30,000 now equal 30 percent of the total value of $100,000 in Frank's traditional IRAs. Thus, 30 percent of the total withdrawal, whether from his deductible or nondeductible IRA, is nontaxable, 70 percent is taxable.

Because the IRS views all your traditional IRAs (except your inherited IRAs) as a single IRA, you have considerable flexibility in making the required withdrawals. You can pull the necessary amount from one IRA or take the total withdrawal from several accounts in any proportion you want. Also, there is no maximum distribution amount. You can always withdraw amounts from your IRA in excess of the RMD. In other words, the required minimum distribution is just that; taxpayers can withdraw a larger amount. Individuals who take larger amounts may, however, risk depleting their retirement portfolio.

RMDs From Other Tax-Deferred Plans. RMDs from 401(k)s, 403(b)s, and Keogh plans are calculated the same way as withdrawals from traditional IRAs, using the same life expectancy tables, but separately from your IRAs. There's no mixing allowed between your traditional IRA and your 401(k) or if you have multiple 401(k)s. Unlike traditional IRAs where balances are added together, you cannot add your IRA and 401(k) balances together to determine the amount of your required minimum distributions. If you have multiple 401(k)s, you must calculate the RMD from each separately. However, if you have another type of employer-sponsored retirement plan, such as a 403(b) plan, you can treat the multiple 403(b) accounts as one. You must still calculate your 403(b) withdrawals separately from your IRA or 401(k) withdrawals. Consult your tax advisor.

Tapping Your Nest Egg

Once you determine your withdrawal strategy, you must decide which assets to tap first: those in your taxable accounts or those in your tax-deferred retirement accounts.

Typically, planners recommend drawing down your taxable accounts, your mutual funds, stocks, and bonds, first, and then turning to your tax-deferred accounts, such as your traditional IRA and your 401(k). This sequence gives the income and gains in your tax-advantaged assets time to grow and compound as long as possible. Try to hold off dipping into your tax-deferred savings until federal law says you have to, basically, the year in which you turn 70 ½. Let your traditional IRA with nondeductible (after-tax) contributions compound longer than your fully taxable, deductible, traditional IRA. Part of the distributions from your nondeductible IRAs are tax-free, reflecting your after-tax contributions. Your tax advisor can fill you in on the details. Then withdraw funds from your tax-deferred accounts funded entirely with deductible contributions. All the withdrawals from these accounts, both the initial investments and the earnings, will be taxable as ordinary income. Leave tax-free distributions from your Roth IRA for last, until you've run through all your other savings.

The general rule of thumb is not always the best strategy. Some people should consider spending their traditional IRAs funded with deductible contributions first. On reaching age 70 ½, IRA owners must take required minimum distributions each year. These distributions are taxed as ordinary income. In a taxable account, distributions are not required. Thus, you may want to consider making withdrawals from your traditional IRAs and emptying them early. The decision hinges on the size of your IRAs. If they are large enough, say $500,000 or more in total, so that your required minimum distributions will bump you into a higher federal income tax bracket, you should consider making withdrawals before you reach age 70 ½ so that even with the RMDs you will stay within a lower federal income tax bracket. Emptying an IRA early is a good idea if thereafter you will have other assets to pay for your retirement needs. If this is your situation, consider the early (pre-age 70 ½) withdrawal of funds from your traditional IRA. Consult you tax advisor.

Planning Suggestions for Your IRAs

Most owners want to avoid depleting their traditional IRAs early. They also want to leave something to their wife (or significant other) or their children. To deal with these two problems, you may want to purchase a fixed immediate annuity with your IRA. This type of annuity must begin distributions within one year and pay the same annual amount for the guaranteed period, typically your life or the joint lives of you and your wife (or significant other). Purchasing an annuity fulfills the RMD rules.

Beware: with a fixed immediate annuity, the payouts do not increase with inflation (unless you opt for an inflation-indexed annuity) or a rise in interest rates. You may want to invest all (or part) of your non-annuitized assets for growth.

If you don't purchase an annuity with your IRA, for example, but take RMDs and go into your 90s, a quick glance at the Uniform Life Table shows that the RMDs become a huge percentage of your tax-deferred retirement accounts. The IRS wants you to use these accounts for your retirement, and not pass them on to your heirs in the form of a tax-sheltered estate. To avoid a huge income tax bill in your 90s, assuming you do not need all of the income generated by the RMDs, consider making large charitable donations of up to 50 percent of your income, roughly speaking, to offset your mandatory withdrawals. Or, purchase a charitable gift annuity with part of your tax-deferred account distributions.

A charitable gift annuity is an annuity purchased from a public charity. The charity makes fixed payouts for the life of one (or two) designated beneficiaries or a term of years. The income payments are backed by the charity's assets, leading most donors to favor large, stable nonprofits, such as universities. Some charities reinsure their gift annuities by buying an annuity from an insurance company to ensure being able to meet their obligations to donors.

With a charitable gift annuity, the donor receives an immediate federal income tax deduction for the present value of what the charity expects to wind up with after paying out the income stream, typically between 20 and 50 percent of the amount contributed, based on the life expectancy of the beneficiary (or beneficiaries) and the anticipated income payments. The older the donor, the greater the income tax deduction and the income payments. The donor's income tax deduction is subject to an annual percentage limit, with a five-year carryover. Part of each income payment represents a tax-free return of principal (to make up for the portion of the deduction not taken) until the donor receives an amount equal to his payment to the charity for the annuity contract. Your tax advisor can fill you in on the details.

Beware: The payout from a charitable gift annuity is fixed and affords no protection from inflation if interest rates rise in the future.

If you decide to go the charitable gift annuity route and want to make substantial contributions, most donors opt to establish annuities with several charities. This strategy provides some diversification if one charity encounters financial difficulties. It also allows donors to allocate their gifts to several different causes. You don't need to shop around because most charities will pay the same annuity rate based on the donor's age.

DEALING WITH YOUR EMPLOYER-SPONSORED RETIREMENT PLAN

For many of us, our largest nest egg resides within our employer's retirement plan. At retirement, there are three basic options: keep the money accumulated in your 401(k) plan; roll it over to an IRA; or take the payout in the form of an annuity. With respect to the first two options, it is generally advisable to roll over the assets, tax free, into a traditional IRA unless there is an investment option in the 401(k) plan that is not available to the retail investor. The disadvantages of staying with your 401(k) plan generally include more limited investment choices than typically available in an IRA, more restricted access to your funds, and limited control over investment fees. Staying with your 401(k) plan may, however, have some advantages including familiarity with the investment choices, protection of your plan assets from creditors, and if you remain an active employee with the company, the ability to borrow from your account and delay mandatory withdrawals beyond age 70 ½. Although a rollover IRA offers more flexibility in designing your portfolio and choosing investments, you may be overwhelmed by the choices. If so, a target-date mutual fund may work for you.

If you have company stock in your 401(k) plan, consult your tax advisor on how to handle it. You may be eligible to take advantage of a little known tax break to defer the capital gain taxes on the net unrealized appreciation until you sell the shares.

Beware: If possible, avoid an overexposure to your employer's stock in your 401(k) plan.

You may want to take all (or a part) of your 401(k) funds in the form of an annuity. If you go the fixed immediate payout route, you need to select the type of annuity payout you want: for your life (or the joint lives of you and a beneficiary) or a term years. The payout is guaranteed for the selected payment period. The lifetime income guarantee isn't valuable if you're in poor health. Because the annuity payouts are typically fixed in amount, they lose purchasing power due to inflation. However, inflation-adjusted payouts are available. With an annuity, you lose flexibility in taking withdrawals as you would with an IRA. Also, an annuity payout leaves nothing for your estate unless you structure the payments to be received by your survivors for a number of years.

If you want to arrange your payout as an annuity, compare your employer's annuity quote with those from other commercial insurance companies. If you want to buy the annuity yourself, first rollover your plan's assets into an IRA and then use these funds to purchase the annuity. If you just take the money out in a lump sum and buy an annuity, you will face a big tax bill. Consult your tax advisor.

You may want to use a two-part strategy. You could annuitize part of your plan's assets and rollover the rest to an IRA. See if your plan offers this option.

DEALING WITH ROTH IRAS

One of the best assets for your kids to inherit is your Roth IRA. Although you aren't required to make any RMDs from your Roth IRA during your lifetime, your children must take tax-free distributions each year once they inherit the account, regardless of their own ages. By following the withdrawal rules, they can squeeze years of tax-free growth from your Roth IRA.

If you are in a higher federal income tax bracket than your heirs, it may make sense to draw down your Roth IRA while you're alive and leave your kids your traditional IRA. If your heirs are in a low federal income tax bracket, the traditional IRA's embedded tax bill may not be onerous.

If you want to make charitable contributions on your death, consider leaving your traditional IRA to a charity and enjoying tax-free Roth IRA withdrawals during your lifetime. Consult your tax advisor for details on how to handle your Roth IRA.

SOME CONCLUDING THOUGHTS ON YOUR NEST EGG

You and your wife (or significant other) ought to agree on a strategy to invest your nest egg and crack it open. Ideally, when it comes to making big financial decisions for your longevity strategy do it together. When you make decisions together, you both have ownership of the results (good or bad) from your choices. Even if you have negative results and must cut your spending, you'll tend to weather the storm better together.

Differences bound, however. One couple I know, the wife thinks she will have a significantly longer life expectancy than her husband, even if both are currently in excellent health. The wife worries about running out of money in her 90s. She expresses concern about living to 100 and outliving her money. Thus, they have vastly different views of a withdrawal strategy. Purchasing a fixed immediate annuity (or periodically, a series of annuities) would offer her a guaranteed lifetime income and the ability to withdraw annually a small part of the annuity principal, if needed.

Strive for equality in retirement financial decision-making regardless of past habits about money and power. There are likely to be fewer excuses about a lack of time. Lack of interest is, of course, another matter. You both need to come up with a sound division of labor for bill paying, handling investments, and tax planning.

No one withdrawal strategy can guarantee protection for your income needs during an extended lifespan, say to age 100. With planning, you can strive to maximize the withdrawal period; provide a measure of comfort in trying stock and bond market periods; and minimize the impact of income taxes, transaction costs, and expenses. However, following the recommendations contained in chapters 9, 10, and 11 you ought to sleep comfortably.

CONCLUSION: THE GREAT BEYOND

As we peer forward into the future, we discern the lurking shadow of death. Do not believe as some do that debilitation, which hopefully will be short, and death are the fate of others. We all will die. No matter how healthfully we eat or how much we exercise not one of us will live forever. Immortality on this earthly plane is impossible. To our dismay, greater longevity creates its own problems, such as chronic illness or Alzheimer's disease.

Yet aging, even successful aging, forces us to contemplate death. What initially comes to mind when you think about death? What will happen on your demise? Perhaps you reflect on your death at 2 a.m. in the morning, when you lie restless in bed or when you have a medical emergency.

As we search beyond the darkness, contemplate your own death. Picture yourself lacking a physical being and not being in this earthly world.

We all live in the shadow of death. At a certain age, you think about your own mortality. It frames your search for your purpose in life, for finding meaning in one's whole story. In a life-threatening experience, the confrontation with death is upon us.

Zack related how he thought about death. It started with a dull thud. Then, intensifying, it grew into an acute sharpness in the chest: angina, not enough oxygenated blood getting to the heart, because an artery was partly clogged. He called 911 and found himself in the back of a speeding ambulance, with a paramedic checking his vitals. Death, he imagined, was creeping up. Suddenly it began to pounce and he was forced to stare it in the face.

An angiogram, a procedure using a tiny camera inserted into the heart, revealed blocked arteries near Zack's heart. His cardiologist told him, "You need bypass surgery right away, first thing tomorrow morning."

Within a few hours his whole family surrounded him, smiling, crying, wishing him love and good luck. He saw the fear in his adult children's eyes. Then he was alone.

He asked the night nurse if he could go to the chapel to meditate and pray. Scrubbed and shaved, he reflected about death—his death. To show himself that he was strong, he began a familiar meditation. He started to feel calm. A benign, but hopeful, tranquility settled over him. He prayed to God. Let the Eternal decide. But he wanted the Divine to know that he would like to stay alive. He thought about the Great Beyond—what would happen to him if he died?

As it turned out the procedure was successful. First, he went to the cardiac recovery unit, then the post-op ward, and, finally, home.

Although Zack beat death, it still lingers in his mind. Death never made a full departure, but he gained a reprieve. He keeps on breathing. Life with all its abundance and its pleasures awaits him. Although for some coming to grips with their mortality can be a chilling experience, as they think of themselves as a speck of dust, for many, like Zack, it was liberating and empowering.

Like Zack, some remain calm when death presents itself. In part, they have a sound philosophy of life and the lust for life that grows out of their philosophy.

Some find solace in their faith. The ability to look on death with serenity reflects a strong belief in the hereafter. They may not be anxious to die, but they're not troubled about dying.

The world's leading religions, Buddhism, Christianity, Hinduism, Islam, and Judaism, see death as a gateway into the next life. They express a belief in the hereafter, a continuation of life after death, an existence following this earthly life. They fill us with hope for some type of survival after death. While our physical form changes, our essence— our soul—is indestructible. Our death is not a finite failure, but a natural end and a new beginning on a different plane. For believers, death no longer seems threatening.

Many today realize the truth of everlasting life but not through one's physical body, which must, of necessity, wear out and die. But the physical body is only a part of our being. After death, it is our soul that experiences eternal life. With our physical senses we cannot, of course, perceive the reality of spirit, the world of immortality.

Some traditions even offer the possibility of reincarnation, providing even greater spiritual comfort. Reincarnation affirms our continuity from one physical life to another earthly existence. Through death and rebirth, each soul draws closer to its true identity and greater perfection. Eventually, it is hoped, we all will become enlightened and achieve eternal bliss.

From a spiritual viewpoint, one can see life as an expression of Divine Goodness. Creation represents an expression of Divine Loving Kindness. God who seeks our happiness could not be our complete and total destroyer on our physical demise. God Who cultivates humanity, with faculties and reason, could not decree the destruction of what the Eternal so carefully nurtured and sustained.

What then is the soul—our essence? Although there are many concepts of the soul, for me, it is that part emanating from God through which divinity expresses itself in our body. Because no mortal eye can see God, no earthly eye can behold one's soul. Just as the soul of nature—the Divine—is everlasting, so the soul of humanity is indestructible and immortal. Our soul is divine-like. This ray of Divine Illumination cannot be snuffed out because it comes from the eternal God. Our soul is immortal because it emanates from an immortal source. God gives each of us our soul—our essence—from the Infinite Divine Spirit. Because God lives eternally, every part of the Divine Spirit, including each soul, has eternal life.

Our body serves as the physical instrument to realize the strivings of our spirit on this earthly plane. We leave it here and are liberated from its imperfections and weaknesses. Viewing God as merciful and compassionate and that we are the Eternal's children, we have no reason to fear death.

Worries about aging, dying, and death serve, however, as a shadow over many lives. Negative beliefs about the nature and consequences of death create many pessimistic thoughts, destroying one=s cheerfulness, contributing to anxiety, and holding one back.

God plans to raise each of us into the world of eternity. Each of us will leave behind our physical body with all its pain and suffering. In the Great Beyond, we live, perhaps reincarnated, and then, ultimately, to a life of spiritual exaltedness.

Despite the reports generated by near death experiences and past life reviews, death represents the final frontier of human knowledge. At present, faith is essential to my position that God has something more in store for us than our physical existence. By faith, I mean a trust that there exists a Supreme Power who sustains, protects, and provides for everyone. This Higher Power, intangible, invisible, Who saturates all reality, is the essence of the universe. This Universal Force is the source of all life and sustenance. Each of us emanates from the Eternal and in the Divine Presence we all will find perpetual shelter.

Those who cherish this type of faith, those who trust in God's goodness, never fear death or worry about what will happen on their physical demise. No matter what clouds hang over the horizon, no matter what uncertainties the future seems to hold, someone of faith trusts that God will care for each of us, thereby casting away our anxieties about death.

Although death is a fact of life, its recognition can propel you to impassioned living. Vow to live more fully, today and everyday. You can impact the quality of your life, even if you can't control the quantity.

Time is a precious commodity. You may have remaining far too little or an overabundance of time. In any event, don't spend your time frivolously or without foresight. Make everyday count. Strive to eliminate everything that doesn't matter. Pare down life to what you enjoy. Focus on what makes you the happiest and discard what tends toward misery.

As longevity is a succession of many days, live for each day. Let each day be a day of achievement; let each day be a day of moderation; let each day be a day of enjoyment.

Find meaning and purpose in your existence through productive activity. Stay active, engaged, and vital. Vow to live a joyful, serene, loving, and forgiving life.

With advanced years, you can attain the much deeper, much finer joys that satisfy the heart and ennoble the mind; you can realize your existential, emotional, physical, and financial well-being.

ABOUT THE AUTHOR

Lewis D. Solomon is a research professor at The George Washington University Law School. He is the author of numerous books including *Bratproofing Your Children: How to Raise Socially and Financially Responsible Kids*, co-authored with his wife, Janet Stern Solomon. He resides in Chevy Chase, Maryland.

NOTES

INTRODUCTION

1. Lee Iacocca, "How I flunked retirement," *Fortune*, June 24, 1996, 50, at 61.

CHAPTER 1

1. Viktor R. Frankl, *Man's Search for Meaning* (New York: Washington Square Press, 1984), 133.
2. Ibid, 16.
3. Ibid, 127.
4. Ibid, 131.
5. Árpád Skrabski et al, "Life Meaning: An Important Correlate of Health in the Hungarian Population," *International Journal of Behavioral Medicine* 12:2 (June 2005): 78-85.
6. Quoted in Glenn Ruffenbach, "In Search of a Purpose," *Wall Street Journal*, November 17, 2007, R8.
7. Robert Hammerman-Rozenberg et al, "Working late: the impact of work after 70 on longevity, health and function," *Aging Clinical Experimental Research* 17:6 (December 2005): 508-513.
8. Frank McCourt, "We All Can Have Second Acts (& Third!)," *Parade*, March 9, 2008, 12, at 13.
9. Quoted in Carol Hymowitz, "Nurturing the Muse: Some of the country's most prominent artists discuss how they foster

creativity in later life," *Wall Street Journal*, March 19, 2001, R17.

10. Adapted from Naomi Stephan, *Finding Your LIFE MISSION: How to Unleash That Creative Power and Live With Intention* (Walpole, NH: Stillpoint, 1989), 197-199.

CHAPTER 2

1. *Now, Discover Your Strengths* (New York: Free Press, 2001), Marcus Buckingham and Ronald O. Clifton.

2. Ibid, 12.

3. Ibid, 25.

4. *Strengths Finder 2.0* (New York: Gallup Press, 2007), Tom Rath.

5. *Don't Retire, REWIRE!: 5 Steps to Fulfilling Work that Fuels Your Passion, Suits Your Personality, and Fills Your Pocket*, Second Edition (New York: Alpha Books, 2007), Jeri Sedlar and Rick Miners, 58, 71-78.

6. Gregory E. Miller and Carsten Wrosch, "You've Gotta Know When to Fold'em: Goal Disengagement and Systemic Inflammation in Adolescence," *Psychological Science* 18:9 (September 2007): 773-777.

7. Gene D. Cohen, *The Creative Age: Awakening Human Potential in the Second Half of Life* (New York: Avon, 2000), 148.

CHAPTER 3

1. Quoted in Scott R. Schmedel, "Making a Difference," *Wall Street Journal*, August 21, 2006, R5, R12.

2. Linda P. Fried et al, "A Social Model for Health Promotion for an Aging Population: Initial Evidence on the Experience Corps Model," *Journal of Urban Health* 81:1 (March 2004): 64-78. See also Jeremy S. Barron et al, "Potential for Intensive Volunteering to Promote the Health of Older Adults in Fair Health," *Journal of Urban Health* 86:4 (July 2009): 641-653.

SECTION II

1. Becca R. Levy et al, "Longevity Increased by Positive Self-Perceptions of Aging," *Journal of Personality and Social Psychology*

83:2 (August 2002): 261-270. See also Becca R. Levy et al, "Age Stereotypes Held Earlier in Life Predict Cardiovascular Events Later in Life," *Psychological Science* 20:3 (March 2009): 296-298.

2.   Glenn V. Ostir, Kenneth J. Offenbacher, Kyriakos S. Markides, "Onset of Frailty in Older Adults and the Protective Role of Positive Affect," *Psychology and Aging* 19:3 (September 2004): 402-408.

CHAPTER 4

1.   *Learned Optimism* (New York: Knopf, 1991), Martin E. P. Seligman.

2.   *Ibid*, 174-182.

3.   Christopher Peterson, Martin E.P. Seligman, George E. Vaillant, "Pessimistic Explanatory Style Is a Risk Factor for Physical Illness: A Thirty-Five-Year Longitudinal Study," *Journal of Personality and Social Psychology* 55:1 (July 1988): 23-27.

4.   Leslie Kamen-Siegel et al, "Explanatory Style and Cell-Mediated Immunity in Elderly Men and Women," *Health Psychology* 10:4 (1991): 229-235.

5.   Bruce S. Jonas and James F. Lando, "Negative Affect as a Prospective Risk Factor for Hypertension," *Psychosomatic Medicine* 62:2 (March-April 2000): 188-196.

6.   John F. Todaro et al, "Effect of Negative Emotions on Frequency of Coronary Heart Disease (The Normative Aging Study)," *American Journal of Cardiology* 92:8 (October 15, 2003): 901-906 and Laura D. Kubzansky and Ichiro Kawachi, "Going to the heart of the matter: do negative emotions cause coronary heart disease?," *Journal of Psychosomatic Research* 48:4-5 (April-May 2000): 323-337.

7.   Christopher Peterson et al, "Catastrophizing and Untimely Death," *Psychological Science* 9:2 (March 1998): 127-130.

8.   H. Koivumaa-Honkanen et al, "Self-reported Life Satisfaction and 20-Year Mortality in Healthy Finnish Adults," *American Journal of Epidemiology* 152:10 (November 15, 2000): 983-991.

9. Numerous articles link depression and coronary heart disease including Koen Van der Kooy et al, "Depression and the risk for cardiovascular diseases: systematic review and met analysis," *International Journal of Geriatric Psychiatry* 22:7 (July 2007): 613-626; Marijke A. Bremmer et al, "Depression in Older Age is a Risk Factor for First Ischemic Cardiac Events," *American Journal of Geriatric Psychiatry* 14:6 (June 2006): 523-530; Heather S. Lett et al, "Depression as a Risk Factor for Coronary Artery Disease: Evidence, Mechanisms, and Treatment," *Psychosomatic Medicine* 66:3 (May-June 2004): 305-315; Lawson R. Wulsin and Bonita M. Singal, "Do Depressive Symptoms Increase the Risk for the Onset of Coronary Disease? A Systematic Quantitative Review," *Psychosomatic Medicine* 65:2 (March-April 2003): 201-210; Reiner Ruguliers, "Depression as a Predictor for Coronary Heart Disease: A Review and Meta-Analysis," *American Journal of Preventive Medicine* 23:1 (July 2002): 51-61; Brenda W.J.H. Penninx et al, "Depression and Cardiac Mortality: Results From a Community-Based Longitudinal Study," *Archives of General Psychiatry* 58:3 (March 2001): 221-227; Daniel E. Ford et al, "Depression Is a Risk Factor for Coronary Artery Disease in Men: The Precursors Study," *Archives of Internal Medicine* 158:13 (July 13, 1998): 1422-1426.

10. Martin Liebetrau, Bertil Steen, Ingmar Skoog, "Depression as a Risk Factor for the Incidence of First-Ever Stroke in 85-Year Olds," *Stroke* 39:7 (July 2008): 1960-1965; Jose J. Arbelaez et al, "Depressive Symptoms, Inflammation, and Ischemic Stroke in Older Adults: A Prospective Analysis in the Cardiovascular Health Study," *Journal of American Geriatrics Society* 55:11 (November 2007): 1825-1830; Glenn V. Ostir et al, "The Association Between Emotional Well-Being and the Incidence of Stroke in Older Adults," *Psychosomatic Medicine* 63:2 (March/April 2001): 210-215; Bruce S. Jonas and Michael E. Mussolino, "Symptoms of Depression as a Prospective Risk Factor for Stroke," *Psychosomatic Medicine* 62:4 (July/August 2000): 463-471; Susan A. Everson et al, "Depressive Symptoms and Increased Risk of Stroke Mortality Over a 29-Year Period,"

Archives of Internal Medicine 158:10 (May 25, 1998): 1133-1138.

11. Briana Mezuk et al, "Depression and Type 2 Diabetes Over the Lifespan: A meta-analysis," *Diabetes Care* 31:12 (December 2008): 2383-2390; Mercedes R. Carnethon et al, "Longitudinal Association Between Depressive Symptoms and Incident Type 2 Diabetes Mellitus in Older Adults: The Cardiovascular Health Study," *Archives of Internal Medicine* 167:8 (April 23, 2007): 802-807; L.A. Palinkas, P.P. Lee, E. Barrett-Connor, "A prospective study of Type 2 diabetes and depressive symptoms in the elderly: The Rancho Bernardo Study," *Diabetic Medicine* 21:11 (November 2004): 1185-1191; Sherita Hill Golden et al, "Depressive Symptoms and the Risk of Type 2 Diabetes: The Atherosclerosis Risk in Communities Study," *Diabetes Care* 27:2 (February 2004): 429-435.

12. R.A. Schovers et al, "Depression and excess mortality: evidence of a dose response relation in community living elderly," *International Journal of Geriatric Psychiatry* 24:2 (February 2009): 169-176; Lawson R. Wulson et al, "Depressive Symptoms, Coronary Heart Disease, and Overall Mortality in the Framingham Heart Study," *Psychosomatic Medicine* 67:5 (September-October 2005): 697-702; Richard Schulz et al, "Association Between Depression and Mortality in Older Adults: The Cardiovascular Health Study," *Archives of Internal Medicine* 160:12 (June 26, 2000):1761-1768; Brenda W.J.H. Penninx, "Minor and Major Depression and the Risk of Death in Older Persons," *Archives of General Psychiatry* 56:10 (October 1999): 889-895; Lawson R. Wulsin, George E. Vaillant, Victoria E. Wells, "A Systematic Review of the Mortality of Depression," *Psychosomatic Medicine* 61:7 (January-February 1999): 6-17; John C. Barefoot and Marianne Schroll, "Symptoms of Depression, Acute Myocardial Infarction, and Total Mortality in a Community Sample," *Circulation* 93:11 (June 1, 1996): 1976-1980.

13. Laura D. Kubzansky et al, "Is Worrying Bad For Your Heart? A Prospective Study of Worry and Coronary Heart Disease in

the Normative Aging Study," *Circulation* 95:4 (February 18, 1997): 818-824.

14. Glenn V. Ostir et al, "Hypertension in Older Adults and the Role of Positive Emotions," *Psychosomatic Medicine* 68:5 (September-October 2006): 727-733.

15. Erik J. Giltay et al, "Dispositional Optimism and Risk of Cardiovascular Death: The Zutphen Elderly Study," *Archives of International Medicine* 166:4 (February 27, 2006): 431-436 and Laura D. Kubzansky et al, "Is the Glass Half Empty or Half Full? A Prospective Study of Optimism and Coronary Hearth Disease in the Normative Aging Study," *Psychosomatic Medicine* 63:6 (November-December 2001): 910-916. But see Hermann Nabi et al, "Positive and negative affect and risk of coronary heart disease: Whitehall II prospective cohort study," *British Medical Journal* 337:7660 (July 2008): 32-45.

16. Glenn V. Ostir et al, "The Association Between Emotional Well-Being and the Incidence of Stroke in Older Adults," *Psychosomatic Medicine* 63:2 (March/April 2001): 210-215.

17. Yoichi Chida and Andrew Steptoe, "Positive Psychological Well-Being and Mortality: A Quantitative Review of Prospective Observational Studies," *Psychosomatic Medicine* 70:7 (September 2008): 741-756.

18. Andrew Steptoe et al, "Dispositional optimism and healthy behaviour in community-dwelling older people: Associations with healthy ageing," *British Journal of Health Psychology* 11:1 (February 2006): 71-84.

19. Andrew Steptoe and Jane Wardle, "Positive affect and biological function in every day life," *Neurobiology of Aging* 26S:1 (December 2005): S108-S112 and Andrew Steptoe, Jane Wardle, Michael Marmot, "Positive affect and health-related neuroendocrine, cardiovascular, and inflammatory processes," *Proceedings of National Academy of Sciences* 102:18 (May 3, 2005): 6508-6512. See also Sheldon Cohen and Sarah Pressman, "Positive Affect and Health," *Current Directions in Psychological Service* 15:3 (June 2006): 122-125 and Sheldon Cohen et al, "Positive Emotional Style Predicts Resistance to Illness After Experimental Exposure to Rhinovirus or Influenza

A Virus," *Psychosomatic Medicine* 68:6 (November-December 2006): 809-815.

20. Glenn V. Ostir et al, "Emotional Well-Being Predicts Subsequent Functional Independence and Survival," *Journal of the American Geriatric Society* (May 2000): 473-478.

21. Toshihiko Maruta et al, "Optimism-Pessimism Assessed in the 1960s and Self-reported Health Status 30 Years Later," *Mayo Clinic Proceedings* 77:8 (August 2002): 748-753 and Toshihiko Maruta et al, "Optimists vs. Pessimists: Survival Rate Among Medical Patients Over a 30-Year Period," *Mayo Clinic Proceedings* 75:2 (February 2000): 140-143. See also Beverly H. Brummett et al, "Prediction of All-Cause Mortality by the Minnesota Multiphasic Personality Inventory Optimism-Pessimism Scale Scores: Study of a College Sample During a 40-Year Follow-up Period," *Mayo Clinic Proceedings* 81:12 (December 2006): 1541-1544.

22. *An Anatomy of an Illness as Perceived by a Patient: Reflections on Healing and Regeneration* (New York: Norton 1979), Norman Cousins.

23. American Psychiatric Association, *Diagnostic and Statistical Manual of Mental Disorders*, Fourth edition (Washington, D.C.: American Psychiatric Association, 2000), 356.

CHAPTER 5

1. Suzanne C. Segerstrom and Gregory E. Miller, "Psychological Stress and the Human Immune System: A Meta-Analytic Study of 30 Years of Inquiry," *Psychological Bulletin* 130:4 (July 2004): 601-630.

2. Sheldon Cohen et al, "Types of Stressors That Increase Susceptibility to the Common Cold in Healthy Adults," *Health Psychology* 17:3 (May 1998): 214-223.

3. Annika Rosengren et al, "Association of psychosocial risk factors with acute myocardial infarction in 11119 cases and 13648 controls from 52 countries (the INTERHEART study): case-control study," *Lancet* 364: 9438 (September 11-17, 2004): 953-962.

4. Charalambos Vlachopoulos et al, "Acute Mental Stress Has a Prolonged Unfavorable Effect on Arterial Stiffness and Wave Reflections," *Psychosomatic Medicine* 68:2 (March/April 2006): 231-237 and Thomas G. Pickering, "Mental Stress As a Causal Factor In the Development of Hypertension and Cardiovascular Disease," *Current Hypertension Reports* 3:3 (June 2001): 249-254.

5. R.S. Wilson et al, "Proneness to psychological distress and risk of Alzheimer disease in a biracial community," *Neurology* 64:2 (January 25, 2005): 380-382 and R.S. Wilson et al, "Proneness to psychological distress is associated with risk of Alzheimer's disease," *Neurology* 61:11 (December 9, 2003): 1479-1485.

6. Bruce Felton, "When Rage Is All the Rage: The Art of Anger Management," *New York Times*, March 15, 1998, Business Section, 12 (quoting Dr. Hendrie Weisinger).

7. Janice E. Williams et al, "Anger Proneness Predicts Coronary Heart Disease Risk: Prospective Analysis From the Atherosclerosis Risk in Communities (ARIC) Study," *Circulation* 101:17 (May 2, 2000): 2034-2039.

8. John C. Barefoot, W. Grant Dahlstrom, Redford B. Williams, Jr., "Hostility, CHD Incidence, and Total Mortality: A 25-Year Follow-Up Study of 255 Physicians," *Psychosomatic Medicine* 45:1 (March 1983): 59-63.

9. Murray A. Mittleman et al, "Triggering of Acute Myocardial Infarction Onset by Episodes of Anger," *Circulation* 92:7 (October 1, 1995): 1720-1725.

10. Ichiro Kawachi et al, "A Prospective Study of Anger and Coronary Health Disease: The Normative Aging Study," *Circulation* 94:9 (November 1, 1996): 2090-2095.

11. Janice E. Williams et al, "The Association Between Trait Anger and Incident Stroke Risk: The Atherosclerosis Risk in Communities (ARIC) Study," *Stroke* 33:1 (January 1, 2002): 13-20.

12. Todd Q. Miller et al, "A Meta-Analytical Review of Research on Hostility and Physical Health," *Psychological Bulletin* 119:2 (March 1996): 322-348.

13. *The Relaxation Response* (New York: William Morrow, 1975), Herbert Benson with Miriam Z. Klipper.

14. Herbert Benson, M.D. with Marg Stark, *Timeless Healing: The Power and Biology of Belief* (New York: Scribner 1996), 127.

15. Adam Clark, Alexander Seidler, Michael Miller, "Inverse association between sense of humor and coronary heart disease," *International Journal of Cardiology* 80:1 (August 2001): 87-88.

16. See Lisa F. Berkman and Thomas Glass, "Social Integration, Social Networks, Social Support, and Health," in *Social Epidemiology*, eds. Lisa F. Berkman and Ichiro Kawachi (New York: Oxford, 2000) and Sheldon Cohen, "Social Relationships and Health," *American Psychologist* 59:8 (November 2004): 676-684.

17. Lisa Berkman and S. Leonard Syme, "Social Networks, Host Resistance, and Mortality: A Nine-Year Follow-Up Study of Alameda County Residents," *American Journal of Epidemiology* 109:2 (February 1979): 186-204.

18. Kate Mary Bennett, "Low level social engagement as a precursor of mortality among people in later life," *Age and Ageing* 31:3 (May 2002): 165-168.

19. Lynne C. Giles et al, "Effect of social networks on 10 year survival of very old Australians: the Australian longitudinal study of aging," *Journal of Epidemiology and Community Health* 59:7 (July 2005): 574-579.

20. Karen A. Ertel, Marie Glymour, Lisa F. Berkman, "Effects of Social Integration on Preserving Memory Function in a Nationally Representative US Elderly Population," *American Journal of Public Health* 98:7 (July 2008): 1215-1220.

21. Annika Rosengren et al, "Stressful life events, social support, and mortality in men born in 1933," *British Medical Journal* 307:6912 (October 30, 1993): 1102-1105. See also Kristina Orth-Gomér, Annika Rosengren, Lars Wilhelmsen, "Lack of Social Support and Incidence of Coronary Heart Disease in Middle-Aged Swedish Men," *Psychosomatic Medicine* 55:7 (February 1993): 37-43.

22. Michael E. McCullough et al, "Religious Involvement and Mortality: A Meta-Analytic Review," *Health Psychology* 19:3 (May 2000): 211-222. See also R.F. Gillum, "Frequency of Attendance at Religious Services and Mortality in a U.S. National Cohort," *Annals of Epidemiology* 18:2 (February 2008): 124-129.

23. Dana E. King et al, "The Relationship between Attendance At Religious Services and Cardiovascular Inflammatory Markers," *International Journal of Psychiatry in Medicine* 31:4 (October 13, 2001): 415-425.

24. Harold G. Koenig et al, "The Relationship between Religious Activities and Blood Pressure In Older Adults," *International Journal of Psychiatry in Medicine* 28:2 (July 1998): 189-213.

CHAPTER 6

1. Loving Kindness Meditation. Adapted from Stephen Levine, *Healing in Life and Death* (New York: Doubleday, 1987), 23-27.

2. *The Healing Power of Doing Good: The Health and Spiritual Benefits of Helping Others* (New York: Fawcett Columbine, 1991), Allan Luks with Peggy Payne.

3. *Ibid*, 17.

4. *Ibid*, 17, 49, 60, 81-83, 105.

5. Doug Oman, Carl E. Thoresen, and Kay McMahon, "Volunteerism and mortality among the community-dwelling elderly," *Journal of Health Psychology* 4:3 (July 1999): 301-316. See generally Doug Oman, "Does Volunteering Foster Physical Health and Longevity?," Elizabeth Midlarsky and Eva Kahana, "Altruism, Well-Being, and Mental Health in Late Life," and Adam S. Hirschfelder with Sabrina L. Reilly, "Rx: Volunteer: A Prescription for Healthy Aging" in *Altruism and Health: Perspectives from Empirical Research*, ed. Stephen G. Post (New York: Oxford University, 2007).

6. Terry Y. Lum and Elizabeth Lightfoot, "The Effects of Volunteering on the Physical and Mental Health of Older People," *Research on Aging* 27:1 (January 2005): 31-55; Nancy Morrow-Howell et al, "Effects of Volunteering on the Well-

Being of Older Adults," *Journal of Gerontology* 58B:3 (November 2003): S137-S145; Carolyn Schwartz et al, "Altruistic Social Interest Behaviors Are Associated With Better Mental Health," *Psychosomatic Medicine* 65:5 (September/October 2003): 778-785.

7. Alex H.S. Harris and Carl E. Thorsen, "Volunteering is Associated with Delayed Mortality in Older People: An Analysis of the Longitudinal Study of Aging," *Journal of Health Psychology* 10:6 (December 2005): 739-752.

8. Loren Toussaint and Jon R. Webb, "Theoretical and Empirical Connections Between Forgiveness, Mental Health, and Well-Being," in *Handbook of Forgiveness*, ed. Everett L. Worthington, Jr. (New York: Routledge, 2005), 353-357.

9. The health benefits of forgiveness are summarized in Charlotte V.O. Witvliet and Michael E. McCullough, "Forgiveness and Health: A Review and Theoretical Exploration of Emotion Pathways," in *Altruism and Health.*

10. Kathleen A. Lawler et al, "A Change of Heart: Cardiovascular Correlates of Forgiveness in Response to Interpersonal Conflict," *Journal of Behavioral Medicine* 26:5 (October 2003): 373-393. See also Kathleen A. Lawler et al, "The Unique Effects of Forgiveness on Health," *Journal of Behavioral Medicine* 28:2 (April 2005): 157-167 and Jennifer P. Friedberg, Sonia Suchday, Danielle V. Shelov, "The impact of forgiveness on cardiovascular reactivity and recovery," *International Journal of Psychophysiology* 65:2 (August 2007) 87-94.

11. Charlotte vanOyen Witvliet, Thomas E. Ludwig, Kelly L. Vander Laan, "Granting Forgiveness Or Harboring Grudges: Implications for Emotion, Physiology, and Health," *Psychological Science* 12:2 (March 2001): 117-122.

12. Loren L. Toussaint et al, "Forgiveness and Health: Age Differences in a U.S. Probability Sample," *Journal of Adult Development* 8:4 (October 2001): 249-257.

13. Adapted from Levine, *Healing in Life and Death*, 98-101.

CHAPTER 7

1. Laurel B. Yates et al, "Exceptional Longevity in Men: Modifiable Factors Associated With Survival Function to Age 90 Years," *Archives of Internal Medicine* 168:3 (February 11, 2008): 284-290.
2. *Ibid*, 286.
3. *Ibid*, 286.
4. *Ibid*, 286.
5. *Ibid*, 286.
6. T. Pischon et al, "General and Abdominal Adiposity and Risk of Death in Europe," *New England Journal of Medicine* 359:20 (November 13, 2008): 2105-2120. See also Emily B. Levitan et al, "Adiposity and Incidence of Heart Failure Hospitalization and Mortality: A Population-Based Prospective Study," *Circulation: Heart Failure* 2:2 (May 2009): 202-208.
7. Leonie K. Heilbronn et al, "Effect of 6-Month Calorie Restriction on Biomarkets of Longevity, Metabolic Adaptation, and Oxidative Stress in Overweight Individuals," *Journal of the American Medical Association* 295:13 (April 5, 2006): 1539-1548 and D. Enette Larson-Meyer et al, "Effect of Calorie Restriction With or Without Exercise on Insulin Sensitivity, B-Cell Function, Fat Cell Size, and Ectopic Lipid in Overweight Subjects," *Diabetes Care* 29:6 (June 2006): 1337-1344.
8. Timothy E. Meyer et al, "Long-Term Caloric Restriction Ameliorates the Decline in Diastolic Function in Humans," *Journal of the American College of Cardiology* 47:2 (January 17, 2006): 398-402.
9. Luigi Fontana et al, "Long-term caloric restriction is highly effective in reducing the risk for atherosclerosis in humans," *Proceedings of the National Academy of Sciences* 101:17 (April 27, 2004): 6659:6663.
10. Luigi Fontana and Samuel Klein, "Aging, Adiposity, and Calorie Restriction," *Journal of American Medical Association* 297:9 (March 7, 2007): 986-994.
11. Yates, "Exceptional Longevity," 286.
12. Kristina Sundquist et al, "Frequent and Occasional Physical Activity in the Elderly: A 12-Year Follow-Up Study of

Mortality," *American Journal of Preventive Medicine* 27:1 (July 2004): 22-27. See also Kristina Sundquist et al, "The long-term effect of physical activity on incidence of coronary heart disease: a 12-year follow-up study," *Preventive Medicine* 41:1 (July 2005): 219-225 and J. Stessman et al, "The Effects of Physical Activity on Mortality in the Jerusalem 70-Year-Olds Longitudinal Study," *Journal of the American Geriatrics Society* 48:5 (May 2000): 499-504; Amy A. Hakim, "Effects of Walking on Mortality among Nonsmoking Retired Men," *New England Journal of Medicine* 338:2 (January 8, 1998): 94-99.

13. The quotations in this paragraph are from Philip Roth, *Exit Ghost* (Boston: Houghton Mifflin, 2007), 67, 109, 103-104.

14. Gerald L. Andriole et al, "Mortality Results from a Randomized Prostate-Cancer Screening Trial," *New England Journal of Medicine* 360:13 (March 26, 2009): 1310-1319.

CHAPTER 8

1. MetLife Foundation Alzheimer's Survey: What American Thinks, May 11, 2006.

2. American Psychiatric Association, *Diagnostic and Statistical Manual of Mental Disorders*, Fourth edition (Washington, D.C.: American Psychiatric Association, 2000), 157.

3. Roth, *Exit Ghost,* 105.

4. Joe Verghese et al, "Leisure Activities and the Risk of Dementia in the Elderly," *New England Journal of Medicine* 348:25 (June 19, 2003): 2508-2516.

5. Robert S. Wilson et al, "Participation in Cognitively Stimulating Activities and Risk of Incident Alzheimer Disease," *Journal of the American Medical Association* 287:6 (February 13, 2002): 742-748.

6. N. Scarmeas et al, "Influence of leisure activity on the incidence of Alzheimer's Disease," *Neurology* 57:12 (December 2001): 2236-2242.

7. Sherry L. Willis et al, "Long-Term Effect of Cognitive Training on Everyday Functional Outcomes in Older Adults," *Journal of*

the American Medical Association 296:23 (December 20, 2006): 2805-2814.

8.   Glenn E. Smith et al, "A Cognitive Training Program Based on Principles of Brain Plasticity: Results from the Improvement in Memory with Plasticity-based Adaptive Cognitive Training (IMPACT) Study," *Journal of American Geriatrics Society* 57:4 (April 2009): 594-603.

9.   R.S. Wilson, " Chronic distress and incidence of mild cognitive impairment," *Neurology* 68:24 (June 2007): 2085-2092.

10.   D.P. Devanand et al, "Depressed Mood and the Incidence of Alzheimer's Disease in the Elderly Living in the Community," *Archives of General Psychiatry* 53:2 (February 1996): 175-182.

11.   A long-term study of 2,812 elderly persons by Shari S. Bassuk, Lisa F. Berkman, David Wypij, "Depression Symptomatology and Incident Cognitive Decline in an Elderly Community Sample," *Archives of General Psychiatry* 55:12 (December 1998): 1073-1081 concluded that depressive symptoms presaged future cognitive losses among those with moderate cognitive impairments. However, the data did not support the hypothesis that depressive symptoms are associated with the onset of rate of cognitive decline among the cognitive intact elderly.

12.   Laura Fratiglioni, Stephanie Paillard-Borg, Bengt Winblad, "An active and socially integrated lifestyle in late life might protect against dementia," *Lancet Neurology* 3:6 (June 2004): 343-353; Marie-Victoria Zunzunegui et al, "Social networks, social integration, and social engagement determine cognitive decline in community-dwelling Spanish older adults, " *Journals of Gerontology* 58B:2 (March 2003): S93-S100; Laura Fratiglioni et al, "Influence of social network on occurrence of dementia: a community-based longitudinal study," *Lancet* 355:9212 (April 15, 2000): 1315-1319; Shari Bassuk, Thomas A. Glass, Lisa F. Berkman, "Social Disengagement and Incident Cognitive Decline in Community-Dwelling Elderly Persons," *Annals of Internal Medicine* 131:3 (August 3, 1999): 165-173.

13.   Karen A. Ertel, M. Maria Glymour, Lisa F. Berkman, "Effects of Social Integration on Preserving Memory Function in a

Nationally Representative US Elderly Population," *American Journal of Public Health* 98:7 (July 2008): 1215-1220.

14. Christophe Tzourio et al, "Cognitive decline in individuals with high blood pressure," *Neurology* 53:9 (December 10, 1999): 1948-1952.

15. Lenore J. Launer et al, "Midlife blood pressure and dementia: the Honolulu-Asia aging study," *Neurobiology of Aging* 21:1 (January-February 2000): 49-55.

16. Annick Fontbonne et al, "Changes in Cognitive Abilities Over a 4-Year Period Are Unfavorably Affected in Elderly Diabetic Subjects: Results of the Epidemiology of Vascular Aging Study," *Diabetes Care* 24:2 (February 2001): 366-370 and A. Ott et al, "Diabetes mellitus and the risk of dementia: The Rotterdam Study," *Neurology* 53:9 (December 10, 1999): 1937-1942.

17. R.A. Whitmer et al, "Central obesity and increased risk of dementia more than three decades later," *Neurology* 71:14 (September 30, 2008): 1057-1063 and Nancy A. West and Mary N. Haan, "Body Adiposity in Late Life and Risk of Dementia or Cognitive Impairment in a Longitudinal Community-Based Study," *Journals of Gerontology* 64A:1 (January 2009): 103-109.

18. Miia Kivipelto et al, "Obesity and Vascular Risk Factors at Midlife and the Risk of Dementia and Alzheimer Disease," *Archives of Neurology* 62:10 (October 2005): 1556-1560.

19. Nikolaos Scarmeas et al, "Physical Activity, Diet, and Risk of Alzheimer's Disease," *Journal of American Medical Association* 302:6 (August 12, 2009): 627-637.

20. Martha Clare Morris et al, "Consumption of Fish and n-3 Fatty Acids and the Risk of Incident Alzheimer Disease," *Archives of Neurology* 60:7 (July 20, 2003): 940-946 and Martha Clare Morris et al, "Fish Consumption and Cognitive Decline With Age in a Large Community Study," *Archives of Neurology* 62:12 (December 2005): 1849-1853. But see O. van de Rest et al, "Effect of fish oil on cognitive performance in older subjects: A randomized, controlled trial," *Neurology* 71:6 (August 2008): 430-438 and Danielle Laurin et al, "Omega-3

fatty acids and risk of cognitive impairment and dementia," *Journal of Alzheimer's Disease* 4:4 (August 2003): 315-322.

21. Stanley Colcombe and Arthur F. Kramer, "Fitness Effects On The Cognition Function Of Older Adults: A Meta-Analytic Study," *Psychological Science* 14:2 (March 2003): 125-130.

22. Eric B. Larson et al, "Exercise Is Associated with Reduced Risk for Incident Dementia among Persons 65 Years of Age and Older," *Annals of Internal Medicine* 144:2 (January 17, 2006): 73-81. See also Danielle Laurin et al, "Physical Activity and Risk of Cognitive Impairment and Dementia in Elderly Persons," *Archives of Neurology* 58:3 (March 2001): 498-504. But see Maureen T. Sturman et al, "Physical Activity, Cognitive Activity, and Cognitive Decline in a Biracial Community Population," *Archives of Neurology* 62:11 (November 2005): 1750-1754.

23. Arthur F. Kramer et al, "Ageing, Fitness and Neurocognitive Function," *Nature* 400:6743 (July 29, 1999): 418-419.

24. Stanley J. Colcombe et al, "Aerobic Exercise Training Increases Brain Volume in Aging Humans," *Journals of Gerontology Series A: Biological and Medical Sciences* 61A:11 (November 2006): 1116-1170.

25. Scarmeas, "Physical Activity, Diet, and Risk of Alzheimer's Disease."

26. Quoted in Joseph Durso, "Mickey Mantle, Great Yankee Slugger, Dies at 63," *New York Times*, August 14, 1995, A1, B7.

CHAPTER 9

1. A. Michael Lipper with Douglas R. Sease, *Money Wise: How to Create, Grow, and Preserve Your Wealth* (New York: St. Martin's, 2008), 105.

INDEX